DOS 6
SureSteps

Yvonne Johnson

que

DOS 6 SureSteps

Copyright © 1993 by Que® Corporation.

All rights reserved. Printed in the United States of America. No part of this book may be used or reproduced in any form or by any means, or stored in a database or retrieval system, without prior written permission of the publisher except in the case of brief quotations embodied in critical articles and reviews. Making copies of any part of this book for any purpose other than your own personal use is a violation of United States copyright laws. For information, address Que Corporation, 11711 N. College Ave., Carmel, IN 46032.

Library of Congress Catalog No.: 93-85044

ISBN: 1-56529-262-6

This book is sold *as is*, without warranty of any kind, either express or implied, respecting the contents of this book, including but not limited to implied warranties for the book's quality, performance, merchantability, or fitness for any particular purpose. Neither Que Corporation nor its dealers or distributors shall be liable to the purchaser or any other person or entity with respect to any liability, loss, or damage caused or alleged to have been caused directly or indirectly by this book.

95 94 93   6 5 4 3 2 1

Interpretation of the printing code: the rightmost double-digit number is the year of the book's printing; the rightmost single-digit number, the number of the book's printing. For example, a printing code of 93-1 shows that the first printing of the book occurred in 1993.

Screen reproductions in this book were created with Collage Plus from Inner Media, Inc., Hollis, NH.

Publisher: David P. Ewing

Associate Publisher: Rick Ranucci

Managing Editor: Corinne Walls

Publishing Plan Manager: Thomas H. Bennett

Marketing Manager: Ray Robinson

Composed in Stone Serif and MCPdigital by Que Corporation.

Title Manager
Charles O. Stewart III

Acquisitions Editor
Sarah Browning

Product Development Specialist
Jim Minatel

Production Editors
Elsa M. Bell
Barb Colter
Jane A. Cramer
J. Christopher Nelson
Joy M. Preacher
Kathy Simpson

Technical Editors
Lynda Fox
Mitch Milam

Book Designer
Amy Peppler-Adams

Indexer
Joy Dean Lee

Production Team
Danielle Bird
Paula Carroll
Laurie Casey
Michelle Greenwalt
Heather Kaufman
Jay Lesandrini
Caroline Roop
Tina Trettin

About the Author

Yvonne Johnson is the president of Corporate Computer Training Center, a PC training company in Louisville, Kentucky. She has been in the computer training and consulting business since 1981 and has written over 50 computer books and manuals about most of the major software programs, including DOS, Windows, Lotus 1-2-3, Quattro Pro, PageMaker, Ventura, dBASE, Paradox, Enable, WordPerfect, MS-Word, Displaywrite, and MultiMate—to name a few. She is considered a leading expert in the computer industry.

Yvonne is noted for her easy-to-understand style of writing and her playful sense of humor, which add a light touch to her books. Readers have commented that her books are such invaluable references that they eventually fall apart from frequent use.

When she is not writing, teaching, and overseeing the training center, Yvonne spends her time at the football field with her husband, watching their two sons (and future Heisman Trophy winners). One day she intends to take up golf again and will probably write a book about it entitled *Why Women Should Always Use a Pink Ball and a Color-Coordinated Golf Bag*.

Readers who would like to pay Mrs. Johnson for her training, consulting, or writing services can contact her in care of Que.

Dedication

To the football dynasty—Richard, Kirk, and Todd

Acknowledgments

I am keenly aware of how much work goes into a book at the publishing company, and I want to acknowledge all the people at Que who have been involved with this book. I especially want to thank Jim Minatel and Barb Colter for the time and effort they gave to the book.

Trademarks

All terms mentioned in this book that are known to be trademarks or service marks have been appropriately capitalized. Que Corporation cannot attest to the accuracy of this information. Use of a term in this book should not be regarded as affecting the validity of any trademark or service mark.

MS-DOS is a registered trademark of Microsoft Corporation.

Contents at a Glance

Introduction

Section One: The Basics

Lesson 1: Getting Acquainted with Your PC

Lesson 2: Taking a Closer Look at DOS

Lesson 3: Working with Files

Section Two: File and Disk Management

Lesson 4: Organizing the Hard Disk

Lesson 5: Commands that Deal with Files

Lesson 6: Commands that Deal with a Disk

Section Three: Customizing and Enhancing Your System

Lesson 7: Commands and Files that Deal with the System

Lesson 8: Backing Up and Restoring Files

Lesson 9: Protecting the PC from Viruses

Lesson 10: Increasing Disk Space with DoubleSpace

Lesson 11: Optimizing Memory and Speed

Section Four: Productivity Tools

Lesson 12: Using the MS-DOS Editor

Lesson 13: Connecting Two PCs with Interlnk

Appendix A: Getting Ready to Use *DOS 6 SureSteps*

Appendix B: Commands Used at the DOS Prompt and in Batch Files

Glossary

Contents

Introduction 1
What Does This Book Contain? 2
    Section One: The Basics 2
    Section Two: File and Disk Management 2
    Section Three: Customizing and Enhancing Your
        System 3
    Section Four: Productivity Tools 4
    Appendixes and Glossary 4
How to Use This Book 4
How Lessons Are Organized 5
Conventions 6

Section 1: The Basics   7

1 Getting Acquainted with Your PC 9
Getting Acquainted with Your Hardware 10
    Turning On the System 11
    Adjusting the Monitor 12
    Using the Disk Drives 13
    Using the Keyboard 16
    Using a Mouse 20
    Using a Printer 21
Getting Familiar with Software 22
Learning the Functions of DOS 23
Booting the PC 24
    Performing a Cold Boot 24
    Performing a Warm Boot 26
    Interrupting the Booting Process 27
Turning Off the System 28
Lesson Summary 29
If You Want to Stop Now 29
From Here 30

2 Taking a Closer Look at DOS 31
Starting and Exiting the DOS Shell 32
Using the DOS Shell 32
    Learning the Parts of the DOS Shell 33
    Moving Around in the DOS Shell 35

>   Using the DOS Shell Menu 37
>   Learning More about Menus and Dialog Boxes 38
>   Changing the Look of the DOS Shell 39
>   Selecting a Different View 41
> Using the Command Prompt 42
> Using Help 43
>   Using Command Prompt Syntax Help 44
>   Using Help in the DOS Shell 45
>   Accessing Help from the Menu 45
>   Accessing Help with F1 46
>   Navigating a Help Screen 47
>   Using Help in Dialog Boxes 49
>   Using Help at the DOS Prompt 50
>   Getting More Detailed Help 51
>   Moving Around 52
>   Using the Menu to Print and Search 53
>   Displaying Cross References 55
> Lesson Summary 56
> If You Want to Stop Now 57
> From Here 57
>
> **3 Working with Files** 59
> Naming a File 60
>   Creating the File Name 60
>   General Rules for File Names 61
>   Identifying Application Default File Extensions 62
> Viewing a List of Files 65
> Using Wild Cards with File Names 68
> Lesson Summary 70
> If You Want to Stop Now 70
> From Here 70
> Your Turn Answers 71

Section Two: File and Disk Management   73

> **4 Organizing the Hard Disk** 75
> Learning More about Directories 76
> Looking at a Typical Root Directory 77
> Changing Directories 79
>   Changing Directories in the DOS Shell 79
>   Changing Directories at the DOS Prompt 80
> Making a Directory 81
>   Making a Directory in the DOS Shell 82

	Making a Directory at the DOS Prompt	83
	Removing a Directory	84
	Removing a Directory in the DOS Shell	84
	Removing a Directory at the DOS Prompt	85
	Viewing the Tree	87
	Deleting the Tree	88
	Lesson Summary	90
	If You Want to Stop Now	91
	From Here	91
5	**Commands that Deal with Files**	**93**
	Viewing a List of Files	94
	Expanding and Changing the Directory View	94
	Changing the Order of Files	96
	Selecting a File	98
	Searching for a File	100
	Copying Files	102
	Copying Files in the DOS Shell	102
	Copying Files with a Mouse	105
	Copying Files at the DOS Prompt	107
	Copying Files and Directories	108
	Moving Files	110
	Replacing Files	112
	Deleting Files	114
	Undeleting Files	116
	Renaming Files	120
	Lesson Summary	122
	If You Want to Stop Now	122
	From Here	123
6	**Commands that Deal with a Disk**	**125**
	Checking a Disk	126
	Using Parameters with CHKDSK	127
	Defragmenting a Disk	129
	Making an Exact Copy of a Disk	131
	Comparing Two Disks	134
	Understanding Disks and Formatting	136
	Formatting a Disk	137
	Using Other Formatting Options	139
	Unformatting a Disk	142
	Naming a Disk and Displaying the Name	145
	Lesson Summary	146
	If You Want to Stop Now	148
	From Here	148

Section Three: Customizing and Enhancing Your System — 149

7 Commands and Files that Deal with the System 151
- Displaying the Version of DOS 152
- Setting the Date 153
- Setting the Time 154
- Setting the Path 155
- Setting the Prompt 158
- Using an AUTOEXEC.BAT File 160
  - Creating a File 161
  - Creating Your Own AUTOEXEC.BAT File 163
- Creating Other Batch Files 166
  - Batch File Commands 168
- Understanding the CONFIG.SYS File 172
- Troubleshooting the CONFIG.SYS File 173
- Lesson Summary 174
- If You Want to Stop Now 175
- From Here 175
- On Your Own Answers 175

8 Backing Up and Restoring Files 177
- Understanding Microsoft Backup 178
- Configuring Microsoft Backup 179
- Performing a Backup 184
- Comparing Backup Copies with Originals 187
- Restoring Files 189
  - Restoring a Backup Set 189
- Making Subsequent Backups 192
  - Selecting the Right Type of Backup 192
  - Establishing a Backup Strategy 192
  - Using Setup Files 193
  - Using Catalogs 195
  - Using Master Catalogs 197
- Using Microsoft Backup from Windows 197
- Lesson Summary 199
- If You Want to Stop Now 200
- From Here 200

9 Protecting the PC from Viruses 201
- Preventing Viruses 202
- Classifying Viruses 203

xii DOS 6 SureSteps

Using Anti-Virus 203
    Configuring Anti-Virus 206
    Displaying Information about Viruses 208
    Recognizing False Alarms 209
Using VSafe 211
Using Anti-Virus with Windows 212
Lesson Summary 214
If You Want to Stop Now 214
From Here 214

10 Increasing Disk Space with DoubleSpace 215
Considering the Advantages and the Disadvantages ... 216
Installing DoubleSpace 217
    Compressing Your Hard Drive 217
    Using Custom Setup to Compress a Disk 220
Maintaining Compressed Drives 223
    Displaying Information about a
       Compressed Drive 223
    Changing the Size of a Compressed Drive 225
    Changing the Compression Ratio 226
    Defragmenting a Compressed Drive 227
    Formatting a Compressed Drive 228
    Deleting a Compressed Drive 229
Compressing Floppy Disks 230
Using Compressed Floppy Disks 232
Troubleshooting 233
Removing DoubleSpace 234
Lesson Summary 237
If You Want to Stop Now 238
From Here 239

11 Optimizing Memory and Speed 241
Distinguishing Types of Memory 242
    Conventional Memory 244
    Upper Memory Area 245
    Extended and Expanded Memory 246
    High Memory Area (HMA) 247
Managing Memory with DOS 248
Using MemMaker 249
    Running the Express Setup 250
    Undoing Changes 253
    Optimizing the Order in CONFIG.SYS and
       AUTOEXEC.BAT 254

    Optimizing System Speed 256
        Cleaning Up Directory Structures 256
        Using Programs for Extended Memory 258
    Lesson Summary 260
    If You Want to Stop Now 260
    From Here 260

Section Four: Productivity Tools   261

12 Using the MS-DOS Editor 263
    Starting the MS-DOS Editor 264
        Editing an Existing File 264
        Creating a New File to Edit 266
    Getting Familiar with the Screen and Menu 268
    Using Help 269
    Entering and Editing Text 271
        Selecting and Editing Blocks of Text 274
        Finding Text 276
        Finding and Changing Text 278
        Setting Bookmarks 280
    Saving a File 280
    Printing a File 281
    Exiting the MS-DOS Editor 283
    Lesson Summary 283
    If You Want to Stop Now 285
    From Here 285

13 Connecting Two PCs with Interlnk 287
    Understanding the Relationship of the Two PCs 288
    Preparing to Use Interlnk 288
    Making and Breaking the Connection 289
    Lesson Summary 290

A Getting Ready to Use *DOS 6 SureSteps* 291
    Preparing to Install DOS 6 292
    Installing the Upgrade 293
    Making a Working Copy of the SureSteps Disk 296

B Commands Used at the DOS Prompt
    and in Batch Files 299
    Commands and Device Drivers Used Only in
        CONFIG.SYS 308

    Glossary 313

    Index 321

Introduction

Microsoft DOS has been the industry standard for many years. The latest version of DOS, version 6, adds more power and more functionality to an already powerful operating system. Not only can you perform all the commands that have always been available, such as copying and deleting files, creating directories, checking the disk, and so on, but now DOS offers disk compression, virus protection, more sophisticated backup, memory optimization, computer linking, and many other new or enhanced features.

This book, *DOS 6 SureSteps*, is designed for people who are new to MS-DOS 6. New users learn the basic DOS commands and the use of the DOS Shell. They also learn more advanced tasks, such as how to use Anti-Virus, DoubleSpace, and MemMaker.

DOS 6 SureSteps provides lessons—ranging from 15 to 60 minutes in length—that begin with basic commands and concepts and move to the more advanced features. The lessons are self-paced and easy to follow—with or without an instructor. You can work your way through the entire book in a linear fashion or choose only the lessons you need.

What Does This Book Contain?

Beginning with the most basic skills, this book guides the new user to proficiency in using DOS. Each lesson builds on the last; however, each lesson also can stand alone. To support the reader, this book supplies added margin notes, tips, and sections that guide you through potential trouble spots.

To make learning DOS 6 easier, this book contains 13 lessons that are divided into four parts. Instructions for installing DOS 6 and a command reference are provided in the appendixes, and a glossary is added for your reference.

Section One: The Basics

This section consists of lessons designed to introduce the new user to DOS. In this section, you learn about hardware and software, DOS installation and booting, how to use the DOS Shell, and so on.

Lesson 1, "Getting Acquainted with Your PC," explains hardware and software terms, the general function of DOS, and how to boot DOS. Lesson 1 provides basic information that is invaluable to anyone who has used a computer very little or not at all.

Lesson 2, "Taking a Closer Look at DOS," introduces the DOS Shell, the command line, and the Help feature. In this lesson, you learn how to start the DOS Shell and use its menus and icons, use the command line for basic commands, and use the many different types of Help that are available.

Lesson 3, "Working with Files," explains what a file is and how to name a file. It also discusses the use of wild card characters in file names.

Section Two: File and Disk Management

This section deals with commands and features that pertain to file and disk management.

Lesson 4, "Organizing the Hard Disk," teaches you how to make directories, change the current directory, remove directories, and view the tree structure of the disk. It also includes a discussion of the new DELTREE command that removes a directory and all its subdirectories.

Lesson 5, "Commands that Deal with Files," covers basic file commands like COPY, MOVE, DELETE, RENAME, and so on. The advanced file commands, REPLACE and UNDELETE, also are explained.

Lesson 6, "Commands that Deal with a Disk," deals with disk commands like FORMAT, UNFORMAT, CHKDSK, DISKCOPY, and DISKCOMP (disk compare). Lesson 6 also explores the new DEFRAG command that cures the disk fragmentation problem.

Section Three: Customizing and Enhancing Your System

This section provides insight on how to use the DOS utility programs to customize, safeguard, and enhance your system. These include Microsoft Backup, Anti-Virus, DoubleSpace, MemMaker, and Interlnk.

Lesson 7, "Commands and Files that Deal with the System," explores the AUTOEXEC.BAT file and the CONFIG.SYS file as well as system commands like VER, DATE, TIME, PATH, and PROMPT.

Lesson 8, "Backing Up and Restoring Files," reviews the procedures for backing up a disk and restoring files to a disk. Lesson 8 also includes a discussion of recommended backup strategies.

Lesson 9, "Protecting the PC from Viruses," explains how to use the Anti-Virus utility to detect and clean viruses from the system.

Lesson 10, "Increasing Disk Space with DoubleSpace," teaches you how to increase the hard disk space available by compressing the disk with DoubleSpace. The lesson also discusses the pros and cons of using DoubleSpace.

Lesson 11, "Optimizing Memory and Speed," introduces the MemMaker utility. It opens with a discussion of the types of memory and then explains how MemMaker can optimize the memory in your system.

Section Four: Productivity Tools

This section deals with two tools that help you to be more productive.

Lesson 12, "Using the MS-DOS Editor," teaches you how to use the text-editing program called MS-DOS Editor. The lesson explores the menus and all the options available in the program, including copying, deleting, moving, saving, and printing.

Lesson 13, "Connecting Two PCs with Interlnk," shows how to connect two computers for the purpose of transferring files.

Appendixes and Glossary

Appendix A, "Getting Ready to Use *DOS 6 SureSteps*," walks through the basic procedure for installing DOS 6. This appendix also explains how to make a working copy of the SureSteps disk included with this book.

Appendix B, "Commands Used at the DOS Prompt and in Batch Files," lists and briefly explains all the DOS 6 commands covered in this book.

The Glossary offers definitions of common computer terms used in this book.

How to Use This Book

This book can be used in classroom situations with an instructor or by one motivated learner. If you are new to DOS, work sequentially through all the lessons. If you have some experience with DOS and need only specific skills, read through the table of contents or the lesson summaries to identify points of interest or areas you want to study. The following table includes suggestions, based on your experience level, on what lessons and learning path might be of most benefit to you.

If you want to...	Do...
Learn about a PC or DOS	Lessons 1, 2, and 3 first. You should continue with the other lessons in the order presented as well.
Learn the basic DOS commands	Lessons 4-7
Learn about the new DOS backup utility	Lesson 8
Detect viruses and protect your PC from them	Lesson 9
Increase your disk space	Lesson 10
Maximize the use of your PC's memory	Lesson 11
Use the MS-DOS Editor for creating and revising files	Lesson 12
Transfer files between two PCs	Lesson 13

The SureSteps disk enclosed with this book supplies various files that are used in the exercises in the lessons. The exercises assume that you will be using the disk in your floppy drive.

■ **Note:** Make a copy of the SureSteps disk before you use if so you can use the original again if necessary. Appendix A, "Getting Ready to Use *DOS 6 SureSteps*," explains how to copy this disk.

How Lessons Are Organized

Every lesson in *DOS 6 SureSteps* teaches you an important part of using the program. Each lesson contains the following elements:

- ■ **Overviews of procedures.** You can review these sections before you start a hands-on exercise oras a reference to help you remember the steps.

- **Your Turn**. These hands-on tutorials provide step-by-step instruction for accomplishing specific tasks, using *real world* examples and working with practice files from the SureSteps disk.

- **If You Have Problems**. These notes provide troubleshooting tips to help you avoid or get out of trouble.

- **On Your Own**. These sections provide more exercises without detailed instructions in order to give you a chance to test your knowledge of specific procedures.

- **Lesson Summary**. This section reviews the basic procedures of the lesson. You can use the lesson summary as a reference.

- **From Here**. This brief section provides a sneak preview of the next lesson or suggests related lessons if you are not using the book in a linear manner.

Conventions

Because you can use a mouse or the keyboard with DOS 6, neither method is really emphasized in the book. Steps are written in a generic way so that you can use the mouse or the keyboard.

In some cases, you may need to use key combinations. In this book, a key combination is joined by a plus sign (+). If the text says to press Alt+F4, for example, you press and hold down the Alt key while you press the F4 key.

In this book, the use of typefaces is purposeful. The book uses the following typefaces:

Typeface	Meaning
Italic type	Used to represent words or phrases defined for the first time and provide emphasis.
Boldface type	Used to represent text that you are instructed to type or keys pressed to make menu selections.
`Special` font	Used to represent screen messages and other on-screen elements.

Section One

The Basics

1. Getting Acquainted with Your PC
2. Taking a Closer Look at DOS
3. Working with Files

SURESTEPS LESSON 1

Getting Acquainted with Your PC

In this lesson, you learn how to do the following:

- Turn on your PC properly
- Use your hardware components
- Boot the system

Lesson time:
30–45 minutes

A complete computer system consists of hardware (physical devices) and software (programs that perform specific tasks). A keyboard and a monitor are classified as hardware, for example, and DOS and Lotus 1-2-3 are classified as software. This lesson explains the fundamentals of using computer hardware and software.

If you have little or no experience with PCs, read this lesson thoroughly. If you are an experienced user but have not used the DOS Shell extensively, skip to Lesson 2. If you are an experienced user and familiar with the DOS Shell, you might want to start with Section Two, Three, or Four of this book. Be sure to read Lessons 8, 9, 10, 11, and 13 because they deal with features that are new in DOS 6.

Getting Acquainted with Your Hardware

The main component of a PC is the system unit. Technically speaking, the *system unit* is the component that contains the "brain" of the PC. Just as the human brain is made up of different areas, the brain of the computer is made up of the CPU (Central Processing Unit), the memory, and, in many cases, a math coprocessing unit.

The CPU is a computer chip that acts like a traffic cop: the CPU directs the flow of information through the computer. It also performs arithmetic and logical functions. The CPU used in the first IBM PC in 1981 was made by Intel, and it was called the 8088 chip. Since then, the CPU has evolved through these changes: the 8086, the 80286, the 80386, the 80486, and the 80586 (also called the Pentium). With each new chip, the processing speed is faster. When the latest chip is on the market, a chip that is two or three versions beyond the latest chip is in the developmental stage.

The memory of a computer consists of RAM (Random Access Memory), ROM (Read Only Memory), cache memory, extended memory, and expanded memory. RAM is used for temporary storage of data or programs during processing. ROM is permanent internal memory containing basic operation instructions for the computer. Extended memory is an extra amount of RAM that is added to the motherboard (the computer's basic computer chip board). Cache memory can be on the motherboard or in the processor itself and is used by the processor to store frequently used data for speedier access. Expanded memory is a special way of configuring and using extended memory that conforms to a memory management specification, typically called the *LIM specification*, named after the primary companies that developed it—Lotus, Intel, Microsoft. Extended and expanded memory are explained in more detail in Lesson 11.

A *math coprocessing unit* is similar to the CPU in that it performs mathematical and logical operations. It actually aids the CPU and increases the computer's processing speed.

All other parts of a PC, including the monitor, keyboard, disk drive, mouse, modem, printer, and so on, are technically considered *peripherals*. (A keyboard, disk drive, and monitor are so essential to the system, however, that they are not commonly considered peripherals.) This lesson presents only the basic peripherals.

Turning On the System

Generally speaking, when you start your PC, you should turn on peripherals before you turn on the system unit. The system unit then can recognize or acknowledge all the peripherals that are attached; however, not all PCs require the peripherals to be turned on first. Some systems have one power switch that turns on all devices at once.

If you have problems...	If you can use one switch for turning on your complete system (from a power bar, for example), you should not have any problems. If you do have problems, such as the printer not working correctly, try turning on all peripherals before you turn on the system

▶Your Turn

If you do not have a switch that turns on all your devices at once, practice turning on your PC by following these steps:

1 Turn on the printer.

2 Turn on the monitor.

3 Turn on the external modem if you have one.

4 Turn on the PC.

If your computer has one power switch, turn it on and check that all attached devices are turned on.

Adjusting the Monitor

Monitors come in several types and sizes. Currently, the most popular monitors are VGA and Super VGA. These monitors are capable of showing 16 and 256 colors (respectively) in standard mode. They also are capable of showing many more colors in other modes.

Regardless of the size or type of monitor that you have, your monitor will probably tilt and swivel so that you can adjust it to a comfortable position for your eyes. If your monitor is difficult to adjust, grasp it with both hands and use a gentle rocking motion to move it. Sometimes it helps if you stand up when you adjust the position of the monitor.

■ **Tip:** Most of the adjustment controls have a slight click at their factory-preset middle positions. This makes it easy to find the middle setting if you want to reset the monitor.

Monitors also have adjustment controls for the brightness and contrast of the display. You should adjust the screen display so that it is not too bright but bright enough that you do not have to strain to see it. The contrast adjustment is used to show a contrast between a normal display and a high- or low-intensity display. Normal text might be a normal green color, for example, whereas bold text is a high-intensity green color. If the contrast is not adjusted properly, you may not be able to see the difference between the two.

Many monitors, especially color monitors, have additional adjustment controls to adjust the vertical size and hold. These controls are adjusted at the factory and seldom need to be changed.

▶ Your Turn

With your computer turned on, follow these steps to adjust your monitor controls:

1 Turn the brightness control to its brightest setting.

2 Turn the brightness control to its lowest setting.

3 Adjust the brightness so that it is comfortable for you.

4 Turn the contrast control to its highest setting.

5 Turn the contrast control to its lowest setting.

6 Adjust the contrast so that it is comfortable for you.

▶ On Your Own

If your monitor has vertical adjustment controls, turn them and watch the effect on the screen.

Using the Disk Drives

Currently, the most common storage media for storing and retrieving programs and user-created data is a magnetic disk. Data can be read from and written to a disk by using the hardware device called a *disk drive*.

The two most common types of disk drives are floppy and fixed (or hard) drives. Floppy drives come in two sizes to accommodate either a 5 1/4-inch disk or a 3 1/2-inch disk. You can insert a floppy disk in the disk drive when you want to use it and then take the disk out and store it when you are finished with it. A fixed drive houses a magnetic hard disk that is sealed in the drive compartment. Unlike floppy disks, most hard disks are not removable, but there are several makes and models of removable hard disks available.

Disk drives are named with letters. Floppy drives are A and B, and the hard drive is usually named C. When you are using a PC program that requires drive information, you must designate the drive with its letter, followed by a colon. If you must refer to drive A, for example, you type the following:

    a:

The *floppy drive* gets its name from the disks that are inserted in the drive; the disks are made of a thin plastic-like material that is very flexible or floppy. The *hard drive* takes its name from the hard metal disk that it houses.

The capacity of a drive is measured in kilobytes (K), megabytes (M, MB, or megs), and gigabytes (G, GB, or gigs). A single *byte* is roughly equivalent to one character, such as an *a* or a *5*. A *kilobyte* equals one thousand bytes; a *megabyte* equals one million bytes; and a *gigabyte* equals one billion bytes. An average one-page letter is approximately 1000 bytes, or 1K.

Floppy drives for 5 1/4-inch disks range from 360K to 1.2M. Drives for 3 1/2-inch disks range from 720K to 1.44M. IBM and several other companies are currently marketing a 2.88M drive for 3 1/2-inch disks, but this size has not gained wide acceptance yet.

The capacity of a disk drive determines the disks that can be used in the drive. Lower-capacity drives cannot read higher-capacity disks, but higher-capacity drives can read lower-capacity disks. A 360K drive cannot use a 1.2M disk, for example, but a 1.2M drive can use a 360K disk. Although high-density drives can read and write to low-capacity disks, the likelihood of error, though slight, is increased if you do not use the disk capacity for which the drive is designed.

■ **Note:** The exposed part of a 3 1/2-inch disk is not really exposed at all. It is covered with a metal sleeve that can be moved back and forth.

Floppy disks must be handled very carefully. You should never touch the exposed part of a disk because the body oil that is deposited on the disk could wipe out data and even make the entire disk unusable. Disks should be stored in clean, dry places. Disks also should be protected from undue pressure, sunlight, and magnetic fields found in such unobtrusive places as telephones and paper clip holders. A 3 1/2-inch disk that has been left in a shirt pocket won't survive a trip through the washing machine very well either.

■ **Note:** A 3 1/2-inch disk cannot be successfully inserted in the wrong direction. It will not lock into place if it is backward.

Disks also must be inserted properly in the disk drives. Floppy disks have a right side and a wrong side. The wrong side of a 5 1/4-inch disk shows where the disk cover has been folded over and attached. The wrong side of a 3 1/2-inch disk has a circular metal disk in the middle. When you insert a disk into a drive that is mounted horizontally in the PC, the right side should face the ceiling. If the disk drive is mounted vertically, the correct side should face your left. The exposed part of the disk should be inserted first.

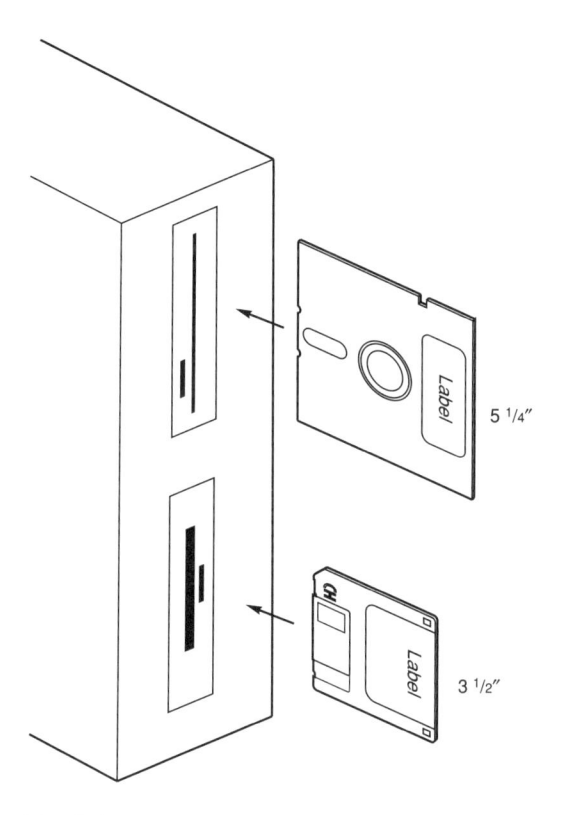

Hard drives range in size from 40M to 4G. When hard drives were first introduced, the size ranged from 10 to 30M, and 30M was more than adequate. Now that people are using more programs and the programs themselves require more room on the drive, an 80M hard drive is common.

Unlike floppy drives, hard drives have no exposed parts to collect fingerprints and other damage. Hard drives are usually located in the safety of the system unit and are very durable. Excessive dust, dirt, smoke, and vibration can damage your hard drive (and other parts of your computer), however, so try to keep the PC environment as clean as possible. Use dust covers or PC furniture that encloses the PC if you are unable to control the environment.

■ **Tip:** Some older hard drives have a special utility for locking or parking the disk to prevent damage when you move the computer. Newer hard drives don't need this and can be damaged by attempts to park them. Check your computer manual to see if your drive needs to be parked when you move the computer.

Getting Acquainted with Your PC: Your Hardware

▶ Your Turn

Follow these steps to become more familiar with floppy disks and disk drives:

1 Locate a 5 1/4-inch disk that does not have important data on it because you are going to destroy the disk in the next step.

2 Cut the disk cover and remove the magnetic disk.

3 Touch the disk and look for your fingerprint.

4 Find a 3 1/2-inch disk and move the sleeve to expose the disk inside, but do not touch the disk; a fingerprint can destroy data or even make the disk totally unusable.

5 If you have a 5 1/4-inch disk drive, insert a different 5 1/4-inch disk with the right side up (for horizontal drives) or facing the left (for vertical drives).

6 Gently push the disk all the way into the drive so that it does not bind on anything as it is being inserted. If the drive has a latch, close the latch.

7 If you have a 3 1/2-inch disk drive, insert a 3 1/2-inch disk with the right side up (for horizontal drives) or facing the left (for vertical drives).

8 Push the disk all the way into the drive. If the drive has a latch, close the latch. If the drive does not have a latch, push the disk in until you hear a click.

▶ On Your Own

Remove the disks and return them to their storage locations.

Using the Keyboard

The keyboard that is currently the most popular is the enhanced 101 keyboard. Unlike older keyboards, it has indicator lights for the Num Lock, Caps Lock, and Scroll Lock keys and two sets of cursor keys. The number and arrangement of the function keys are different, too. Older keyboards have ten function keys arranged in two vertical rows on the left side of the keyboard. The new enhanced keyboards have twelve function keys arranged in one horizontal row across the top of the keyboard.

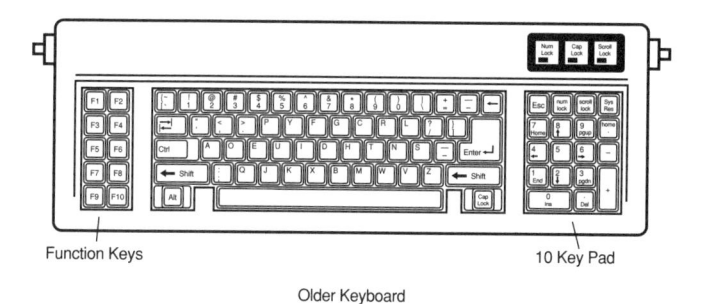

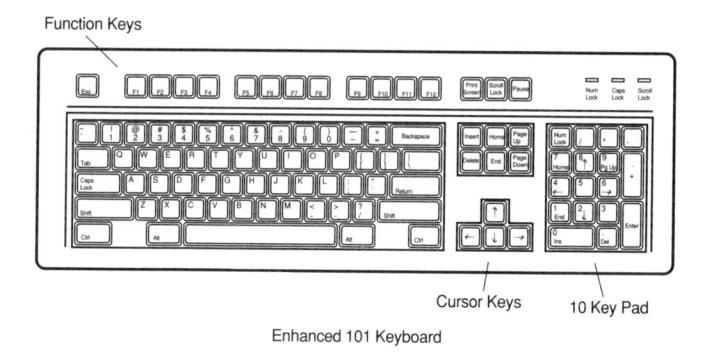

Older Keyboard

Enhanced 101 Keyboard

Function keys are special keys that can be assigned different functions. The function of a key depends on the program that is being used. Lotus 1-2-3 uses the F2 key to edit a cell, for example. WordPerfect uses this key to initiate a search.

In most programs, the Ctrl key and the Alt key modify the use of other keys. Alt+B might activate boldfacing in a program, for example. When you use Ctrl and Alt with other keys, you must use them like you do the Shift key; that is, you must press the Ctrl or Alt key first and hold it down while you press the other key.

You can generally use the Enter key to execute a command. In word processing programs, it also is used to end a short line, such as the last line in a paragraph or a salutation like "Dear Sir." The Enter key is sometimes referred to as the Return key.

In most programs, the Esc key cancels a command before the Enter key is pressed. This key is usually located by itself on the keyboard to help the user avoid accidentally pressing the key.

The Caps Lock key locks the alphabetic keys in uppercase. When Caps Lock is on, you must press Shift with a key to get lowercase. Caps Lock does not affect any keys except the alphabetic keys, so if you press the colon/semicolon key when Caps Lock is on, for example, you get a semicolon, not a colon. To get a colon when Caps Lock is on, you must press the Shift key with the colon/semicolon key.

The Num Lock key controls the keys on the 10-key number pad on the far right side of the keyboard. When Num Lock is on, the numbers work. When Num Lock is off, the cursor keys work. The Shift key can be used in combination with the number and cursor keys to reverse the effect of the Num Lock key. If the Num Lock key is on, for example, you can still use the up arrow if you press Shift with it.

The Scroll Lock key locks the cursor on a line. When the Scroll Lock is on, pressing the up or down arrow causes the screen to scroll. This key is used in spreadsheet programs such as Lotus 1-2-3 but rarely in other programs.

On the enhanced keyboard, the cursor keys are located on the 10-key number pad and between the number pad and the four rows of typing keys. On older keyboards, the cursor keys are on the 10-key number pad only. As mentioned previously, if you want to use the cursor keys on the number pad, you must turn off Num Lock. The cursor keys that are not on the number pad are never affected by the Num Lock key. The up-, down-, left-, and right-arrow keys move the cursor up, down, left, and right, respectively.

■ **Note:** Some keyboards have the words Page Up and Page Down on the keys rather than Pg Up and Pg Dn.

Other special keys also move the cursor. The Home, Pg Up, Pg Dn, and End keys move the cursor in larger increments. The increment depends on the program in use. The Home key might move the cursor to the top of the screen in one program, for example, or to the beginning of the line in another program. These keys have two locations on the enhanced keyboard.

The Del and Ins keys also have two locations on the enhanced keyboard. Generally speaking, the Del key deletes the character at the position of the cursor, and the Ins key toggles between the Insert mode and the Overtype mode. When the keyboard is in the Insert mode, you can insert a character at the position of the cursor. When the keyboard is in the Overtype mode, a character types over the character at the position of the cursor.

■ **Note:** Some keyboards have the words Delete and Insert on the keys rather than Del and Ins.

The Print Screen key prints the contents of the screen. This key is useful when you want to remember what is on-screen, and you have no other way of printing it.

■ **Note:** Some keyboards have the words PrntScrn or PrtScrn on the keys rather than Print Screen.

▶ Your Turn

Try the following steps to practice using some of the special keys on the keyboard. (If you have been following the exercises in this lesson, your computer should be on. If it is not running, turn it on and wait for the C prompt. If your PC takes you directly into a program, perform the keystrokes necessary to return to the C prompt.)

1. Type the DOS command **dir**. When executed, this command lists the files on drive C.

2. Press Enter to execute the command. A list of files appears.

3. Type the DIR command with the typographical error **der**.

4. Press Esc to cancel the command. Notice that the cursor drops down to the next line, but the C prompt is not displayed on the new line.

5. Type **dir** again and then press Enter. The same list of files reappears.

6. Press Caps Lock.

7. Type **NOW IS THE TIME 1 2 3** and then press Esc. Notice that Caps Lock does not work like Shift when you press a key that has two different characters (for example, the keys 1, 2, and 3 on the top row).

■ **Tip:** You learn about the DIR command in Lesson 3.

Getting Acquainted with Your PC: Your Hardware

8 Hold down the Shift key and type **now**. Notice that the Shift key reverses the effect of Caps Lock.

9 Hold down the Shift key and press the number keys 1, 2, and 3 on the top row of the keyboard. Notice that the characters !, @, and # are displayed.

10 Press Caps Lock to turn it off.

11 Press Num Lock to turn it on if it is not on.

12 Type **1 2 3** from the 10-key number pad and then press Esc.

■ **Note:** If you are using a laser printer, you may have to force the page to eject.

13 Make sure that your printer is turned on and press Print Screen. The contents of the screen are then printed.

Using a Mouse

A mouse is a device that operates a pointer on-screen. The pointer is a rectangle if you are using the monitor's text mode or an arrow if you are using the monitor's graphic mode.

Graphic mode cursor   Text mode cursor

To use a mouse effectively, you must learn these actions—point, click, double-click, and drag. To point with a mouse, you roll the mouse until you have moved the pointer to the desired location. To point to a menu option, for example, you move the mouse until the pointer is on the option.

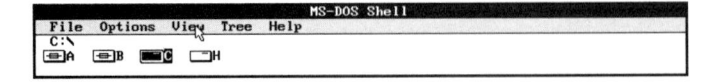

DOS 6 SureSteps

Although the mouse may have two or three buttons, the left mouse button is used almost exclusively with most programs. Clicking the left mouse button makes a selection. When you point to a menu option and then click the mouse, for example, you select the menu option.

Double-clicking (that is, rapidly clicking the left mouse button twice in succession) selects and executes a command. To open a file in some programs, for example, you can double-click the file name rather than click the file name to select it and then click the OK button to open it.

Dragging the mouse consists of holding down the left mouse button continuously while you move the mouse. This action is used very little in the DOS program.

It is not practical to use the mouse at this point. You use a mouse in Lesson 2.

■ **Tip:** Most computer mice are designed for right-handed use. If you are left-handed, you can buy a mouse designed for left-handed users; your primary button will be the right button rather than left. With most mice for right-handed users, you can switch the roles of the left and right buttons, however. Consult your mouse manual for more information.

■ **Tip:** The mouse seems to have a better grip if you use a mouse pad.

Using a Printer

Various types of printers are available for PCs. The different types include daisywheel printers, dot-matrix printers, inkjet printers, and laser printers. It is not within the scope of this book to describe the way all the different printers work. You should refer to the manual that came with your printer to learn about it.

It is very important that your printer is assembled and configured correctly, however. If it is not, your software will not be able to produce the desired results. If you do not have the tractor feeds positioned correctly, for example, you will not get the margins that you have set in your program when you print a file.

▶ On Your Own

Study your printer manual and get to know your printer well. If you have a laser printer with a control panel, learn how to make the proper settings. If your printer has dip switches, make sure that all the switches are set correctly. Practice

Getting Acquainted with Your PC: Your Hardware

loading ribbon or cartridges. Make sure that paper guides and tractor feeds are aligned correctly and that paper bins are attached correctly.

Getting Familiar with Software

Software is the term for programs that perform specific tasks. Software can be broken down into two categories—system software and application software.

System software is the basic set of instructions used by the computer to operate and manage components of the system. DOS is an example of system software. Other examples include OS/2, UNIX, and XENIX. (Windows is not a true operating system because it cannot boot the PC.) In other aspects, however, it is comparable to both an operating system and several different kinds of application programs.

Application software is designed for general use in several broad categories. The categories are listed here with examples of some of the popular programs:

Communications and E-mail

ccMail, Lotus Notes, CrossTalk

Database Management

dBASE IV, Paradox, FoxPro, R:Base

Desktop Publishing

PageMaker, Ventura Publisher

Graphics

CorelDRAW!, Freehand

Graphing

Harvard Graphics, Freelance

Integrated

Enable, Symphony, MS-Works

Project Management

Harvard Project Manager, TimeLine, Lotus Agenda, MS-Project

Spreadsheets

    Lotus 1-2-3, Excel, Quattro Pro

Utilities

    Norton Utilities, PC Tools, Stacker

Word Processing

    WordPerfect, Word, Ami Pro

Programs that have narrower functions like accounting, sales, inventory, and so on, are referred to as *vertical market software*. These packages are designed with a particular market in mind rather than for broad, general use.

▶ On Your Own

Survey the software that is installed on your PC or in your possession. Notice the category for each program. List the types of software you might need in the future.

Learning the Functions of DOS

Remember that DOS is an example of system software. In fact, it is the most widely used system software today. The name DOS is an acronym for **D**isk **O**perating **S**ystem which explains the function of DOS very well. DOS operates the PC system completely. It manages the input and output of information; it manages the hardware devices attached; and it controls the way the PC uses other programs.

Notice some of the specific tasks that DOS performs. The first task that DOS performs on a regular basis is the starting or *booting* of the PC. This routine is explained thoroughly later in this lesson in the section called "Booting the PC."

After the booting task is performed, you may go on to perform many other tasks but never knowingly call on DOS. You may go straight into the WordPerfect program, for example, and begin to create word processing documents. Even though you are not knowingly using DOS, every time you type a character, retrieve, save, print, copy, or delete a file, and so on, you are using the DOS program. DOS is performing its tasks in the background.

At other times, you may purposely use the DOS commands to perform housekeeping chores—chores that organize the hard disk and keep the disk tidy by keeping it free of errors, deleting unwanted files, and using storage space efficiently. You also might use the utility commands of DOS that back up files, search for viruses, compress files to free more disk space, manage memory more efficiently, and connect two computers so that you can exchange files.

Later lessons in this book discuss the "housekeeping" commands and the utility commands in more detail and give you an opportunity to learn and practice all these commands.

Booting the PC

The term *boot* simply means to start. You can boot the PC, boot DOS, boot Lotus, and so on. This bit of computer jargon comes from the old saying "to pull yourself up by your bootstraps." In your mind's eye, picture the old computer pioneers waxing nostalgic and saying, "Let's call *starting* the computer 'booting.' My great-grandpa used to say he got *started* by pulling himself up by his bootstraps." The computer pioneers liked the term booting so much that they called one of the system programs the Bootstrap Loader and they called the drive that contains DOS the *bootstrap drive*.

Performing a Cold Boot

When you turn on your computer, you are performing a *cold boot*. A cold-booted computer checks the hardware to see that everything is in working order before it does anything else. This equipment check is called a Power On Self Test (POST). Then the Bootstrap Loader looks for two programs called IO.SYS and MSDOS.SYS. These are hidden system files created when DOS formats the disk. The Bootstrap Loader looks for these two programs in drive A first. If the drive is empty, the program looks on drive C. If a disk is in drive A and the disk is not a DOS disk, DOS displays an error message.

You should remove the disk and press any key to continue. The PC will look in drive A again and then in drive C.

The IO.SYS file initializes any hardware devices that are attached to the system. Then the file reads the MSDOS.SYS program and the CONFIG.SYS file (if there is one). Finally, the IO.SYS program loads the DOS file called COMMAND.COM in memory. COMMAND.COM looks for the AUTOEXEC.BAT file and follows the instructions in the file (if there is one). When COMMAND.COM is being loaded into memory, your monitor displays this message:

```
Starting MS-DOS. . .
```

When DOS is loaded, a C prompt should be displayed. Due to a specific command in the AUTOEXEC.BAT file, the C prompt can have many different appearances, but it usually looks like this:

```
C:\>
```

■ **Note:** You can set up your computer to begin running a program immediately after booting, and then you do not see the C prompt at all.

▶ Your Turn

Before practicing the cold boot, turn your computer off and wait ten seconds so that the computer chips have time to "relax." Turning a computer off and right back on again can blow the circuitry in a computer chip.

1 Turn on all your computer peripherals (monitor, printer, modem, and so on).

2 Turn on the system itself and listen for a beep. Most computers beep when the POST has been successfully completed.

3 Watch for the light to come on in drive A. This means that the PC is looking for the DOS program in the drive.

Getting Acquainted with Your PC: Booting the PC

If you have problems... If drive A is not empty, DOS displays this message:

```
Non-system disk or disk error.
Replace and strike any key when ready.
```

Remove the disk in drive A and press any key.

4 Watch for the light to come on in drive C.

5 Look for the C prompt when DOS is loaded.

Performing a Warm Boot

A *warm boot* is performed when the computer is already turned on and DOS is restarted. A warm boot can be performed by pressing Ctrl+Alt+Del or by pressing the Reset button if your PC has one. Because the computer itself is not restarted, the POST is not performed, but the PC looks for DOS on drive A and then drive C. The CONFIG.SYS file and the AUTOEXEC.BAT file are read into memory again. When you have made changes to either of these files, you must perform a warm boot for the changes to become effective.

A warm boot is easier on the computer because the power isn't shut off as it is in a cold boot. The drive doesn't stop and then start, and the chips don't cool and heat up; this saves wear and tear on the system. A warm boot is preferred when the system locks up. Sometimes a warm boot will not restart the computer, however, and you must turn it off and then back on again.

✖ Warning: A warm boot clears the computer's memory, so it is not a good idea to perform a warm boot when information is still in memory that has never been saved. Unless your computer is locked up, you should not do a warm boot unless you are at the DOS prompt.

▶ **Your Turn**

Your computer should still be on. Practice the warm boot by following these steps:

1 Press Ctrl+Alt+Del. Notice that the POST is not performed.

2 Watch for the light to come on in drive A.

3 Watch for the light to come on in drive C.

4 Turn your computer off and wait ten seconds.

5 Unplug the keyboard.

6 Start the computer and, during the POST, look for an error message indicating that there is a problem with the keyboard.

7 Turn off the PC and wait ten seconds.

8 Plug in the keyboard.

9 Start the computer again.

Interrupting the Booting Process

Remember that during the booting process DOS loads the instructions in the CONFIG.SYS file and the AUTOEXEC.BAT file. If your system is not working properly and you suspect that the problem could be due to faulty instructions in either or both of these files, you can bypass both files when you boot. Alternatively, you can make DOS prompt you before it executes each command in the CONFIG.SYS and then you can choose to execute all or none of the commands in the AUTOEXEC.BAT files.

To bypass both files, warm boot the PC. When DOS begins to load, press the F5 key or press and hold down the Shift key.

When you bypass these two files, your computer probably will not operate the way it did before, but the problem you were having may be solved. If this is the case, you have positive proof that something in either the AUTOEXEC.BAT file or the CONFIG.SYS file is causing the problem.

If you want to test the commands in the CONFIG.SYS file one at a time, warm boot the PC and press F8 when DOS begins to load.

■ **Tip:** During the line-by-line confirmation process, you can press Esc to process all the rest of the lines in the file without prompting, or you can press F5 to bypass all the remaining lines in the file.

Pressing F8 causes DOS to display each line in the CONFIG.SYS file and to wait for you to confirm the use of the line with **y** for Yes or **n** for No. When DOS has displayed all the commands in the CONFIG.SYS file, it asks you if you want to process the AUTOEXEC.BAT file. If you respond with **y** for Yes, all the commands in the AUTOEXEC.BAT file are executed.

▶ Your Turn

Even though you may not have any problems with your system, practice bypassing the AUTOEXEC.BAT and the CONFIG.SYS files with this exercise:

1 Press Ctrl+Alt+Del.

2 When you see `Starting MS-DOS. . .` on your monitor, press F5. DOS responds with this message:

   `MS-DOS is bypassing your CONFIG.SYS and AUTOEXEC.BAT files.`

3 Press Ctrl+Alt+Del.

4 When you see `Starting MS-DOS. . .` on your monitor, press F8. DOS then displays the first line in the CONFIG.SYS file.

5 Type **y** for each command that is displayed in the CONFIG.SYS file.

6 Type **y** to process the AUTOEXEC.BAT file.

Turning Off the System

There is no correct order for turning off a system. The only recommendation is that you should not turn off the system unit when a disk drive is being accessed. In some cases, however, even this recommendation must be disregarded—if a disk drive seems to be hung up and the PC will not stop reading the disk, for example. If you turn off the system unit when data is being written to disk, you lose data.

In most cases, it is better not to turn off the system unit while a file is printing. The file may not finish printing.

▶ Your Turn

Follow these steps to turn off your computer:

1. Make sure that no disk drive lights are on.
2. Turn off all devices in any order.

Lesson Summary

To	Do this
Turn on your PC	Turn on all the peripherals first and then turn on the system unit.
Adjust the monitor	Adjust the brightness and contrast controls.
Cold boot the PC	Turn on the system.
Warm boot the PC	Press Ctrl+Alt+Del or press the Reset button.
Bypass the loading of AUTOEXEC.BAT and CONFIG.SYS	Perform a cold or warm boot. When you see the message `Starting MS-DOS. . .`, press F5.
Execute the commands one line at a time in the CONFIG.SYS file	Perform a cold or warm boot. When you see the message `Starting MS-DOS. . .`, press F8.
Turn the system off	Make sure that the disk drive is not being accessed. Turn the power off on all devices.

If You Want to Stop Now

If you want to stop now, you are ready to do so; your system should be turned off. If you did not do the last Your Turn, go back and follow the steps to turn off your computer.

From Here

After working with the basics, you should be ready to roll up your sleeves and get into more hands-on activities with DOS. The next lesson introduces the command line, the DOS Shell, and the Help feature.

Taking a Closer Look at DOS

SURESTEPS LESSON 2

In this lesson, you learn how to do the following:

- Start and exit the DOS Shell
- Use the DOS Shell
- Use the DOS Command Prompt
- Access Help in the DOS Shell
- Access Help at the DOS prompt

Lesson time:
30–45 minutes

DOS has two user interfaces—one is the command line and the other is the DOS Shell. Until DOS 4 was introduced, the only interface with DOS was the command line. Users had to memorize dozens of DOS commands with multiple variations as well as the proper syntax for each command and variation.

The experienced users who go back to earlier versions of DOS may feel that the DOS commands are second nature to them. Fortunately, DOS still performs its tasks from the command line. Less experienced users may prefer the DOS Shell interface, however, because it is menu-driven and therefore easier to use.

Starting and Exiting the DOS Shell

To start the DOS Shell if you are using a color monitor, simply type **dosshell** at the DOS prompt and press Enter. If you are using a monochrome monitor, type **dosshell/b** at the DOS prompt and press Enter.

To exit the DOS Shell, press Alt+F4 or F3. You then return to the DOS prompt.

▶ Your Turn

If you have not already done so, turn on the PC and wait for DOS to load. If the C prompt is not displayed, execute whatever keystrokes are necessary to return to the C prompt. Then follow these steps:

1 Type **dosshell** (or **dosshell/b**) and then press Enter. A screen appears, displaying the computer's directory tree and files. The directory tree and files displayed on your screen will not match the figure.

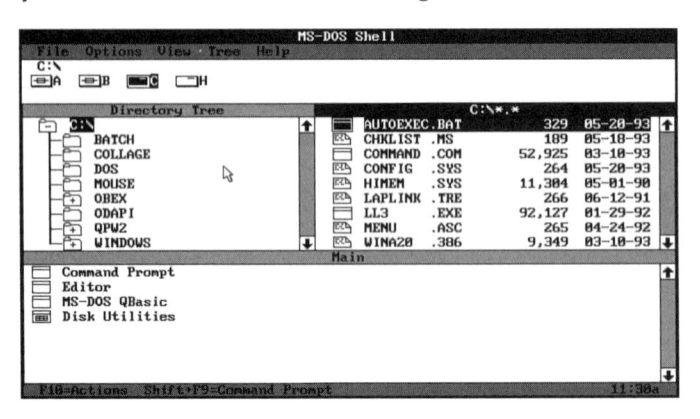

■ **Note:** Your DOS Shell may be in text mode. The figure shows the DOS Shell in graphics mode. Changing the view is discussed in detail later in this lesson.

2 Press Alt+F4. You should see the C prompt on-screen again.

Using the DOS Shell

Using the DOS Shell is the primary focus of this book. It is the interface that users find easier because it uses the

32   DOS 6 SureSteps

Graphical User Interface (GUI). The *GUI* (pronounced "gooey") uses icons (pictures) and visual effects as well as menus to guide the user.

Learning the Parts of the DOS Shell

The DOS Shell is composed of several areas. The title bar, displaying MS-DOS Shell, is at the top of the screen. Under the title bar is the menu bar which has these options—**File, Options, View, Tree,** and **Help.**

Directly below the File option on the menu bar, the DOS Shell displays the current drive and directory. On the next line is the list of drives that are available on your system. The current drive letter and icon are highlighted.

Below the drives are two boxes. The box on the left shows the directory tree (the organization of the disk). If the term *directory* is unfamiliar to you, just think of a directory as a separate holding area for files—like a file drawer in a filing cabinet. (Lesson 4 deals with directories in great detail.) The File List box on the right shows all the files in the current directory. (A *file* contains either a program or work that you have done, such as a letter or a spreadsheet.)

Below the two boxes is the Program List which may have the Main group displayed or the Disk Utilities group displayed. Notice that the title bar for the Program List tells you whether the Main group or the Disk Utilities group is displayed.

By default, the Main group includes Command Prompt, MS-DOS Editor, MS-DOS QBasic, and Disk Utilities. The user can add other options to the group as well. The Disk Utilities group may include Main, Disk Copy, MS Anti-Virus, Backup Fixed Disk, Restore Fixed Disk, Quick Format, Format, and Undelete. The user can add other options to this group also. All the default commands and utilities (except MS-DOS QBasic) are discussed in detail in later lessons.

■ **Note:** The list of items in the Disk Utilities group reflects the programs you installed when you installed DOS 6.

At the bottom of the screen, below the Program List, is the status bar which displays messages from the DOS Shell, shortcut keys, and the current time.

Taking a Closer Look at DOS: Using the DOS Shell

▶ Your Turn

Practice using the DOS Shell by following these steps:

1 Start the DOS Shell again. This screen appears:

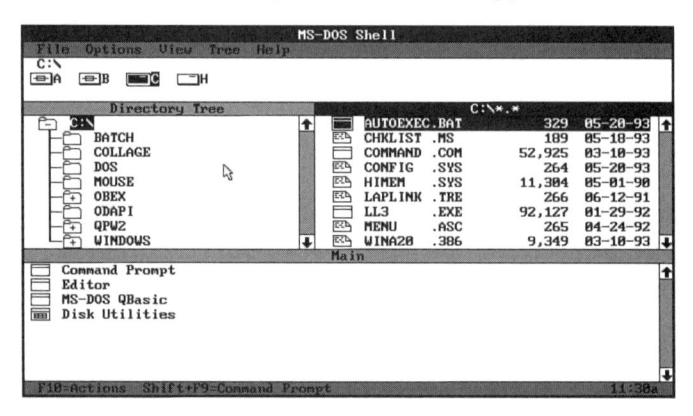

```
                        MS-DOS Shell
File  Options  View  Tree  Help
C:\
 A    B    C    H
      Directory Tree                    C:\*.*
  C:\                          AUTOEXEC.BAT    329   05-20-93
    BATCH                      CHKLIST  .MS    189   05-18-93
    COLLAGE                    COMMAND  .COM 52,925  03-10-93
    DOS                        CONFIG   .SYS    264  05-20-93
    MOUSE                      HIMEM    .SYS 11,304  05-01-90
    OBEX                       LAPLINK  .TRE    266  06-12-91
    ODAPI                      LL3      .EXE 92,127  01-29-92
    QPW2                       MENU     .ASC    265  04-24-92
    WINDOWS                    WINA20   .386  9,349  03-10-93
                              Main
    Command Prompt
    Editor
    MS-DOS QBasic
    Disk Utilities

F10=Actions  Shift+F9=Command Prompt                    11:30a
```

2 Notice the Directory Tree box on the left and the File List box on the right.

3 Notice the Program List at the bottom of the screen. That looks like this figure if it has the Main group displayed:

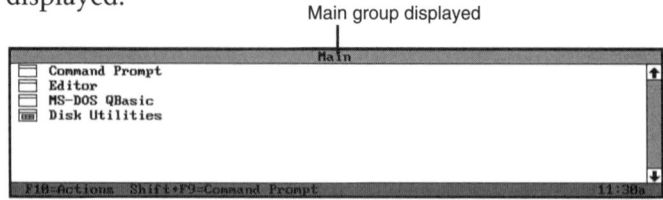

Main group displayed

```
                              Main
    Command Prompt
    Editor
    MS-DOS QBasic
    Disk Utilities


F10=Actions  Shift+F9=Command Prompt                    11:30a
```

If the Disk Utilities group is displayed, the Program List looks similar to this figure:

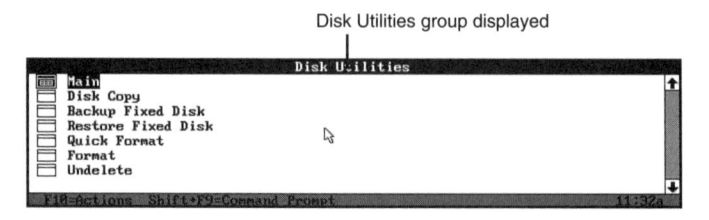

Disk Utilities group displayed

```
                         Disk Utilities
    Main
    Disk Copy
    Backup Fixed Disk
    Restore Fixed Disk
    Quick Format
    Format
    Undelete

F10=Actions  Shift+F9=Command Prompt                    11:32a
```

34 DOS 6 SureSteps

Moving Around in the DOS Shell

To move from one area of the DOS Shell to another, use the Tab key or click the left mouse button in the desired area. If you press the Tab key repeatedly, it moves from the row that lists the drives to the left box, to the right box, and finally to the Program List. Pressing Shift+Tab moves the cursor in the opposite direction.

You can use the up and down arrows or the Pg Up and Pg Dn keys to move the cursor up and down in either of the boxes, in the Program List, and in pull-down menus. The left and right arrows can be used to move from drive to drive on the line that lists the drives or from menu option to menu option in the menu bar.

Notice in the figure that the two boxes in the middle of the screen have scroll bars.

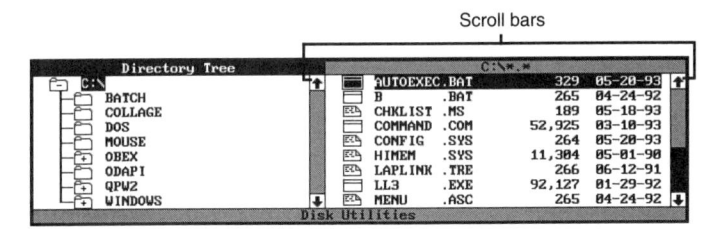

Scroll bars

If your computer has a mouse, you can use the scroll bars in either box to scroll a list that is too long to display completely in the box. To scroll up or down, click the left mouse button repeatedly on the arrow at the top or bottom of the bar. You also can drag the box in the scroll bar to scroll in larger increments than line by line.

▶ Your Turn

Practice moving around the DOS Shell by using these keystrokes:

1 If you have exited the DOS Shell, start it again.

2 Insert the SureSteps disk in drive A or B, whichever is appropriate.

3 Press the Tab key several times until you have moved to each area of the DOS Shell and returned to the line that lists the drives.

4 Using the left arrow, move the cursor to the drive that holds the SureSteps disk and then press Enter. Notice that DOS reads the drive and the information in the boxes changes.

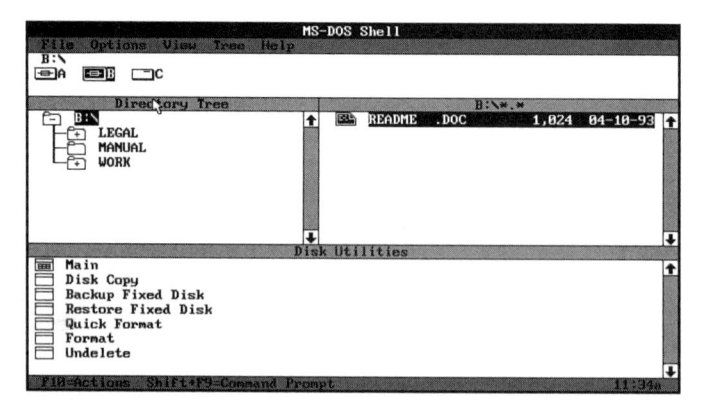

5 Press Tab. You should be in the Directory Tree box.

6 Press the down arrow to move to the MANUAL directory. Notice that the list of files has changed in the right box.

7 Press Tab. You should be in the right box.

8 Use the down arrow to move the cursor to the file called CHAP3.ASC.

9 Press Tab. You should be in the Program List.

10 Move the cursor to Main or Disk Utilities (whichever is displayed) and then press Enter. You then see the new group.

11 Press Enter to return to the previous group.

▶ On Your Own

If you have a mouse, continue by double-clicking the drive C icon. Notice the changes in the Directory Tree and File List boxes. Then click the first directory listed in the Directory Tree box. Notice the changes in the File List box.

Click the second directory listed in the Directory Tree box. Notice the changes in the File List box. Click a file name in the right box. Notice how the file looks when it is selected.

Double-click Main or Disk Utilities (whichever is displayed in the Program List) to display the group options. Double-click Main or Disk Utilities (whichever is now displayed in the Program List) to display the group options. Click the drive icon for the drive that holds the SureSteps disk.

■ **Tip:** If you insert a different disk in a floppy drive that has already been read by the DOS Shell, you must force DOS to read the new disk; otherwise, DOS simply displays the contents of the disk you removed. To force DOS to read the new disk, select the drive icon and press Enter or double-click the drive icon.

Using the DOS Shell Menu

To access a menu option, press Alt or F10, move the cursor to the option, and then press Enter. Alternatively, you can access the menu and type the hot key for an option. (The *hot key*, usually the first character, is emphasized on-screen with an underline or a highlighted character.) If you are using a mouse, you can click the left mouse button on the desired menu option. Choosing an option from the menu displays a pull-down menu with more options.

▶ Your Turn

To explore the menu options, follow these steps:

1 Move the cursor to the File List box on the right and press Alt.

2 Type **f** to select the File option.

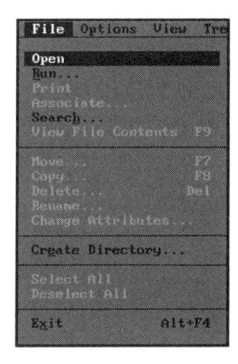

Taking a Closer Look at DOS: Using the DOS Shell

3 Press the right arrow to see the Options pull-down menu.

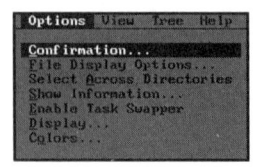

```
Options  View  Tree  Help
Confirmation...
File Display Options...
Select Across Directories
Show Information...
Enable Task Swapper
Display...
Colors...
```

4 Press the right arrow to see the View pull-down menu.

5 Press the right arrow to see the Tree pull-down menu.

6 Press the right arrow to see the Help pull-down menu.

7 Press the right arrow to return to the File pull-down menu.

8 Press Esc.

Learning More about Menus and Dialog Boxes

Some menu options on the pull-down menus have keyboard shortcuts listed beside them. Menu options that are followed by an ellipsis (. . .) display a dialog box when they are chosen. *Dialog boxes* are special menus that can have buttons, text boxes, and check boxes. You can use the Tab key to move around in a dialog box.

A bullet in front of a menu option indicates that option is currently selected or active. Sometimes certain options are not available when a menu is pulled down. If you do not have a file selected, for example, the Copy option is not available on the File pull-down menu. If you are using a color monitor, options that are not available are dimmed. If you are using a monochrome monitor, options that are not available do not have a hot key or they are absent from the menu.

▶ Your Turn

Follow these steps to become familiar with some of the different types of menus and their features.

1 Pull down the Options menu and choose File Display Options. Because this option is followed by an ellipsis, a dialog box opens.

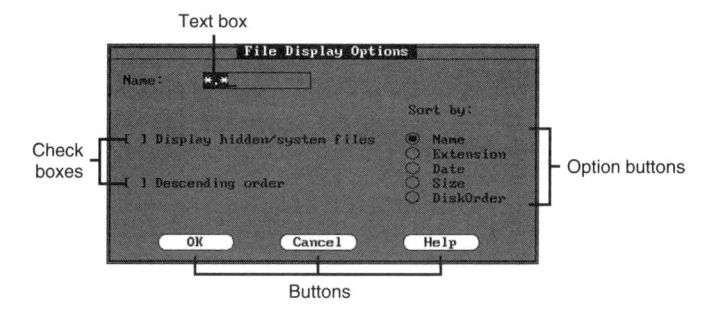

[Diagram: File Display Options dialog box with labels — Text box (Name field), Check boxes (Display hidden/system files, Descending order), Option buttons (Sort by: Name, Extension, Date, Size, DiskOrder), and Buttons (OK, Cancel, Help).]

2 Select the Name text box and type ***.exe**.

3 Select either of the check boxes on the left. To select a check box, move the cursor to the box and press the spacebar.

4 Select any of the five option buttons on the right.

5 Choose Cancel to leave this dialog box without executing any of the changes you made.

6 Pull down the Options menu and choose Select Across Directories if it is not already selected. A bullet indicates that it is selected.

7 Pull down the Option menu again. The bullet to the left of Select Across directories indicates that this option is selected.

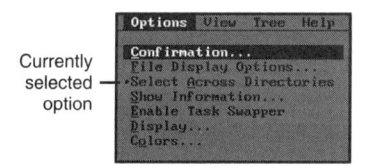

[Diagram: Options menu showing Confirmation..., File Display Options..., •Select Across Directories, Show Information..., Enable Task Swapper, Display..., Colors... — with "Currently selected option" label pointing to Select Across Directories.]

■ **Note:** When default text is highlighted in a text box, it will be replaced with new text that is typed. If you move the cursor, the highlighting is removed and the original text will remain unless you press Backspace or Del.

8 Click anywhere outside the menu or press Esc to exit the menu.

Changing the Look of the DOS Shell

The DOS Shell can be displayed in text mode or graphic mode. The text mode is the default. The graphic mode looks more like a Windows application. After you have selected a mode, it becomes the default mode; that is, if you change to the graphic mode, every time you start the DOS Shell, it is in the graphic mode. To change the Screen Display mode of the DOS Shell, take these steps:

1 Pull down the **Options** menu and choose **Display**. DOS displays a dialog box showing all the possible modes for your monitor.

2 Select the desired mode.

3 Choose OK to change the mode.

▶ Your Turn

Experiment with all the modes by following these steps:

1 Pull down the **Options** menu and choose **Display**. You then see a screen similar to this:

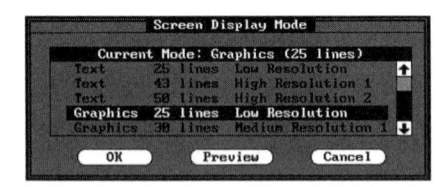

```
               Screen Display Mode
          Current Mode: Graphics (25 lines)
     Text       25 lines  Low Resolution
     Text       43 lines  High Resolution 1
     Text       50 lines  High Resolution 2
     Graphics   25 lines  Low Resolution
     Graphics   30 lines  Medium Resolution 1
        OK         Preview        Cancel
```

2 Highlight a text option by moving the cursor to the option or clicking the option.

3 Choose Preview to see what the display option looks like.

4 Highlight a graphics option.

5 Choose Preview.

6 Experiment with other options that are available.

7 Highlight the display option that you like best.

8 Choose OK.

Selecting a Different View

DOS allows you to select the parts of the DOS Shell that you want to view. You can change to the following views:

- Single File List
- Dual File List
- All Files
- Program/File Lists (the default view)
- Program List

To change the view of the DOS Shell, take these actions:

1 Pull down the View menu.

2 Select the desired view.

▶ Your Turn

Change the view of the DOS Shell with these steps:

1 Pull down the View menu and choose Single File List. You then see a screen similar to the following figure:

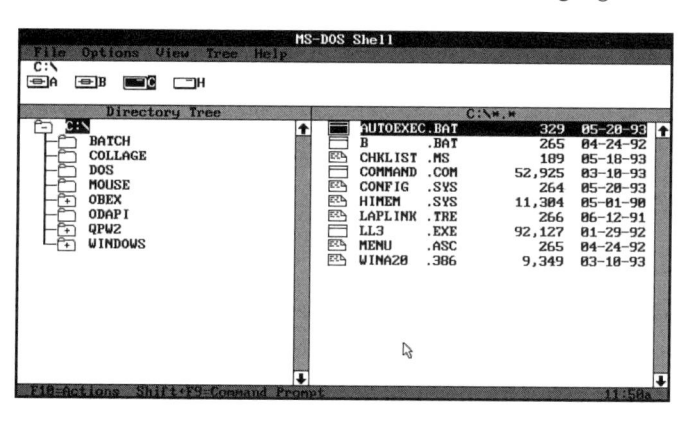

Reminder: The directories and files on your computer will be different.

2 Pull down the View menu and choose Dual File List.

3 Press Tab three times.

Taking a Closer Look at DOS: Using the DOS Shell

4 Move the cursor to the icon for drive C and then press Enter. (Notice that the upper half of the screen shows files in the floppy drive and the lower half shows files in drive C.)

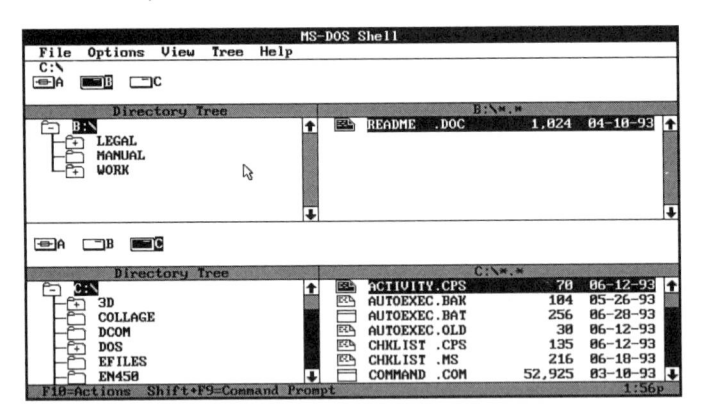

▶ **On Your Own**

There are three other view modes you can choose. Choose each one to see how they differ, and then return to the Program/File List mode.

Using the Command Prompt

■ **Note:** Adding commands to groups in the Program List is an advanced topic not covered in this book.

Unless you add more DOS commands to groups in the Program List, some DOS commands cannot be performed from the DOS Shell. The commands must be issued at the DOS prompt. If you are using the DOS Shell, you can exit to the DOS prompt by displaying the Main group in the Program List and selecting Command Prompt. The DOS prompt reflects the drive and directory that was selected in the DOS Shell. If the drive A icon and the root directory are selected in the DOS Shell, the DOS prompt is A:\>.

After you arrive at the DOS prompt, you can enter the desired commands. If you want to return to the DOS Shell, type **exit** and then press Enter.

▶ Your Turn

Practice going to the DOS prompt from the DOS Shell by using these steps:

1. Select the drive C icon.

2. Display the Main group in the Program List if it is not already displayed.

3. Select Command Prompt. DOS exits the DOS Shell and displays the Command Prompt.

4. Type **dir** and then press Enter. A list of files appears.

5. Type **dir/w** and then press Enter. DOS displays the same list of files in a wide format.

6. Type **cls** and then press Enter. The screen clears.

7. Type **ver** and then press Enter. Your screen should display the message MS-DOS Version 6.00.

■ **Note:** If you know you want to use the DOS prompt to enter several commands after you have booted the PC, don't start the DOS Shell and then go to the Command Prompt. This would be like going from Kentucky to Indiana by way of Atlanta!

Using Help

DOS 6 has a very extensive Help system. Because the *User's Guide* is very brief, it is obvious that Microsoft expects the user to rely heavily on the Help system.

DOS has three levels of Help. Listed in order of their completeness, they are the following:

- Command Prompt Syntax Help
- DOS Shell Help
- DOS Prompt Help

Each level of Help has its own advantage. Command Prompt Syntax Help gives immediate information on two basic subjects—what the command does and how to type the command properly. DOS Shell Help is more visual and covers broader topics. Command Prompt Help contains the most complete information, and the information can be printed.

Using Command Prompt Syntax Help

Regardless of whether you have arrived at the DOS prompt by booting DOS or through the DOS Shell, the Command Prompt Syntax Help feature works the same. If you are uncertain of a command's proper *syntax*—that is, the exact way it should be typed—you can see a brief description of the command's syntax by typing the command followed by /? at the DOS prompt. To see the proper syntax of the COPY command, for example, type **copy/?**.

▶ Your Turn

Display the DOS prompt by whatever method you choose, and then follow these steps to practice using Command Prompt Syntax Help. The commands for which you display Help information in this exercise are explained fully in Lesson 5.

1 Type **copy/?** and then press Enter. A screen containing the following Help information appears:

```
B:\>c:

C:\>copy/?
Copies one or more files to another location.

COPY [/A | /B] source [/A | /B] [+ source [/A | /B] [+ ...]] [destination
 [/A | /B]] [/V]

  source       Specifies the file or files to be copied.
  /A           Indicates an ASCII text file.
  /B           Indicates a binary file.
  destination  Specifies the directory and/or filename for the new file(s).
  /V           Verifies that new files are written correctly.

To append files, specify a single file for destination, but multiple files
for source (using wildcards or file1+file2+file3 format).

C:\>
```

2 Type **del/?** and then press Enter.

3 Type **ren/?** and then press Enter.

Using Help in the DOS Shell

When you are using the DOS Shell, you can access Help in several different ways—with the pull-down menu, by pressing F1, or by selecting a Help button in a dialog box. If you use the menu, you can select the Help topic that you want. If you press F1, DOS displays the Help topic that corresponds to the task that you are doing; this is called *context-sensitive Help*. If you select a Help button, DOS displays information about the current dialog box.

Accessing Help from the Menu

To access Help from the menu, choose the **Help** pull-down menu. Choose any of the following options to get Help:

- Index
- Keyboard
- Shell Basics
- Commands
- Procedures
- Using Help

When you choose the Index option, DOS presents several Help topics—the same topics that are listed individually in the pull-down menu. It is faster to select the topic from the Help pull-down menu than to choose Index and then select the topic.

▶ Your Turn

Start the DOS Shell and practice using Help by following these steps:

1 Pull down the **Help** menu and choose **Index**. This screen appears:

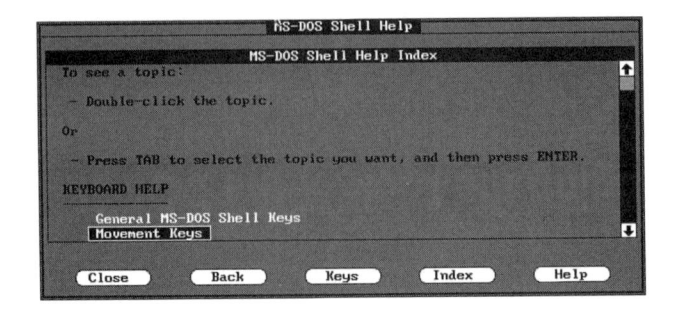

2 Press Pg Dn.

3 Press Tab three times to select the topic Program List keys and then press Enter. This screen displays:

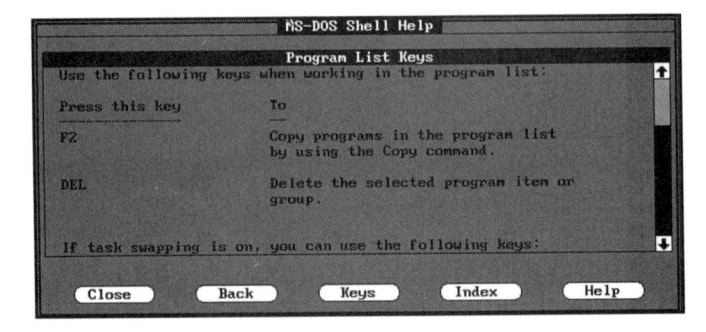

4 After reading the screen, press Esc.

Accessing Help with F1

By pressing F1, you can display immediate Help about the current context. If you choose Copy from the File pull-down menu and then press F1, for example, DOS displays Help concerning copying files.

▶ Your Turn

Try these steps to see how F1 works:

1 Move the cursor to the File List box on the right and then press F1. This screen appears:

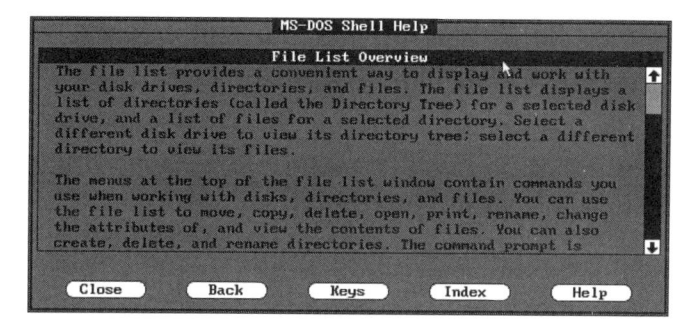

2 Press Tab to move to the Close button and then press Enter.

3 Move the cursor to the Program List box and then press F1 to display Help about the Program List.

4 Press Tab to move the cursor to the Close button and then press Enter.

Navigating a Help Screen

To scroll the information in a Help screen line by line, use the up or down arrow or click the mouse on the arrows at either end of the scroll bar. To move the information one screen at a time, use the Pg Up and Pg Dn keys or use the mouse to drag the scroll box.

Each button displayed at the bottom of a Help screen performs a specific task.

- The Index button displays the Help Index from which you can select another topic.
- The Back button returns to the previous topic.
- The Keys button displays Help on using the keyboard.
- The Help button gives general information about using Help.
- The Close button exits the Help feature.

■ **Tip:** You also can press Esc to exit Help.

Taking a Closer Look at DOS: Using Help

▶ Your Turn

To become comfortable with moving around on the Help screens and using the buttons, try these steps:

1 Pull down the **Help** menu and choose Index.

2 Press the down arrow six times.

3 Press the up arrow six times.

4 Press Pg Dn five times. This takes you to the last screen on this topic. Notice that the last screen is marked with a bullet.

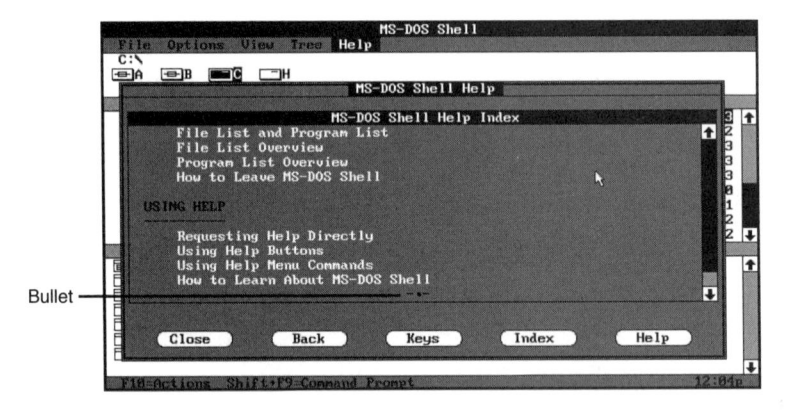

5 Press Pg Up three times and then press Esc.

▶ On Your Own

Pull down the Help menu again and choose Commands to display the Help screen for commands. Press Tab three times. This should move the cursor to the Keys button. Press Enter to display Keyboard Help. Press Shift+Tab to move to the Back button and then press Enter. Notice that you have returned to Commands Help. Press Shift+Tab to move to the Close button and then press Enter.

▶ On Your Own

If you have a mouse, practice using it by pulling down the Help menu and choosing Index. Click the arrow at the bottom of the scroll bar several times to scroll the Help information. Then click the arrow at the top of the scroll bar several times to scroll the Help information in the other direction. Drag the scroll box to scroll the Help information. Click or drag until you return to the top of the first Help screen. Double-click the topic Movement Keys to display a new Help topic and then click the Back button. Notice that you have returned to MS-DOS Shell Help Index. Click the Help button. Click the Back button and then click the Close button to exit Help.

Using Help in Dialog Boxes

Most dialog boxes have a Help button which, when selected, displays information about the command in progress or the dialog box itself. If the dialog box does not have a Help button, you can press F1 to display the Help information.

▶ Your Turn

To practice using Help in dialog boxes, follow these steps:

1 Pull down the Options menu and choose Confirmation to display this dialog box:

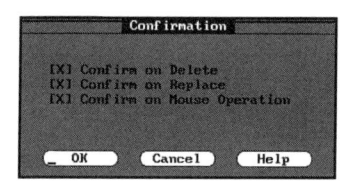

```
        ┌─────── Confirmation ───────┐
        │                            │
        │  [X] Confirm on Delete     │
        │  [X] Confirm on Replace    │
        │  [X] Confirm on Mouse Operation │
        │                            │
        │   ( OK )  ( Cancel ) ( Help ) │
        └────────────────────────────┘
```

2 Choose the Help button to display Help about the Confirmation options.

3 Choose Close to exit Help.

Taking a Closer Look at DOS: Using Help

4 Choose Cancel to exit the Confirmation dialog box.

5 Pull down the File menu and then choose **Run** to display a dialog box.

6 Press F1 to display Help information on running a file.

7 Choose Close to exit Help.

8 Choose Cancel to exit the dialog box.

Using Help at the DOS Prompt

■ **Tip:** When the Command Reference is displayed, you can move quickly to a command by typing the first letter of the command. If several commands begin with the same letter as the command you want, continue typing the first letter until the desired command is highlighted.

If you are at the DOS prompt and you want to display Help information for any command, type **help**, followed by the command. To see information on the COPY command, for example, type **help copy**. To select a Help topic from a list of commands, type **help** and then use the mouse to click on the desired command or use the cursor keys to move to the desired command and then press Enter.

▶ Your Turn

Try your hand at selecting a Help topic by following these steps:

1 Return to the DOS prompt.

2 Type **help** and then press Enter to display the Help Command Reference shown here:

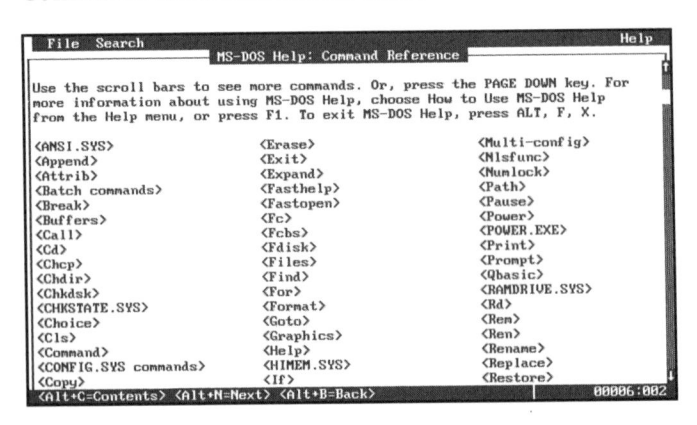

```
┌─File  Search─────────────────────────────────────────────────────Help─┐
│                     ─MS-DOS Help: Command Reference─                   │
│ Use the scroll bars to see more commands. Or, press the PAGE DOWN key. For │
│ more information about using MS-DOS Help, choose How to Use MS-DOS Help │
│ from the Help menu, or press F1. To exit MS-DOS Help, press ALT, F, X. │
│                                                                        │
│  <ANSI.SYS>              <Erase>                <Multi-config>         │
│  <Append>                <Exit>                 <Nlsfunc>              │
│  <Attrib>                <Expand>               <Numlock>              │
│  <Batch commands>        <Fasthelp>             <Path>                 │
│  <Break>                 <Fastopen>             <Pause>                │
│  <Buffers>               <Fc>                   <Power>                │
│  <Call>                  <Fcbs>                 <POWER.EXE>            │
│  <Cd>                    <Fdisk>                <Print>                │
│  <Chcp>                  <Files>                <Prompt>               │
│  <Chdir>                 <Find>                 <Qbasic>               │
│  <Chkdsk>                <For>                  <RAMDRIVE.SYS>         │
│  <CHKSTATE.SYS>          <Format>               <Rd>                   │
│  <Choice>                <Goto>                 <Rem>                  │
│  <Cls>                   <Graphics>             <Ren>                  │
│  <Command>               <Help>                 <Rename>               │
│  <CONFIG.SYS commands>   <HIMEM.SYS>            <Replace>              │
│  <Copy>                  <If>                   <Restore>              │
│<Alt+C=Contents> <Alt+N=Next> <Alt+B=Back>                    00006:002 │
└────────────────────────────────────────────────────────────────────────┘
```

If you have problems...	Other programs may use the HELP command to display Help information. If the DOS Command Reference does not appear when you enter the HELP command, change to the DOS directory by typing **CD\DOS** and then pressing Enter. Then enter the HELP command again.

3 Type **e** three times to select the third command that begins with *e* and then press Enter.

4 Pull down the File menu and choose Exit.

Getting More Detailed Help

The information displayed by Help at the DOS prompt is more detailed than the information displayed by the DOS Shell. Most commands have three sections of information—Syntax, Notes, and Examples.

All Help screens open to the Syntax section. This section tells you what the command does and how to type the command correctly. If the command has variations, called *parameters* and *switches*, these also are listed and explained. The Notes section may contain discussions of special circumstances, possible error messages, parameter limitations, and so on. The Examples section gives several examples of the command and explains what each example does.

To display the Notes or Examples section, click Notes or Examples. (If you are using a keyboard, make sure that the cursor is on the top line of the Help screen. Move the cursor to the name of the desired section either by pressing Tab or using the left or right arrows, and then press Enter.)

▶ **Your Turn**

These steps walk you through the process of displaying the different sections of the Help information:

1 Type **help copy** and then press Enter. This screen appears:

Taking a Closer Look at DOS: Using Help

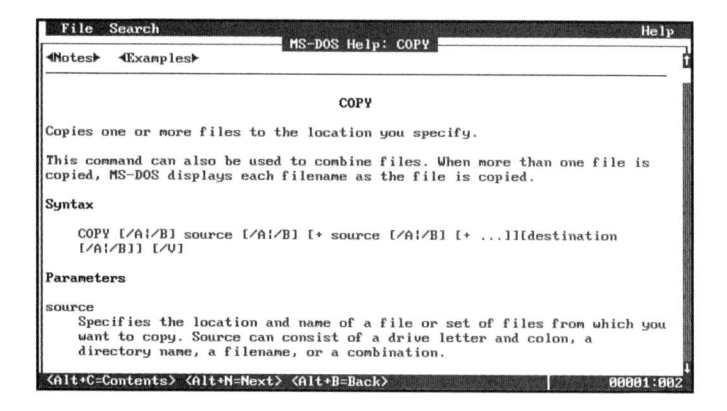

```
 File  Search                                          Help
               MS-DOS Help: COPY
 ◄Notes► ◄Examples►

                           COPY
 Copies one or more files to the location you specify.

 This command can also be used to combine files. When more than one file is
 copied, MS-DOS displays each filename as the file is copied.

 Syntax

     COPY [/A|/B] source [/A|/B] [+ source [/A|/B] [+ ...]][destination
     [/A|/B]] [/V]

 Parameters

 source
     Specifies the location and name of a file or set of files from which you
     want to copy. Source can consist of a drive letter and colon, a
     directory name, a filename, or a combination.

 <Alt+C=Contents> <Alt+N=Next> <Alt+B=Back>                      00001:002
```

2 Select Notes. Read the information displayed on-screen.

3 Select Examples. Read the information displayed on-screen.

4 Pull down the File menu and then choose Exit to leave the Help feature and return to the DOS prompt.

Moving Around

To scroll the information in a Help screen line by line, use the up or down arrow or click the mouse on the arrows at either end of the scroll bars. To move the information a screen at a time, use the Pg Up and Pg Dn keys or use the mouse to drag the scroll box.

To move to the Help screen for the next command listed in the Command Reference, press or click Alt+N. To move to the Help screen for a command that is not listed next, press or click Alt+C to redisplay the list of commands. Then select the desired command from the list. If you display a Help screen for a different command, you can return to the previous Help screen by pressing or clicking Alt+B.

▶ Your Turn

Try these steps to practice scrolling:

1 Type **help copy** and then press Enter to display the Help information for the COPY command.

2 Press the down arrow until you reach the end of the information.

3 Press the up arrow until you return to the top of the Help screen.

4 Press Pg Dn.

5 Press Pg Up.

6 Pull down the File menu and then choose Exit.

▶ On Your Own

If you have a mouse, display the Help screen on the COPY command and practice using the scroll bars.

Using the Menu to Print and Search

Because you have already learned to use the menu in the DOS Shell, you should not have any problems using the menu in the DOS Prompt Help screens. You probably have already noticed that this menu has only two options—File and Search.

The File pull-down menu has two options—Print and Exit. You are already familiar with the Exit option. The Print option prints the section of Help that is currently displayed (Syntax, Notes, or Examples). The output can be sent to a file or a printer. If you send the output to a file, you must give the file a name.

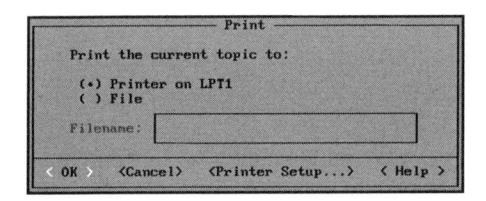

```
┌─────────────── Print ───────────────┐
│ Print the current topic to:         │
│                                     │
│   (•) Printer on LPT1               │
│   ( ) File                          │
│                                     │
│   Filename:                         │
│                                     │
│  < OK >  <Cancel>  <Printer Setup...>  < Help > │
└─────────────────────────────────────┘
```

■ **Note:** If you have difficulty printing, you may have to run the program called PRINT.EXE.

■ **Tip:** To create your own printed documentation supplement, use the print option to send all the Help sections of a command (Syntax, Notes, and Examples) to a file. Revise the file and add your own notes.

Taking a Closer Look at DOS: Using Help

The Search pull-down menu also has two options—Find and Repeat Last Find. To find a particular word or phrase that is used in any Help information screen, follow these steps:

1. Pull down the Search menu and then choose Find to display a dialog box.

2. In the dialog box, type the desired text.

3. Select Match Upper/Lowercase and Whole Word if appropriate.

   (When you select Match Upper/Lowercase, Help looks for text that exactly matches the capitalization that you have used. When you select Whole Word, Help doesn't find the text that you have typed unless it is a complete word.

4. Choose OK.

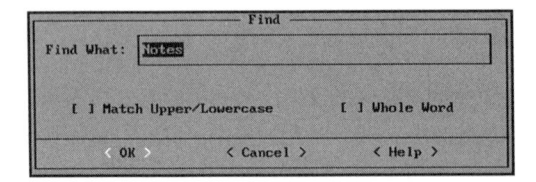

While Help is searching for the text, the status line displays the message Searching - press Esc to cancel. If DOS finds the text quickly, the message appears on-screen too briefly to be seen. If you want to cancel the search, press Esc.

To search for the next occurrence of the text that you entered, press F3 or pull down the Search menu and choose Repeat Last Find. If there is no other occurrence of the word or phrase, DOS remains on the last occurrence that was found.

If you type a word or phrase that cannot be found, DOS indicates that it cannot find a match.

▶ Your Turn

You should still have the DOS prompt displayed. Follow these steps to practice using the Search feature:

1 Type **help** and then press Enter to display the Help screen.

2 Pull down the Search menu and choose Find to display this dialog box:

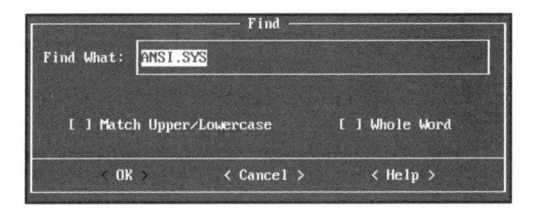

3 Type **device driver** and then press Enter.

4 Press F3 and the MS-DOS Help: Device Driver screen appears.

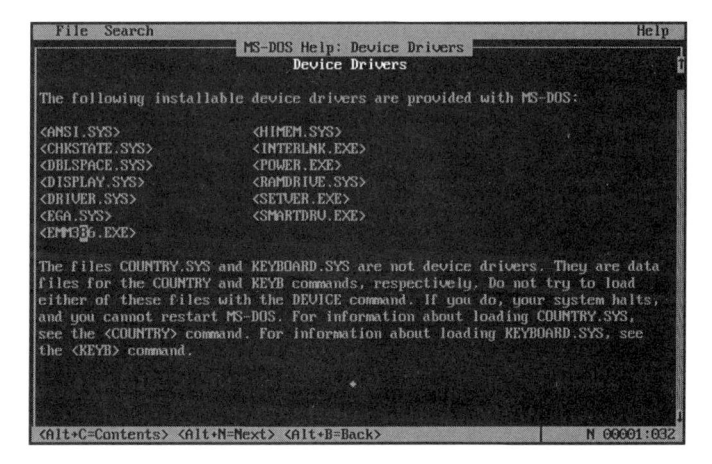

5 Press Alt+B twice to return to the previous Help screen.

6 Pull down the File menu and choose Exit.

Displaying Cross References

Cross references for related topics are found in Help topics that are displayed from either the command line or the DOS Shell. A cross reference is listed in a different color on color monitors and is highlighted on monochrome monitors.

Tab and Shift+Tab move the cursor forward or backward to cross references within a Help topic. To actually display the

Taking a Closer Look at DOS: Using Help

Help topic that is cross-referenced, you must move the cursor to the cross reference and then press Enter or click the cross reference. After displaying a cross reference, you can return to the previous topic by using the Back button.

▶ Your Turn

Follow these steps to practice using cross references:

1. Type **help xcopy** and then press Enter to display the XCOPY Help information.
2. Press Tab three times.
3. Press Enter to see the topic on COPY.
4. Press Alt+B to return to Help for XCOPY.
5. Pull down the File menu and choose Exit.

▶ On Your Own

If you are curious about specific menu options, dialog boxes, or commands, use DOS Help from the command line or the DOS Shell to find out about these topics.

Lesson Summary

To	Do this
Start the DOS Shell	At the DOS prompt, type **dosshell** or, if you are using a monochrome monitor, type **dosshell/b** and then press Enter.
Change the look of the DOS Shell	Pull down the **Options** menu, choose Display, then select the desired display, and choose OK.

To	Do this
Move the cursor to different parts of the DOS Shell	Press Tab or Shift+Tab or click the desired area.
Use the Command Prompt from the DOS Shell	Display the Main group in the Program List. Select Command Prompt.
Use the Command Prompt	Type the desired command and then press Enter.
Use Command Prompt Syntax Help	At the DOS prompt, type the command followed by /?.
Use DOS Shell Help	Pull down the **Help** menu and select a topic.
Use Command Prompt Help	At the DOS prompt, type **help**, press Enter and then select a Help topic or type **help** followed by the desired command and press Enter.

If You Want to Stop Now

If you want to stop now, make sure that you are at the DOS prompt. If you are at the prompt, you are ready to use any other programs you are familiar with or to turn off the computer.

From Here

In this lesson, you learned about the DOS Shell, the Command Prompt, and the Help feature. With this knowledge, you are ready to proceed to Lesson 3, which explains files—the basic storage unit for computer work.

Working with Files

SURESTEPS LESSON 3

In this lesson, you learn how to do the following:

- Name a file
- Recognize extensions
- Use wild cards
- View a list of files

Lesson time:
15–25 minutes

In previous lessons, you learned that you can use a file to store a program or some kind of work that you have created such as a letter, a spreadsheet, a graph, a database, and so on. In this lesson, you learn more about file names and extensions. You also learn how to use wild card characters with file names. If you are already familiar with file names and the use of wild cards, you should skip to Lesson 4.

Naming a File

The user gives a file its name while still in the program that created the file. Generally, programs require that a file be given a name when it is created or saved. DOS 6 has only a few simple rules for naming a file, but the DOS user must follow those rules.

Creating the File Name

■ **Note:** Some programs, such as WordPerfect, allow file names longer than eight characters. WordPerfect assigns a legal DOS name to every file that has a long name, however.

The name that you give a file can have one to eight characters and may be followed by a period and one to three characters. Technically speaking, the first part of the name (before the period) is called the *file name*. The optional characters after a period are called the *extension*. The complete designation of a file is called the *file specification*. Many programs automatically assign an extension to a file name. Microsoft Word assigns the extension DOC, for example. Some programs don't let the user change the extension because the program does not recognize any extensions but its own. Other programs give you the option of using the default extension assigned by the program or using an extension of your own. Still other programs do not assign extensions at all but allow you to use them if you want.

▶ Your Turn

Familiarize yourself with valid file names by following these steps:

1 Look at the following examples of typical file specifications:

letter.doc
budget
smith.1
smith.2
sales.wk1
client.dbf
format.com

wp.exe
1.bat
report.txt
names.asc
finalbid

2 Notice that no file name is longer than eight characters.

3 Notice that some files do not have extensions.

4 Notice that no extension is longer than three characters.

General Rules for File Names

Certain rules apply to the creating of a file name:

- A file name must be unique—that is, no other file that is stored in the same directory can have the same name.
- A file name cannot contain spaces.
- You cannot use the following characters in a file name:

    *   +   \   /   <   >   ,   .   "   :   ;   = |

■ **Note:** The period is used to separate the file name from the extension. No additional periods may be used.

▶ Your Turn

Look at the following file specifications and determine if the specification is valid. If the specification is not valid, list the reason why it is invalid. You can find the answers to the exercise at the end of this lesson.

Specification	Valid (Y/N)	Reason, If Invalid
smithlttr.doc	_____	_____
ltr:8-22.doc	_____	_____
letter	_____	_____
ltr two.sam	_____	_____
sales.1.wk1	_____	_____

> *continues*

> continued

Specification	Valid (Y/N)	Reason, If Invalid
budget1.ssf	_____	_____
list_dbf	_____	_____
list2.dbf	_____	_____
list.dbf1	_____	_____

Identifying Application Default File Extensions

As you become more familiar with file extensions and application programs, you will be able to identify what programs created certain files with a considerable degree of accuracy. Table 3.1 lists default extensions used by some of the popular programs:

Table 3.1. Default File Extensions

Database Management	Extensions
dBASE IV	DBF, NDX
Paradox (DOS)	TBL, DB
Paradox (Windows)	DB
FoxPro	DBF
R:BASE	RBF

Desktop Publishing	
PageMaker 5	PM5
Ventura Publisher	CAP, CHP, CIF, GEN, PUB, STY, VGR

Graphics

CorelDRAW!	CDR
Freehand	FH3, FT3

Graphing

Harvard Graphics (DOS)	CH3
Harvard Graphics (Windows)	PRS
Freelance	DRW, CH1, CHT, FCG, FCT

Integrated

Enable	WPF, SSF, DBF, TPF
Symphony	WR1, PRN, PIC, CCF, CTF, APP, MLB
MS-Works	WPS, WDB, DBF, PCX, WCM

Project Management

Harvard Project Manager	PRJ
TimeLine	T$0

Spreadsheets

Lotus 1-2-3 (DOS)	WKS, WK1
Excel	XLS, XLC
Quattro Pro (DOS)	WQ1
Quattro Pro (Windows)	WB1

Word Processing

WordPerfect (DOS)	Does not use extensions
WordPerfect (Windows)	WPG, WWK

> continues

Table 3.1. Continued

Word Processing	
Word	DOC
Ami Pro	SAM

Certain file extensions have special meanings. A file with an extension of EXE, for example, is an *executable file*—that is, one that contains a program. If you type the name of the file at the DOS prompt, the program is booted. A file with the extension of COM contains one or more commands that will be executed; for example, the DOS file called FORMAT.COM executes the FORMAT command. The DOS file called COMMAND.COM contains several commands that can be executed—COPY and DELETE are two of them. A file with a BAT extension contains a *batch* of DOS commands. If you enter the name of a BAT file at the DOS prompt, the DOS commands in the file are executed. Although it is by no means a standard, the extension ASC is usually associated with an ASCII file.

▶ Your Turn

■ **Note:** Remember that some programs let users assign extensions to files. You will not be able to identify the program for every SureSteps disk file.

Using Table 3.1, examine the SureSteps disk accompanying this book to see if you can determine which programs created the files. The answers are printed at the end of this lesson. Insert the SureSteps disk in the appropriate drive and then follow these steps:

1. At the DOS prompt, type **a:** or **b:** (for whichever drive contains the SureSteps disk) and then press Enter.
2. Type **dosshell** (or **dosshell/b**) and then press Enter.
3. Press Ctrl+*. (This keystroke expands all the directories in the directory tree so that you can see them.)

■ **Note:** If you use the * on the top row of the keyboard, you also must press the Shift key.

DOS 6 SureSteps

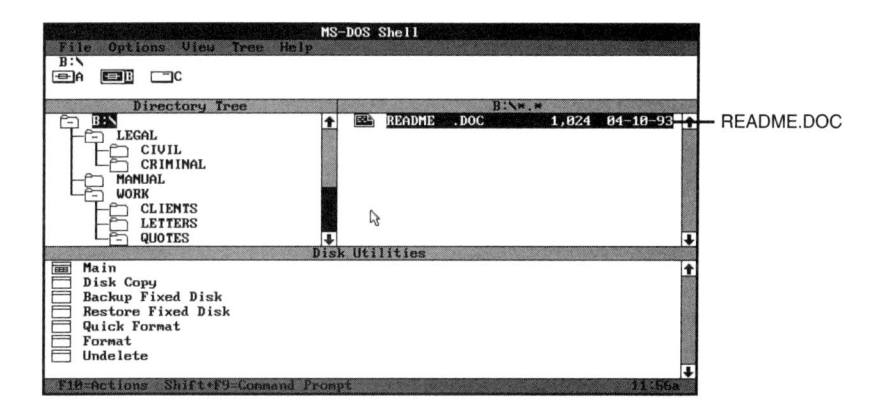

[Screenshot of MS-DOS Shell with callout pointing to README.DOC]

4 Look at the File List box. What program might have created the file called README.DOC?

5 Move the cursor to the MANUAL directory in the Directory Tree box.

6 What program do you think created the files listed in the File List box?

7 Move the cursor to the WORK directory.

8 What program might have created these files?

9 Continue moving the cursor to each directory and try to determine what program may have created each file.

Viewing a List of Files

In this lesson and in Lesson 2, you viewed lists of files primarily in the DOS Shell. In one of the exercises in Lesson 2, however, you used a command from the DOS prompt that displayed a list of files, the DIR command.

The DIR command is one of the most basic and often-used commands. When used by itself, the DIR command lists all the files in a directory.

The following list gives three other ways you can use DIR to control the way the information is displayed on-screen:

- Use the /W parameter, DIR /W, to display the files in a wide version. This version does not include as much information about each file, so more files can be displayed on-screen at one time.

Working with Files: *Viewing a List of Files* **65**

- Use the /P parameter, DIR /P, to see all the file information but to pause the display when the screen is full. Press any key to see another full screen and continue pressing any key until all the files have been displayed.

- Use the DIR command followed by a file name to display information about the specified file.

▶ Your Turn

Follow these steps to practice viewing files on the SureSteps disk:

1. Go to the DOS prompt. (You should have an A or B prompt. If not, type **a:** or **b:** and press Enter.)

2. Type **cd \manual** and then press Enter. This command moves you into the directory called MANUAL. Changing directories is discussed in more detail in Lesson 4.

3. Type **dir** and then press Enter to display the directory.

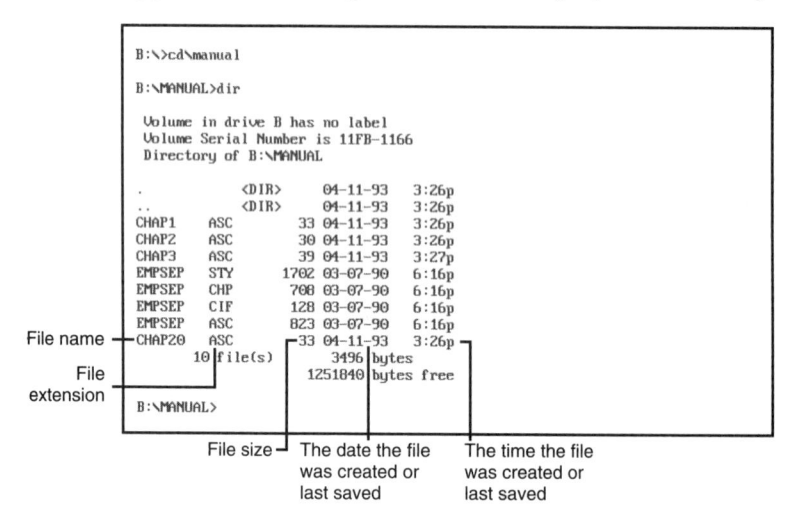

```
B:\>cd\manual

B:\MANUAL>dir

 Volume in drive B has no label
 Volume Serial Number is 11FB-1166
 Directory of B:\MANUAL

.            <DIR>        04-11-93   3:26p
..           <DIR>        04-11-93   3:26p
CHAP1    ASC        33   04-11-93   3:26p
CHAP2    ASC        30   04-11-93   3:26p
CHAP3    ASC        39   04-11-93   3:27p
EMPSEP   STY      1702   03-07-90   6:16p
EMPSEP   CHP       708   03-07-90   6:16p
EMPSEP   CIF       128   03-07-90   6:16p
EMPSEP   ASC       823   03-07-90   6:16p
CHAP20   ASC        33   04-11-93   3:26p
       10 file(s)       3496 bytes
                     1251840 bytes free

B:\MANUAL>
```

File name → CHAP20
File extension
File size → The date the file was created or last saved
The time the file was created or last saved

4 Type **dir /w** and then press Enter to view the directory in the wide version, as in the following figure:

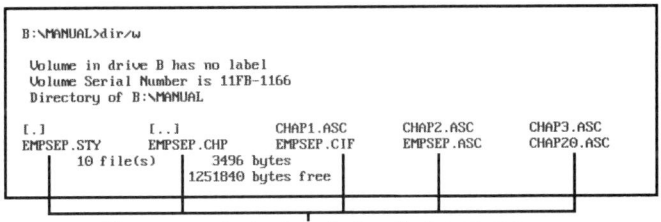

```
B:\MANUAL>dir/w

 Volume in drive B has no label
 Volume Serial Number is 11FB-1166
 Directory of B:\MANUAL

[.]              [..]             CHAP1.ASC        CHAP2.ASC        CHAP3.ASC
EMPSEP.STY       EMPSEP.CHP       EMPSEP.CIF       EMPSEP.ASC       CHAP20.ASC
        10 file(s)          3496 bytes
                         1251840 bytes free
```

File names and extensions displayed in five columns

5 Type **c:** and then press Enter.

6 Type **cd \dos** and then press Enter.

> **If you have problems...** If your PC displays the message Bad command or file name, you don't have a directory called DOS. If you know the name of the directory that stores the DOS program, type **cd **name where *name* is the name of the DOS directory. Then press Enter.

7 Type **dir /p** and then press Enter to display the first screen of the directory listing. The file list on your screen may be slightly different.

```
 Volume in drive C has no label
 Volume Serial Number is 1ACB-4818
 Directory of C:\DOS

.            <DIR>        01-11-93   9:03a
..           <DIR>        01-11-93   9:03a
DBLSPACE BIN       51214  03-10-93   6:00a
FORMAT   COM       22717  03-10-93   6:00a
NLSFUNC  EXE        7036  03-10-93   6:00a
COUNTRY  SYS       17066  03-10-93   6:00a
KEYB     COM       14983  03-10-93   6:00a
KEYBOARD SYS       34694  03-10-93   6:00a
ANSI     SYS        9065  03-10-93   6:00a
ATTRIB   EXE       11165  03-10-93   6:00a
CHKDSK   EXE       12907  03-10-93   6:00a
EDIT     COM         413  03-10-93   6:00a
EXPAND   EXE       16129  03-10-93   6:00a
MORE     COM        2546  03-10-93   6:00a
EDLIN    EXE       12642  11-11-91   5:00a
MSD      EXE      158470  03-10-93   6:00a
QBASIC   EXE      194309  03-10-93   6:00a
RESTORE  EXE       38294  03-10-93   6:00a
SYS      COM        9379  03-10-93   6:00a
Press any key to continue . . .
```

Message indicating that DOS pauses before showing the next screen

Working with Files: *Viewing a List of Files* **67**

8 Press any key to continue the listing.

9 Repeat Step 8 until the DOS prompt is returned.

Using Wild Cards with File Names

A *wild card* is a character that can represent one or several characters in a file specification. DOS uses two wild card characters:

> ? (the question mark) can stand for one character.

> * (the asterisk) can stand for any number of characters.

Wild cards are generally used as a shortcut when entering DOS commands at the DOS prompt. The wild card combination *.* means all files. Be very careful when you use this combination with the ERASE command!

■ **Note:** When the asterisk wild card is used, trailing characters are ignored. For example, *2.bat represents all files that have an extension of BAT. If you want only those BAT files with the last character of 2 in the file name, you must use this representation: ???????2.bat.

▶ Your Turn

The following steps illustrate the use of wild cards with the DIR command. Their use with other commands is similar.

1 Go to the DOS prompt. (You should have an A or B prompt. If not, type **a:** or **b:** and press Enter.)

2 Type **cd \manual** and then press Enter. This command moves you into the directory called MANUAL. Changing directories is discussed in more detail in Lesson 4.

3 Type **dir *.asc** and then press Enter. Your screen should look like the following figure:

68   DOS 6 SureSteps

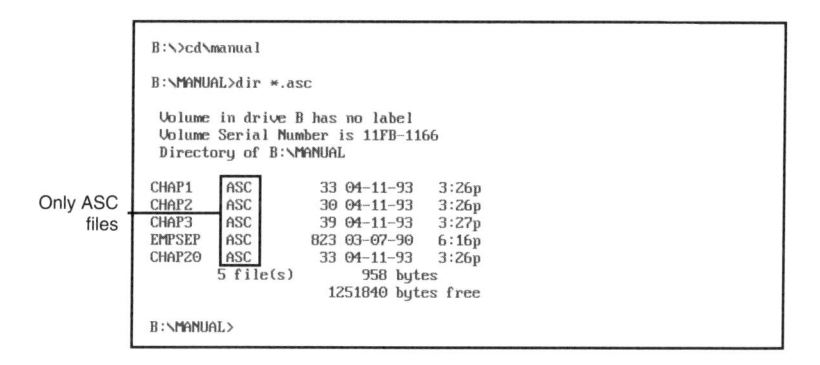

```
B:\>cd\manual

B:\MANUAL>dir *.asc

 Volume in drive B has no label
 Volume Serial Number is 11FB-1166
 Directory of B:\MANUAL

CHAP1    ASC       33 04-11-93   3:26p
CHAP2    ASC       30 04-11-93   3:26p
CHAP3    ASC       39 04-11-93   3:27p
EMPSEP   ASC      823 03-07-90   6:16p
CHAP20   ASC       33 04-11-93   3:26p
        5 file(s)        958 bytes
                     1251840 bytes free

B:\MANUAL>
```

Only ASC files

4 Type **dir c*.asc** and then press Enter. DOS displays only the files that start with *c* and have an extension of *asc*.

5 Type **dir chap?.asc** and then press Enter. DOS displays only the files that start with *chap*, followed by one character and an extension of *asc*.

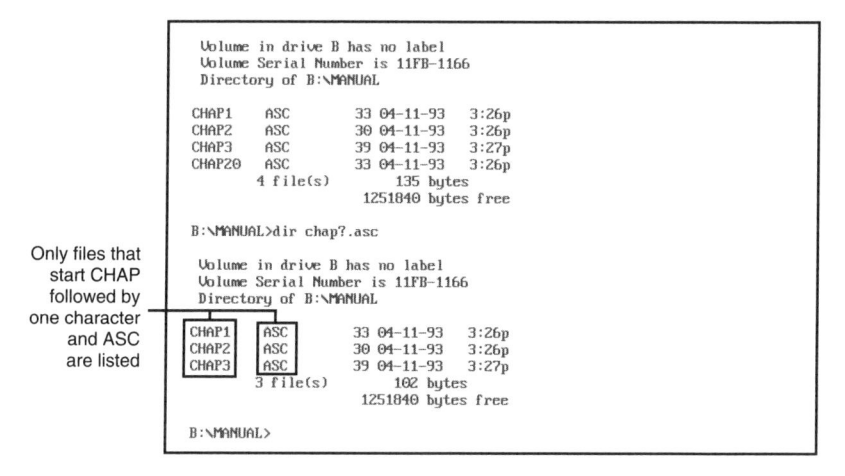

```
 Volume in drive B has no label
 Volume Serial Number is 11FB-1166
 Directory of B:\MANUAL

CHAP1    ASC       33 04-11-93   3:26p
CHAP2    ASC       30 04-11-93   3:26p
CHAP3    ASC       39 04-11-93   3:27p
CHAP20   ASC       33 04-11-93   3:26p
        4 file(s)        135 bytes
                     1251840 bytes free

B:\MANUAL>dir chap?.asc

 Volume in drive B has no label
 Volume Serial Number is 11FB-1166
 Directory of B:\MANUAL

CHAP1    ASC       33 04-11-93   3:26p
CHAP2    ASC       30 04-11-93   3:26p
CHAP3    ASC       39 04-11-93   3:27p
        3 file(s)        102 bytes
                     1251840 bytes free

B:\MANUAL>
```

Only files that start CHAP followed by one character and ASC are listed

6 Type **dir empsep.*** and then press Enter. DOS displays only the files that have a file name of *empsep* with any extension.

Working with Files: *Using Wild Cards with File Names*

Lesson Summary

To	Do this
Name a file	Use a unique name of no more than eight characters for the file name, no more than three characters for the extension, and no spaces or any of these characters: * + \ / < > , . " : ; = |
Represent all characters in a file name	Use an asterisk (*)
Represent one character in a file name	Use a question mark (?)
See a list of files at the DOS prompt	Type **dir** and press Enter

If You Want to Stop Now

If you have been following the exercises in this lesson, you should be at the DOS prompt. You can turn your PC off if you want to stop now.

From Here

If you understand the information in this chapter, you understand the basics of working with files. You are now ready to continue with Lesson 4 so that you can apply these basic skills and learn how to organize the hard disk.

Your Turn Answers

Answers for Using a File Extension:

Specification	Valid	Reason, If Invalid
smithlttr.doc	no	Uses more than 8 characters in file name
ltr:8-22.doc	no	Uses an illegal character (:)
letter	yes	
ltr two.sam	no	Uses a space
sales.1.wk1	no	Uses an additional period
budget-1.ssf	yes	
list_dbf	yes	
list2.dbf	yes	
list.dbf1	no	Uses more than 3 characters in extension

Answers for Identifying Application Default File Extensions:

Directory	Program
B:\	Word
CIVIL	Unknown
CRIMINAL	Unknown
MANUAL	Ventura
WORK	Enable
CLIENTS	dBASE or Enable
LETTERS	Ami Pro, Word, WordPerfect
RETAIL	Enable and Lotus 1-2-3
WHOLESL	Lotus 1-2-3

Section Two

File and Disk Management

2

4. Organizing the Hard Disk
5. Commands that Deal with Files
6. Commands that Deal with a Disk

4
SURESTEPS LESSON 4

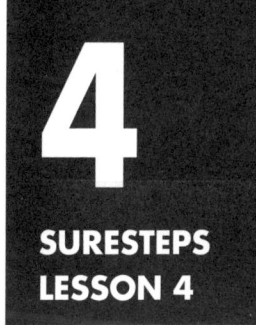

Organizing the Hard Disk

In this lesson, you learn how to do the following:

- Change directories
- Make a directory
- Remove a directory
- View the tree
- Delete the tree

In earlier lessons, you learned that a directory is a separate holding area for files on a disk, much like a file cabinet drawer is a holding area for printed files. In this lesson, you learn more about directories and how to manipulate them.

Lesson time:
30–45 minutes

Learning More about Directories

Every disk has a main directory called the *root*, which is represented by the backslash (\). Because a hard disk is so big, it must be organized into more manageable segments called directories. If users could store all their files in the root, finding a file would be a nightmare.

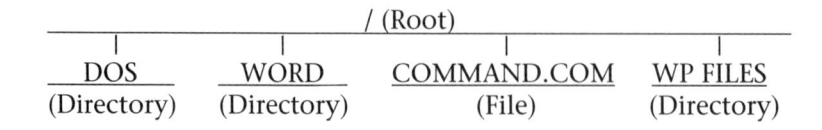

■ **Note:** Even if the 200 files occupy only one-third of the total disk space, DOS does not allow you to store any more files on the disk.

DOS sets a limit on how many files you can store. This limit varies with the size of the drive and the versions of DOS, but the number of files you can store in the root of a hard disk is approximately 200.

Directories have no limit to the number of files they can store. Because a directory is really considered a file, however, you are limited to approximately 200 directories in the root of a hard disk. If you are afraid that you need more than 200 directories, you can make directories within directories.

■ **Note:** The terms directory and subdirectory are used interchangeably in the computer industry. Technically speaking, the root is the only directory and all others are subdirectories. The term directory is used in this book almost exclusively for directories under the root and often for directories within a directory.

Some people call a directory within a directory a *subdirectory*. The directory that contains another directory is called the *parent*.

Generally, a hard disk has directories for programs and separate directories for the files that are created by the programs. A hard disk may have a directory called WORD, for example, and one called WPFILES. The WORD directory might store the word processing program called MS Word, and the WPFILES directory might store the word processing files created by Word. The WORD and WPFILES directories can both be on the same level under the root or the WPFILES directory can be created inside the WORD directory.

These two figures show two typical organizations of hard disks:

```
                        / (Root)
     |            |           |              |
    DOS         WORD      COMMAND.COM     WP FILES
 (Directory) (Directory)     (File)       (Directory)
```

DOS 6 SureSteps

```
                    / (Root)
        |              |              |
      DOS            WORD         COMMAND.COM
   (Directory)    (Directory)       (File)
                      |
                   WP FILES
                  (Directory)
```

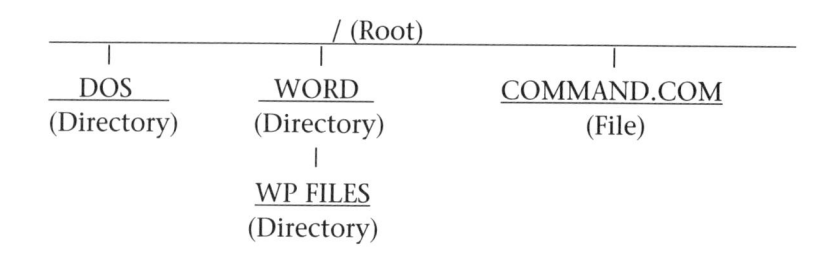

▶ Your Turn

Practice your organizational skills by following these steps:

1 Suppose that you have these program: DOS, WordPerfect (a word processing program), Quattro Pro (a spreadsheet program), and dBASE IV (a database program). You use the WordPerfect program to write letters, and Quattro Pro and dBASE IV to track sales.

2 Decide how you would organize the programs and data files on a hard disk.

Looking at a Typical Root Directory

In Lessons 2 and 3, you have been looking at typical root directories, but the emphasis has been on other things. Many times you have used the DOS Shell to display the files on the SureSteps disk, and you have seen the directories listed in the Directory Tree box. Remember that the Directory Tree box, which shows the organization of the hard disk, is displayed when you start the DOS Shell.

▶ Your Turn

To display the organization of the SureSteps disk, insert the disk into your floppy drive and follow these steps:

1 Access the DOS prompt by turning your computer on or returning to the DOS prompt from your current activity.

2 Type **a:** or **b:** (the drive in which the SureSteps disk is inserted) and then press Enter.

3 Start the DOS Shell.

4 Press **Ctrl+*** to expand the display of the directory tree.

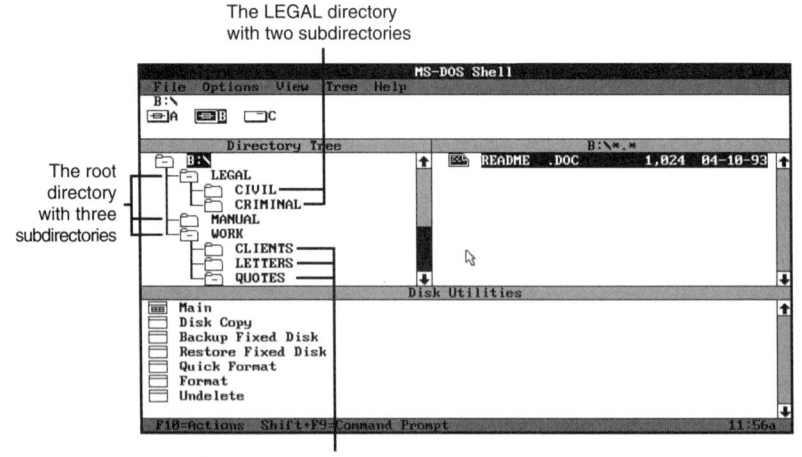

```
                    The LEGAL directory
                    with two subdirectories
                              |
┌─────────────────────────────────────────────────────────────┐
│                         MS-DOS Shell                        │
│ File  Options  View  Tree  Help                             │
│ B:\                                                         │
│ ⊜A  ⊜B  ☐C                                                  │
├─────────────────────────────────────────────────────────────┤
│       Directory Tree              B:\*.*                    │
│  ┌─ B:\                    ↑   README  .DOC  1,024  04-10-93│
│  ├─ LEGAL                                                   │
The root │  │  ├─ CIVIL                                       │
directory├─ │  └─ CRIMINAL                                    │
with three  ├─ MANUAL                                         │
subdirectories└─ WORK                                         │
│     ├─ CLIENTS                                              │
│     ├─ LETTERS                                              │
│     └─ QUOTES                                               │
├─────────────────────────────────────────────────────────────┤
│                      Disk Utilities                         │
│  ▦ Main                                                     │
│  ▤ Disk Copy                                                │
│  ▤ Backup Fixed Disk                                        │
│  ▤ Restore Fixed Disk                                       │
│  ▤ Quick Format                                             │
│  ▤ Format                                                   │
│  ▤ Undelete                                                 │
│ F10=Actions  Shift+F9=Command Prompt              11:56a    │
└─────────────────────────────────────────────────────────────┘
           The WORK directory with three subdirectories
```

5 Scroll the list of directories.

Notice that the root directory has three directories, the LEGAL directory has two subdirectories, the WORK directory has three subdirectories, and the QUOTES directory has two subdirectories.

▶ On Your Own

Use the DOS Shell to explore the organization of your hard disk. See if you can determine whether a directory contains a program or data files. When you have finished, select the icon for the floppy drive in which the SureSteps disk is inserted.

Hint: Directory names and file names help you determine the type of directory.

Changing Directories

The directory in which you are located is called the *current directory*. To move to a different directory, you change directories. If you are going to perform several commands in the same directory, you probably will find that changing to that directory is more convenient than working from another directory.

Changing Directories in the DOS Shell

Changing directories is easy if you are using the DOS Shell. You simply display the directories that you want to see in the Directory Tree box and then highlight the directory name by moving the cursor to the name or clicking the name.

▶ Your Turn

You have changed directories several times in previous lessons, but try the following steps to remind yourself of the process:

1 Select the Directory Tree Box by using the TAB key to reach it or by clicking it.

2 Scroll down to the RETAIL directory and highlight it. You have changed the directory.

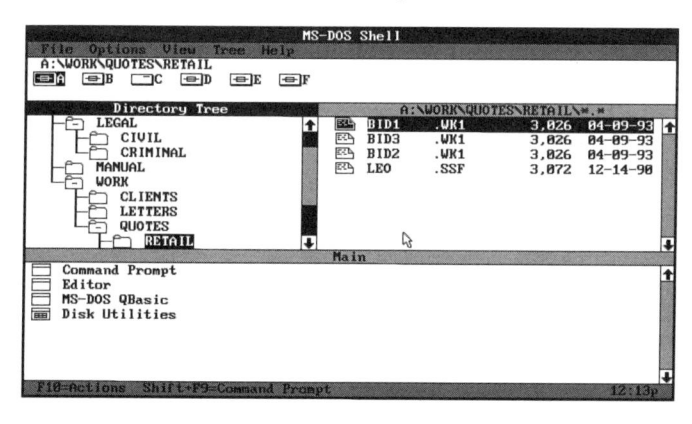

Reminder: You should still be looking at the drive in which the SureSteps disk is inserted.

Organizing the Hard Disk: Changing Directories

3 Highlight the MANUAL directory. You have changed directories again.

4 Pull down the File menu and choose Exit. Notice that the DOS prompt reflects the last directory that was current when you exited.

Changing Directories at the DOS Prompt

Even though this book focuses primarily on the DOS Shell commands, in this lesson the commands used at the DOS prompt also are discussed. The reason for this slight departure is to give you a better feel for the path of a file. The *path* of a file identifies its exact location by listing its directories.

The path of a file is a very basic concept that is easily overlooked when using the DOS Shell. Because the DOS Shell is so visual and because you can search through directories so easily, it isn't difficult to find a file. If you aren't using the DOS Shell, however, specifying the location of a file can be very difficult if you do not understand the path concept.

Reminder: The backslash key refers to the root.

To change directories at the DOS prompt, use the CD command. (*CD* stands for *change directories*.) To change from the root of the current drive to the WORK directory (which is one level under the root), for example, type **cd work** and then press Enter. (You also can type **cd \work**, but if you are in the root directory, you don't have to type the backslash.) To change to the RETAIL directory from the root of the current drive, you must list the path in the command so that DOS can find the directory. You must type **cd work\quotes\retail** and then press Enter. You cannot simply type **cd retail** because DOS would look for RETAIL directly under the root, and the RETAIL directory is three levels under the root.

▶ **Your Turn**

Try these steps to practice changing directories at the DOS prompt:

80 DOS 6 SureSteps

1 Type **cd ** and then press Enter.

2 Type **cd work** and press Enter. Your DOS prompt then should be A:\WORK> or B:\WORK>.

Reminder: You should still be looking at the disk drive in which the SureSteps disk is inserted.

If you have problems...	If your DOS prompt doesn't match the examples given, you should temporarily fix the problem so that you can continue in this lesson. Type **prompt pg** at the DOS prompt and then press Enter. To permanently change the prompt, you must revise the AUTOEXEC.BAT file and revise or add the PROMPT command. This task is discussed in Lesson 7.

3 Type **cd \manual** and then press Enter. Your DOS prompt should now be A:\MANUAL> or B:\MANUAL>.

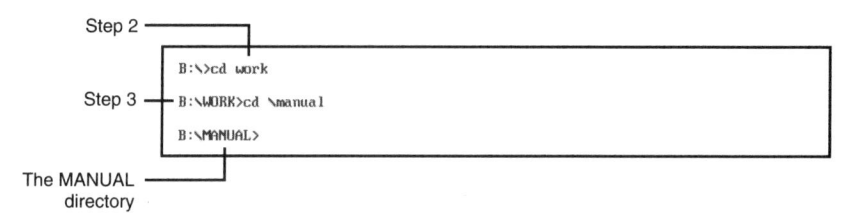

```
Step 2 ──┐
         B:\>cd work
Step 3 ──┼─ B:\WORK>cd \manual
         B:\MANUAL>
The MANUAL
  directory
```

Notice that the path in step 3 begins with the backslash. The backslash is necessary because you are in the WORK directory when you type the command. If you don't include the backslash, DOS starts looking in the WORK directory for the MANUAL directory, and it will not be able to find it because WORK is not the parent directory.

Making a Directory

Directories are usually created in one of two ways—by the user or by a program installation routine. When you install a program on your hard drive, many times the installation process creates a directory to store the program. Normally, the installation routine either asks you for a directory name or it asks you to accept the name that it wants to use. When the DOS 6 upgrade program is installed, for example, it asks you if you approve of the directory name DOS.

Organizing the Hard Disk: Making a Directory

When the user makes a directory, a special command is used. Like most commands, the command can be selected from the DOS Shell menu or typed at the DOS prompt.

Making a Directory in the DOS Shell

To create a file from the DOS Shell menu, follow these steps:

1 Highlight the directory in the Directory Tree box that will be the parent directory.

2 Pull down the File menu and choose Create Directory. A dialog box appears.

3 Type the name that you want to use for the directory.

4 Choose OK.

▶ Your Turn

At the DOS prompt, follow these steps:

1 Start the DOS Shell.

2 Press Ctrl+* to expand the directory tree.

3 Select the Directory Tree box.

4 Highlight the WORK directory in the Directory Tree box.

5 Pull down the File menu and choose Create Directory to display this dialog box:

```
              Create Directory
  Parent name: B:\WORK
  New directory name. .  [            ]



        [  OK  ]   [ Cancel ]   [ Help ]
```

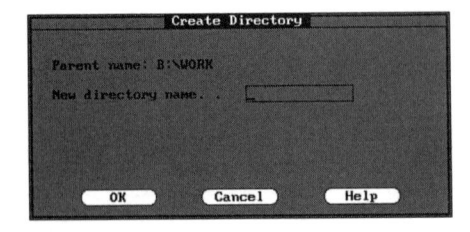

6 Type **mydir**.

7 Choose OK. Notice that the new directory is shown in the Directory Tree box.

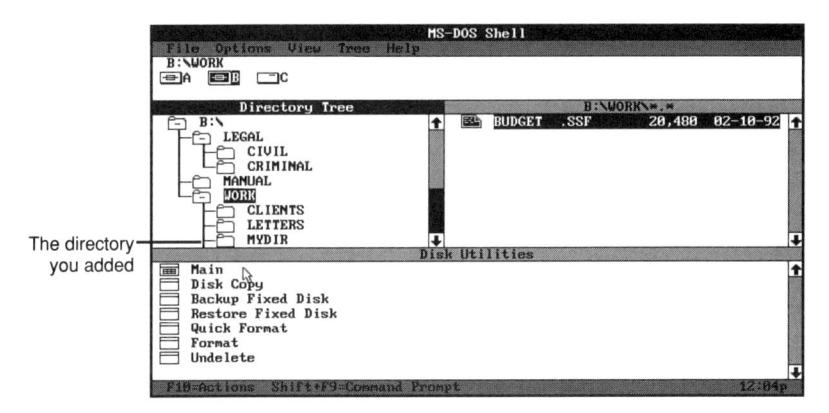

■ **Tip:** Because a directory is really a file, the rules for naming a file also apply to naming a directory. Most people do not use extensions in directory names. It is acceptable to do so but not recommended.

The directory you added

Making a Directory at the DOS Prompt

To create a directory from the DOS prompt, you can type **md**, followed by the path and the name of the directory, or you can change to the parent directory and type **md**, followed by the directory name. (*MD* stands for *m*ake *d*irectory.)

▶ Your Turn

Make sure that the icon for the SureSteps disk drive is selected and exit the DOS Shell. Follow these steps to create another directory using the MD command:

1 Type **cd ** and then press Enter.

2 Type **md mydata** and then press Enter.

3 Type **dir** and then press Enter. The new directory should be listed with the other directories and files. The order of files on your screen may not match the figure exactly.

■ **Note:** Many novice users expect the DOS prompt to change to the new directory name when a directory is created. Remember that the DOS prompt only changes if you move into the directory by using the CD command.

Organizing the Hard Disk: Making a Directory at the DOS Prompt   **83**

```
B:\>cd\

B:\>md mydata

B:\>dir

 Volume in drive B has no label
 Volume Serial Number is 11FB-1166
 Directory of B:\

MYDATA       <DIR>      06-11-93  12:24p
WORK         <DIR>      04-09-93   1:22p
MANUAL       <DIR>      04-11-93   3:26p
LEGAL        <DIR>      04-21-93   8:23p
README   DOC     1024   04-10-93   4:04p
       5 file(s)         1024 bytes
                      1250816 bytes free

B:\>
```

New directory → MYDATA

Removing a Directory

If a directory is no longer needed, you should remove it from the disk. If you purchase an upgrade for a program that is already on your disk, for example, the new program is usually installed in a new directory. The old program in the old directory is no longer needed and should be removed. By removing unnecessary files from the disk, you not only free disk space, you increase the speed of the system. Disk access is faster on a disk with fewer files and directories.

Before you can remove a directory, however, one or two conditions must be met—the directory must have no files stored in it (including other directories), and, if you are using the DOS prompt, the directory to be removed cannot be the current directory.

Removing a Directory in the DOS Shell

To remove a directory in the DOS Shell, follow these steps:

1 Erase all files in all subdirectories in the directory.

2 Remove all subdirectories in the directory.

3 Erase all the files in the directory.

4 Select the Directory Tree box.

5 Highlight the desired directory and press Del. A confirmation box appears.

6 Choose Yes to confirm the deletion.

▶ Your Turn

In this exercise, you remove one of the directories you created earlier on the SureSteps disk. Because the directory you are removing contains no directories or files, it is ready to be removed. (In Lesson 5, you learn how to erase files that may be stored in a directory.) Return to the DOS Shell, make sure that the directory tree of the SureSteps disk is displayed, and then follow these steps:

1 Expand all levels of the tree.

2 Select the Directory Tree box.

3 Scroll down to the directory named MYDIR, select it, and press Del. This dialog box is displayed:

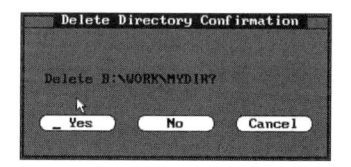

4 Choose Yes.

Removing a Directory at the DOS Prompt

To remove a directory using the DOS prompt, follow these steps:

1 Erase all files in all subdirectories in the directory.

2 Remove all subdirectories in the directory.

3 Erase all the files in the directory.

4 Change to another directory if the directory to be removed is the current directory.

Organizing the Hard Disk: Removing a Directory

5 Type **rd**, followed by a space, and the path and name of the directory to be removed, and then press Enter. The DOS prompt returns with no verification that the command has been executed.

▶ Your Turn

In this exercise, you remove the directory that you created earlier on the SureSteps disk. The directory is empty, so it's ready to remove. Exit to the DOS prompt, make sure that the DOS prompt reflects the drive in which the SureSteps disk is inserted, and follow these steps:

1 Type **cd ** and press Enter.

2 Type **rd \mydata** and press Enter.

3 To see whether the directory has been removed, type **dir** and then press Enter. This figure shows the directory listing:

```
B:\>cd\

B:\>rd mydata

B:\>dir

 Volume in drive B has no label
 Volume Serial Number is 11FB-1166
 Directory of B:\

WORK         <DIR>     04-09-93   1:22p
MANUAL       <DIR>     04-11-93   3:26p
LEGAL        <DIR>     04-21-93   8:23p
README   DOC      1024 04-10-93   4:04p
        4 file(s)       1024 bytes
                     1251840 bytes free

B:\>
```

If you have problems... If you try to remove a directory that still has files or subdirectories in it, you get the following message:

Invalid path, not directory,

or directory not empty

Remember to erase all files in subdirectories and then remove the subdirectories before you remove the directory.

DOS 6 SureSteps

Viewing the Tree

Tree is a term that you have seen in several previous lessons. The DOS Shell has a box called the Directory Tree. You probably have deduced that *tree* refers to the structure of a directory. Obviously, the picture of a directory tree is tied to the term *root*, the designation of the main directory.

When you look at the directories listed in the DOS Shell Directory Tree box, you are looking at the tree or the structure of the disk. As you have seen, the structure can be displayed in a compressed form or an expanded form. A fully expanded view of the tree shows all the directories at every level.

To see the tree at the DOS prompt, type **tree** and press Enter. To see all the file names when the directories are listed, type the /F parameter with the TREE command like this: **tree/f**. Then press Enter.

Reminder: You have been using Ctrl+* to fully expand the tree.

■ **Tip:** When you use the TREE command with the /F parameter, the display probably scrolls for several screens if you have lots of files. To make the screen pause when it is full, type the command like this: **tree /f|more**. When the screen pauses, press any key to continue.

▶ **Your Turn**

You should still be at the DOS prompt that reflects the drive in which the SureSteps disk is inserted. Follow these steps to see the tree:

1 Type **cd ** and press Enter.

2 Type **tree** and press Enter. Your screen should look like this:

```
B:\>tree
Directory PATH listing
Volume Serial Number is 11FB-1166
B:.
├──WORK
│   ├──QUOTES
│   │   ├──RETAIL
│   │   └──WHOLESL
│   ├──LETTERS
│   └──CLIENTS
├──MANUAL
└──LEGAL
    ├──CIVIL
    └──CRIMINAL

B:\>
```

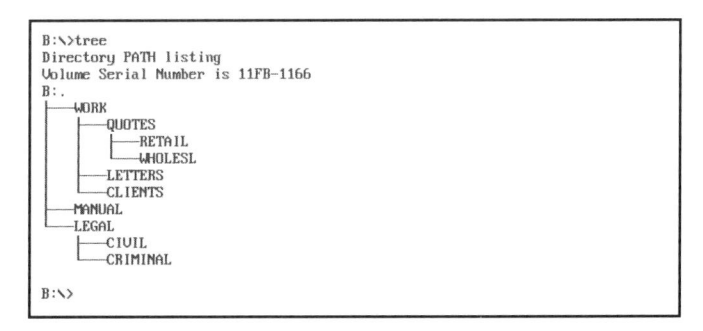

3 Type **tree/f** and press Enter. Your screen should show all the directories and the files in each directory. The display scrolls if it has too much information for one screen.

Organizing the Hard Disk: Viewing the Tree **87**

■ **Note:** The vertical bar (|) is usually locked on the backlash key.

4 Type **tree/f|more** and press Enter. This command pauses when the screen fills and stops the scrolling. Your screen should look like the following figure:

```
Directory PATH listing
Volume Serial Number is 0B60-0EFE
A:.
    README.DOC
├──WORK
│       BUDGET.SSF
│      ─QUOTES
│       ├──RETAIL
│       │      LEO.SSF
│       │      BID2.WK1
│       │      BID3.WK1
│       │      BID1.WK1
│       │
│       └──WHOLESL
│              PRICES.WK1
├──LETTERS
│       PPIHIST.DOC
│       DISCLOSE
│       Q&A.ASC
│       NOTE.SAM
─ More ─
```

5 Press any key to continue.

▶ On Your Own

Refresh your memory of the Directory Tree in the DOS Shell by starting the DOS Shell and then looking at the directory of the hard disk. Expand the directory to display all levels.

Deleting the Tree

A new command added to DOS 6 can delete the entire tree or branches of the tree (or directories) without first having to erase the files or remove the directories. This command is the DELTREE command. It should be used very carefully because it is very destructive. By using it, you can delete hundreds of files.

The DELTREE command is used at the DOS prompt. There is no corresponding command in the DOS Shell.

You may be wondering when you would use such a command. Consider the example used earlier. You just bought the upgrade to a program that you have been using on the hard disk. Because the upgrade installs the new version in a new directory, you want to delete the directory that holds the old version. This directory, named PROG, has six subdirectories that hold specific program files. Without the DELTREE command, you would have to erase all the files in the subdirectories, remove those subdirectories, then erase all the files in the PROG directory, and finally remove it. You would have to issue a minimum of 14 commands to accomplish this task. With the DELTREE command, the same task is accomplished with one command. Remember that DELTREE is a two-edged sword. It is as dangerous as it is helpful.

To delete a directory and all the files and directories under it, follow these steps:

1 Type **deltree**, followed by the path and name of the directory, and then press Enter. DOS displays a warning message.

2 When DOS warns you that all files and directories will be deleted, type **y** for Yes and press Enter.

▶ Your Turn

To delete the LEGAL directory, its directories CIVIL and CRIMINAL, and the files they contain, follow these steps:

1 Type **deltree legal** and then press Enter. DOS displays this message:

```
Delete directory "legal" and all its subdirectories?[yn]
```

Before you complete the next step, make sure that the DOS prompt reflects the drive in which the SureSteps disk is inserted. If the DOS prompt reflects a different drive which happens to have a directory called LEGAL, that directory will be deleted.

If you have problems...	If you are in the wrong drive or directory, type **n**, then change to the correct one, and start the process.

2 Type **y** and press Enter.

Organizing the Hard Disk: Deleting the Tree **89**

Lesson Summary

To	Do this
Change directories	In the DOS Shell, expand the Directory Tree box if necessary. Highlight the desired directory. At the DOS prompt, type **cd**, followed by the path and directory name. Press Enter.
Make a directory	In the DOS Shell, highlight the parent directory in the Directoy Tree box. Pull down the File menu and choose Create Directory. Type the directory name and choose OK. At the DOS prompt, type **md**, followed by the path and directory name. Press Enter.
Remove a directory	Whether you are using the DOS Shell or the DOS prompt, you must first erase all files and remove all directories in the desired directory. In the DOS Shell, highlight the desired directory. Press Del. Choose Yes. At the DOS prompt, make sure that the desired directory is not the current directory. Type **rd**, followed by the path and the name of the directory. Press Enter.
View the Tree	In the DOS Shell, expand the directory by pressing Ctrl+*. At the DOS prompt, type **tree** and press Enter.
Delete the tree	At the DOS prompt, type **deltree** followed by the path and directory name. Press Enter. Type **y** and press Enter.

If You Want to Stop Now

If you want to stop now, you can turn off the PC or use another program.

From Here

In this lesson, you learned how to organize the hard disk. You are now ready to learn about commands that deal with files. Continue with Lesson 5.

Commands that Deal with Files

In Lesson 1, you learned that working with files is one of the main functions of DOS. There are many housekeeping chores that DOS must perform in order to maintain your files. By using DOS commands, you can keep track of the files that you have—deleting, copying, and renaming them when necessary. You can move the files to different locations for better organization, and you can even search for files that you have misplaced.

SURESTEPS LESSON 5

In this lesson, you learn how to do the following:

- View a list of files
- Search for files
- Copy and move files
- Copy files and directories at the same time
- Replace a file
- Delete and undelete files
- Rename files

Lesson time:
40–50 minutes

Viewing a List of Files

■ **Note:** The DOS Shell always lists the directories and files for the root of the current drive. If you are in C:\DOS when you boot the DOS Shell, DOS lists the directories and files in the root of drive C, not those in the DOS directory.

Knowing the location of your files is important so that you can work with them. When you start the DOS Shell, the root and the directories of the *current drive* are listed for you in the Directory Tree box on the left. In this box, the cursor is automatically positioned on the root directory, and all the files in the root are listed in the File List box on the right.

▶ Your Turn

Follow these steps to view the list of files on the SureSteps disk:

1 Start your computer if you have not already done so.

2 Insert the SureSteps disk in drive A or B (whichever is appropriate).

3 If you inserted the SureSteps disk in drive A, type **a:** and then press Enter. If you inserted the disk in drive B, type **b:** and then press Enter.

■ **Note:** Do not be concerned if your screen doesn't match the figure. Several different views of the DOS Shell are available. These views are discussed later in this lesson.

4 Type **dosshell** and press Enter. Your screen should look similar to this:

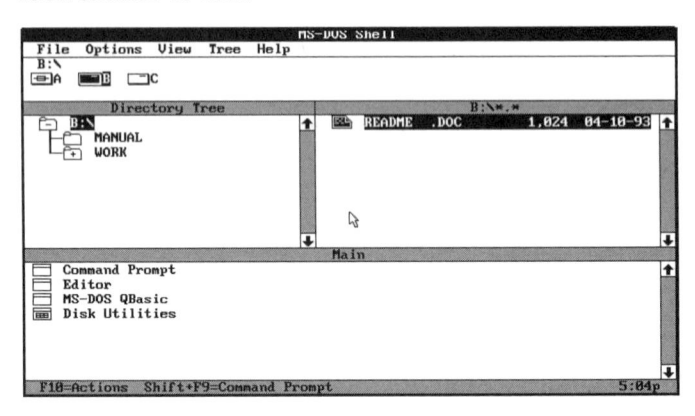

```
                              MS-DOS Shell
 File  Options  View  Tree  Help
 B:\
 ▣A  ▣B  ▢C
 ─────────── Directory Tree ───────────  ──── B:\*.* ────
        B:\                              ▨ README  .DOC    1,024  04-10-93
        ├─ MANUAL
        └─ WORK




                                        ─── Main ───
        ▢ Command Prompt
        ▢ Editor
        ▢ MS-DOS QBasic
        ▥ Disk Utilities


 F10=Actions  Shift+F9=Command Prompt                              5:04p
```

Expanding and Changing the Directory View

When the DOS Shell is first started, all the directories on a disk are collapsed—that is, DOS does not show any

DOS 6 SureSteps

directories below the first level under the root. You may notice a plus sign (+) beside a directory name in the left box. The plus sign indicates that there are subdirectories within the directory. You can expand the view of a directory by selecting the directory, pulling down the Tree menu, and then choosing Expand One Level, Expand Branch, or Expand All. When a directory is expanded, the plus changes to a minus. You also can expand or collapse one directory at a time by clicking the plus or minus (or by typing a plus or minus when the cursor is positioned on the plus or minus).

To see the files in a different directory on the same drive, select the desired directory in the box on the left by clicking the directory name or by moving the cursor to the directory name.

To see the directories and the files for other drives, select the desired drive from the list above the two boxes. To see the files on drive C, for example, select the drive C icon.

■ **Tip:** The keyboard shortcut to expand all levels is Ctrl+*. You have used this shortcut several times in preceding exercises.

▶ **Your Turn**

Follow these steps to practice displaying directories and files:

1 Select the Directory Tree box.

2 Pull down the Tree menu and choose Expand All. Your screen should look like this:

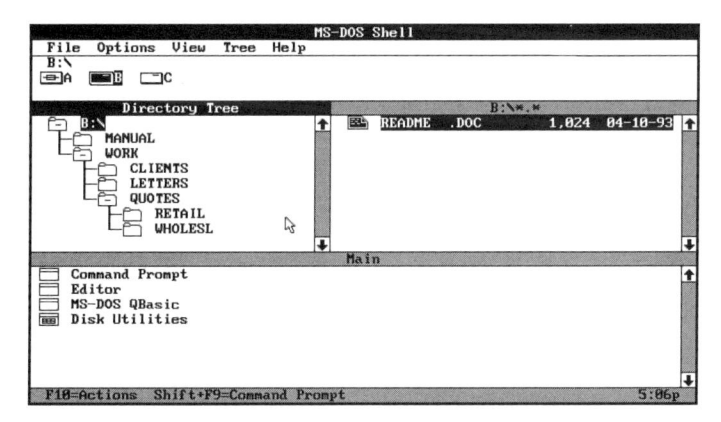

3 Select the RETAIL directory. Notice the change in the box on the right.

Commands that Deal with Files: *Viewing a List of Files*

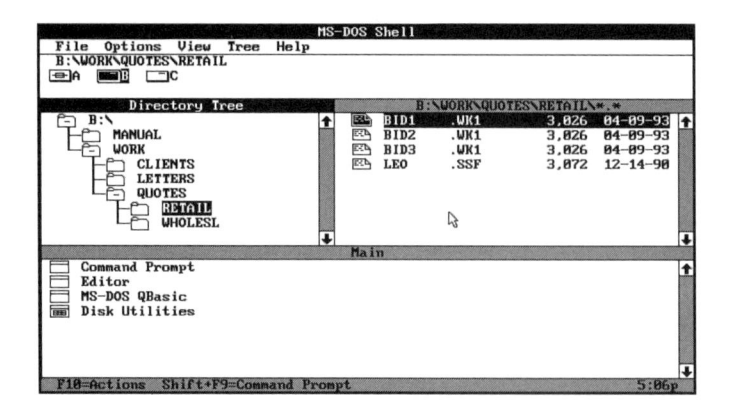

```
                    MS-DOS Shell
 File  Options  View  Tree  Help
 B:\WORK\QUOTES\RETAIL
 ▄A  ▄B  ▄C
        Directory Tree                       B:\WORK\QUOTES\RETAIL\*.*
    B:\                              BID1    .WK1    3,026  04-09-93
      MANUAL                         BID2    .WK1    3,026  04-09-93
      WORK                           BID3    .WK1    3,026  04-09-93
        CLIENTS                      LEO     .SSF    3,072  12-14-90
        LETTERS
        QUOTES
          RETAIL
          WHOLESL
                              Main
 Command Prompt
 Editor
 MS-DOS QBasic
 Disk Utilities

 F10=Actions  Shift+F9=Command Prompt                          5:06p
```

4 Select the drive C icon.

5 Select one of the directories displayed. Notice the change in the box on the right.

6 Select the drive A or B icon (the drive in which the SureSteps disk is inserted). Notice the change again.

Changing the Order of Files

Files that are listed in the box on the right are sorted alphabetically by file name. DOS also can list the files in order (either ascending or descending) by extension, date, size, or disk order (the order in which files are stored on the disk). To change the order of the file listing, follow these steps:

1 Pull down the Options menu and choose File Display Options to display a dialog box.

2 Select the desired order from the dialog box and then choose OK.

▶ Your Turn

Follow these steps to change the order of the file display:

1 Select the LETTERS directory.

2 Pull down the Options menu and choose File Display Options. This dialog box appears:

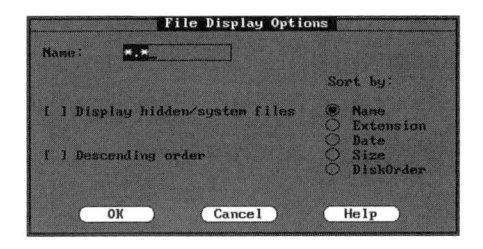

3 Select Size.

4 Choose OK. The files are now ordered by size with the smallest files listed first.

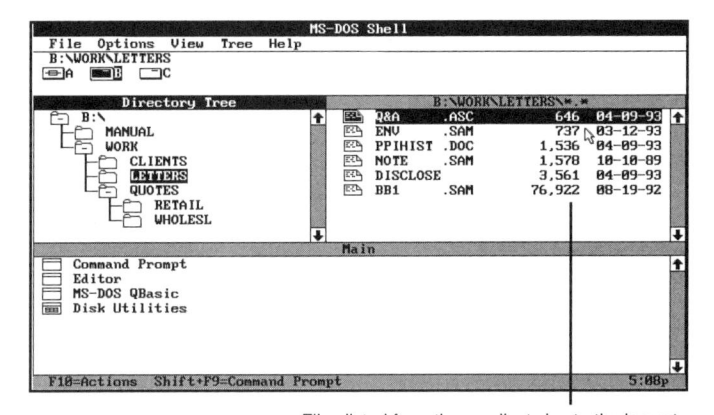

Files listed from the smallest size to the largest

■ **Note:** Hidden files are usually files that are essential to the operation of a program. By default, they are not displayed in file listings, but you can display them by choosing Display Hidden/System Files from the File Display Options dialog box. Because users do not need to interact with hidden files in any way, it is generally best not to include them in the file listings.

5 Pull down the Options menu and choose File Display Options.

6 Select Date.

7 Select Descending order.

8 Choose OK. The files are now listed by date, with the newest files listed first.

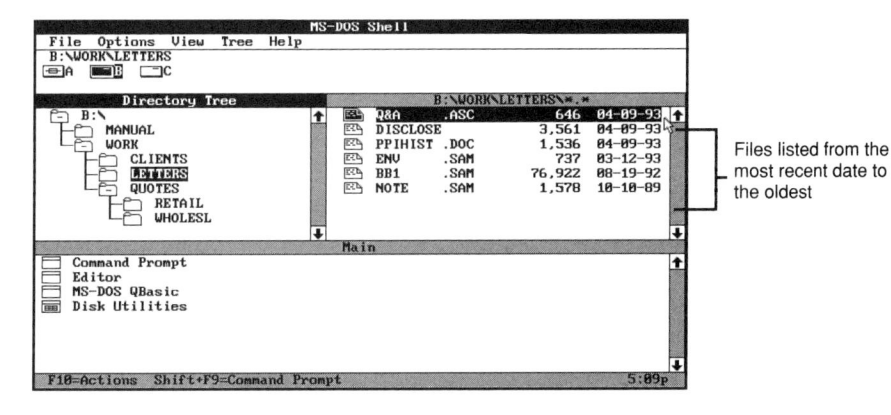

Files listed from the most recent date to the oldest

Commands that Deal with Files: *Viewing a List of Files*

9 Pull down the Options menu and choose File Display options.

10 Return settings to Size and deselect the Descending Order check box.

Selecting a File

Most of the commands discussed in this lesson require you to select files. You may have to select all files, one file, a group of files that are listed together, or a group of files that are not listed together (non-contiguous files).

To select all files displayed, pull down the File menu and choose Select All or press Ctrl+/. To deselect all files, pull down the File menu and choose Deselect All or press Ctrl+\.

To select individual files or groups of files, use the mouse or the keyboard. If you are using the text mode for the DOS Shell, a selected file has an arrow beside it. If you are using the graphic mode, a selected file is highlighted in reverse video.

The following table lists the methods for selecting files by using the mouse or the keyboard:

■ **Note:** The keyboard method for selecting a single file and the mouse method for selecting non-contiguous files are toggles; you can select or deselect a file with the same method.

To Select	With the Mouse	With the Keyboard
One file	Click the file name	Move the cursor to the file or press Shift+F8 to turn on the Add mode, then move the cursor to the file name and press the space bar, and press Shift+F8 again to turn off the Add mode.
A group of files	Click the first file and hold down the Shift key while you click the last file in the group.	While in the Add mode, position the cursor on the first file name and then hold down the Shift key as you move the cursor down to the last file name in the group.

To Select	With the Mouse	With the Keyboard
Non-contiguous files	Hold down the Ctrl key as you click each of the desired file names.	While in the Add mode, move the cursor to each file name and press the space bar.

▶ Your Turn

Position the cursor in the File List box and use these steps to practice selecting files:

1 Move the cursor to Q&A.ASC if it is not already there.

2 Press Shift+F8.

3 Hold down the Shift key and move the cursor down to PPIHIST.DOC. Notice that three files are selected. Your screen should look like this:

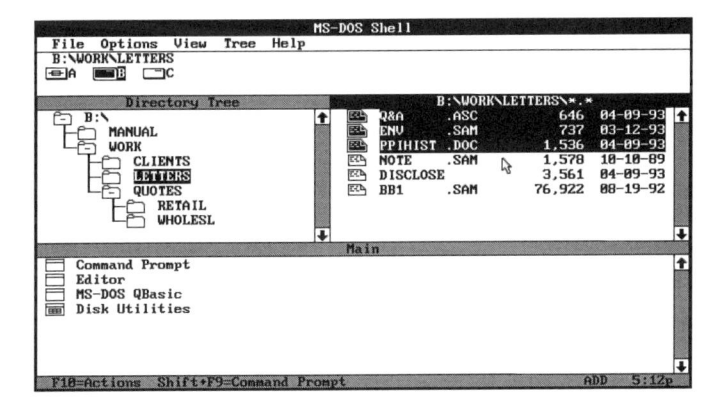

```
                              MS-DOS Shell
 File  Options  View  Tree  Help
 B:\WORK\LETTERS
 ⇨A  ⇨B  ☐C
┌─────────── Directory Tree ──────────┬──────── B:\WORK\LETTERS\*.* ────────┐
│ ┌─ B:\                             ↑│  Q&A       .ASC       646  04-09-93 ↑│
│ │  ├─ MANUAL                       ││  ENV       .SAM       737  03-12-93 │
│ │  └─ WORK                         ││  PPIHIST   .DOC     1,536  04-09-93 │
│ │      ├─ CLIENTS                  ││  NOTE      .SAM     1,578  10-10-89 │
│ │      ├─ LETTERS                  ││  DISCLOSE           3,561  04-09-93 │
│ │      ├─ QUOTES                   ││  BB1       .SAM    76,922  08-19-92 │
│ │      └─ RETAIL                   ││                                     │
│ │          └─ WHOLESL              ││                                     │
│                                   ↓││                                    ↓│
├──────────────────── Main ───────────────────────────────────────────────┐
│  Command Prompt                                                        ↑│
│  Editor                                                                 │
│  MS-DOS QBasic                                                          │
│  Disk Utilities                                                         │
│                                                                        ↓│
 F10=Actions  Shift+F9=Command Prompt                      ADD      5:12p
```

4 Release the Shift key and move the cursor to the file DISCLOSE.

5 Press the space bar. You have selected a block of files and a non-contiguous file.

6 Press Shift+F8 again to turn off Add mode. The files are still selected until you take another action (by moving the cursor down, for example).

***Commands that Deal with Files:** Copying Files*

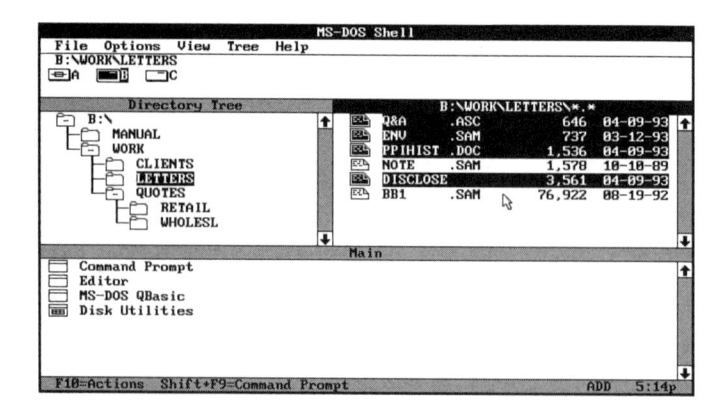

```
                        MS-DOS Shell
      File  Options  View  Tree  Help
      B:\WORK\LETTERS
      ⊡A  ■B  ☐C
                  Directory Tree              B:\WORK\LETTERS\*.*
      ┌─ B:\                              ↑    Q&A     .ASC       646  04-09-93  ↑
      │  ├─ MANUAL                             ENV     .SAM       737  03-12-93
      │  └─ WORK                               PPIHIST .DOC     1,536  04-09-93
      │        ├─ CLIENTS                      NOTE    .SAM     1,578  10-10-89
      │        ├─ LETTERS                      DISCLOSE         3,561  04-09-93
      │        └─ QUOTES                       BB1     .SAM    76,922  08-19-92
      │              ├─ RETAIL
      │              └─ WHOLESL
                                         ↓                                       ↓
                                       Main
      ☐ Command Prompt                                                           ↑
      ☐ Editor
      ☐ MS-DOS QBasic
      ▤ Disk Utilities



      F10=Actions  Shift+F9=Command Prompt                       ADD     5:14p
```

▶ On Your Own

If you have a mouse, practice selecting one file, a block of files, and non-contiguous files.

Searching for a File

At one time or another, every computer user has created a file and forgotten where it was stored. With the SEARCH command, DOS can search the entire disk, including all directories, to find the file for you. To search for a file, follow these steps:

1 Select the desired drive.

2 Pull down the File menu and choose Search to display a dialog box. Make sure that Search Entire Disk is selected in the dialog box.

3 Type the name of the file and choose OK.

If the file exists, DOS displays the path of the file in every location. After studying the information that DOS gives you, you can return to the DOS Shell by pressing Esc. If you want to search for multiple files or if you are uncertain of the exact file name, you can use wild cards in the Search dialog box.

▶ Your Turn

Follow these steps to locate the file called BID1.WK1 on the SureSteps disk. (Make sure that you have selected the drive in which the SureSteps disk is inserted.)

1. Pull down the File menu and choose Search to display a dialog box.

2. Type **bid1.wk1**.

3. Make sure that Search Entire Disk is selected. The dialog box should look like this:

```
                    Search File
Current Directory is B:\
Search for. .  bid1.wk1_
         [X] Search entire disk

     OK        Cancel       Help
```

4. Choose OK. DOS displays the path like this:

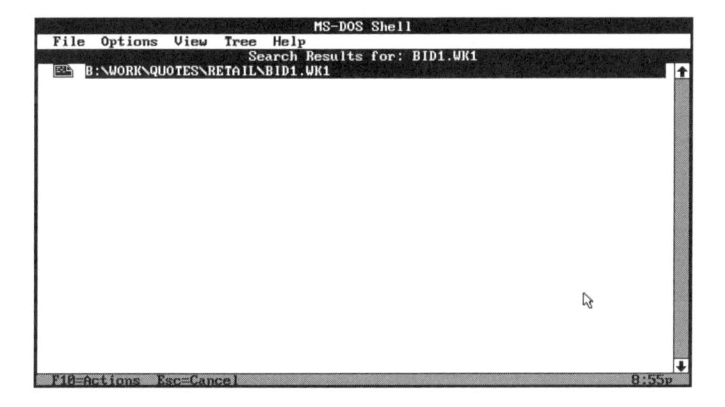

```
                         MS-DOS Shell
File  Options  View  Tree  Help
                    Search Results for: BID1.WK1
    B:\WORK\QUOTES\RETAIL\BID1.WK1




F10=Actions  Esc=Cancel                              8:55p
```

5. After DOS displays the path, press Esc to return to the DOS Shell.

▶ On Your Own

Use the SEARCH command to find any files that you have lost in the past. Remember that you can use wild cards if you do not know the exact file names. If you know the file name starts with *B* and has an extension of DOC, for example, you can search for B*.DOC.

Copying Files

■ **Note:** You cannot copy a file to a disk if the file is larger than the capacity of the disk. In this case, you must use the BACKUP command explained in Lesson 8.

You can probably think of several good reasons why you would want to copy a file. You might want to copy a file so that you can revise it. You might want to copy a file from your hard disk at work and revise it on your PC at home, or you might want to make a copy of a file as a backup.

Copying files has some different and useful options when done at the DOS prompt rather than the DOS Shell. The next sections look at these two different means of copying.

Copying Files in the DOS Shell

Copying files by using the DOS Shell is very simple and quick. This method should satisfy most of your copying needs. To copy a file or files, follow these steps:

1 Select the files.

2 Pull down the File menu and choose Copy or use the keyboard shortcut F8. A dialog box appears.

3 Make sure that the file in the From box is the one you want and then type the destination in the To box.

■ **Note:** If you attempt to copy a file to a different directory that has a file with the same name, DOS asks you to confirm that you really want to complete the copying.

The To prompt displays the current path. If you have selected only one file and you want to copy the file back to the current path, press the right arrow and type a backslash (\) and a different file name. Alternatively, you can simply type the new file name; as soon as you begin to type, the path that was displayed disappears, but it is used for the destination.

If you want to copy to a new path and keep the same file name, type only the path. To copy to a new path with a new file name, type the path and the name.

4 Press Enter or click OK to copy the files.

▶ Your Turn

Display the file listing (with all levels expanded) of the drive in which the SureSteps disk is inserted and then follow these steps to practice copying files:

1. Select the LETTERS directory to view.
2. Select the file called PPIHIST.DOC
3. Pull down the File menu and choose Copy.

> **If you have problems...** If the COPY command is not available on the pull-down menu, your cursor was not positioned in the box on the right or you have not successfully selected a file.

4. Type **ppihist2.doc** and choose OK. This figure must appear before you choose OK:

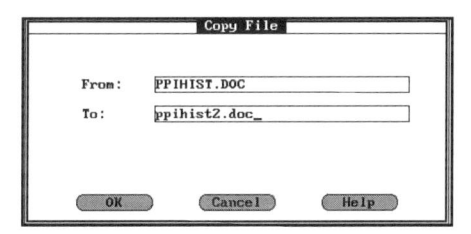

Notice that the new file name is listed in the display.

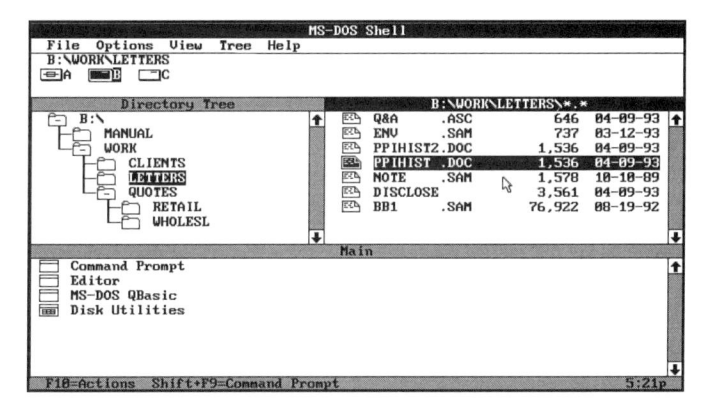

5. Choose OK.
6. Pull down the File menu and choose Copy.

Commands that Deal with Files: *Copying Files*

7 Type **c:** and choose OK to copy PPIHIST.DOC to the root of C.

8 Use the keyboard shortcut F8 to display the Copy dialog box.

9 Type **c:\ppihist2.doc** and choose OK to copy the PPIHIST.DOC file to the root of C and give it a different name.

10 Select the drive C icon to display the files on drive C.

11 Select the directory C:\.

The two files that you copied to drive C should be listed in the box on the right. (You may have to scroll down to see them.) The directories and file names will be different for each user.

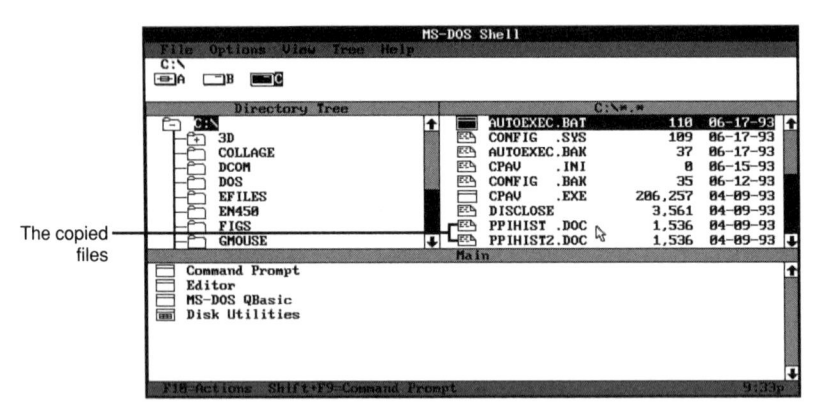

```
                              MS-DOS Shell
 File  Options  View  Tree  Help
 C:\
 [=]A  [=]B  [=]C
            Directory Tree                          C:\*.*
      C:\                            AUTOEXEC.BAT     110   06-17-93
        3D                           CONFIG   .SYS   109   06-17-93
        COLLAGE                      AUTOEXEC.BAK    37    06-17-93
        DCOM                         CPAV     .INI    0    06-15-93
        DOS                          CONFIG   .BAK   35    06-12-93
        EFILES                       CPAV     .EXE  206,257 04-09-93
        EM450                        DISCLOSE        3,561 04-09-93
        FIGS                         PPIHIST  .DOC   1,536 04-09-93
        GMOUSE                       PPIHIST2 .DOC   1,536 04-09-93
                                    Main
   Command Prompt
   Editor
   MS-DOS QBasic
   Disk Utilities

 F10=Actions  Shift+F9=Command Prompt                          9:33p
```

The copied files

12 Select the icon of the drive in which the SureSteps disk is inserted, redisplaying the files.

13 Select PPIHIST.DOC in the LETTERS directory.

14 Press F8 to copy the file.

15 Type **c:** and choose OK. The Replace File Confirmation dialog box appears. The directories and file name will be different with each user.

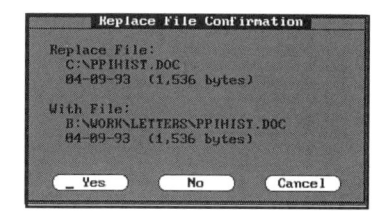

16 Choose Yes.

If you have problems... DOS does not allow you to copy a file to the same location unless you give it a new name. If you attempt to do so, you see the Copy File dialog box.

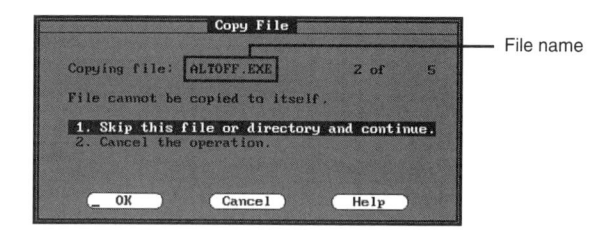

Copying Files with a Mouse

If you have a mouse, you can use it to copy a file. Follow these steps:

1 Select the file to be copied.

2 Press and hold down Ctrl and then click on the file name to highlight the file name and icon.

3 Drag the cursor to the new directory name or drive icon.

4 Release the mouse button and then release Ctrl. DOS then displays a confirmation dialog box.

5 Choose Yes to confirm the copy.

If you want to copy a file by dragging it from a directory in one drive to a directory in another drive, change the view of the DOS Shell to **D**ual File Lists and display one drive at the top and the other drive at the bottom.

▶ Your Turn

■ Note: If you do not have a mouse, practice the step by using the keyboard to copy a file.

The following steps help you get comfortable with using the mouse to copy files:

1 Select the drive in which the SureSteps disk is inserted and expand all levels of the tree, if necessary.

2 Select the RETAIL directory.

3 Hold down Ctrl and then click on BID1.WK1.

4 Continue holding down Ctrl and then drag the file to the WHOLESL directory.

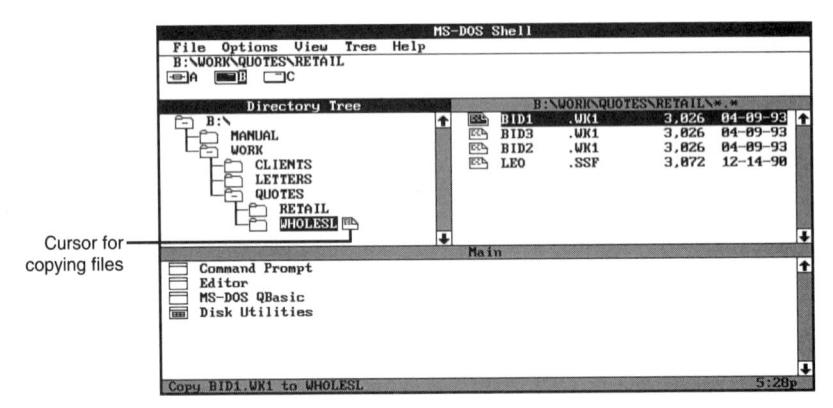

```
                        MS-DOS Shell
File  Options  View  Tree  Help
B:\WORK\QUOTES\RETAIL
⊟A  ■B  ⊟C
            Directory Tree                     B:\WORK\QUOTES\RETAIL\*.*
        B:\                           ↑    BID1   .WK1    3,026  04-09-93  ↑
          MANUAL                           BID3   .WK1    3,026  04-09-93
          WORK                              BID2   .WK1    3,026  04-09-93
            CLIENTS                         LEO    .SSF    3,072  12-14-90
            LETTERS
            QUOTES
              RETAIL
              WHOLESL
                                           Main
        Command Prompt                                                      ↑
        Editor
        MS-DOS QBasic
        Disk Utilities

Copy BID1.WK1 to WHOLESL                                            5:28p
```

Cursor for copying files

5 Release the mouse button and then release Ctrl. DOS displays a confirmation dialog box.

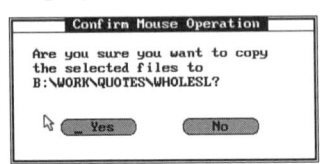

```
┌─ Confirm Mouse Operation ─┐
│ Are you sure you want to copy │
│ the selected files to         │
│ B:\WORK\QUOTES\WHOLESL?       │
│                               │
│    ( Yes )      ( No )        │
└───────────────────────────────┘
```

If you have problems... If the dialog box asks you to confirm a move rather than a copy, you pressed or released Ctrl at the wrong time. Choose No in the dialog box and try again from step 3.

6 Choose Yes to copy the file.

Copying Files at the DOS Prompt

The main advantage of using the DOS prompt to copy files is that you can copy a group of files and give the files new names, which you cannot do in the DOS Shell.

To copy files at the DOS prompt, type **copy** [*source*] [*destination*]. For the [*source*], type the name of the file or files to be copied; for the [*destination*], type the name of the file or files to which the file is to be copied. You can use wild cards to specify more than one file. If you are copying files from a directory other than the one you are in, include the path with the name of the file.

▶ **Your Turn**

Practice using the COPY command at the DOS prompt to copy files by following these steps:

1 Display the Main group in DOS Shell and choose Command Prompt to go to the DOS prompt. You exit the DOS Shell temporarily and then the DOS prompt is displayed. The prompt should correspond to the drive in which the SureSteps disk is inserted.

2 If you have an A prompt, type the following command and then press Enter:

    copy \work\letters\bb1.sam a:

If you have a B prompt, type the following command and press Enter:

    copy \work\letters\bb1.sam b:

DOS then displays the message 1 file(s) copied. This command copies the file BB1.SAM to the root directory.

■ **Tip:** Type the command ***copy bb1.sam b:*** if the current directory is B:\WORK\LETTERS.

```
Microsoft(R) MS-DOS(R) Version 6
        (C)Copyright Microsoft Corp 1981-1993.

B:\WORK\QUOTES\RETAIL>copy \work\letters\bb1.sam b:\
        1 file(s) copied

B:\WORK\QUOTES\RETAIL>
```

Commands that Deal with Files: *Copying Files*   **107**

3 Type **copy \work or \letters*.sam a:*.dup** (or type **copy \work\letters*.sam b:*.dup** if you have a B prompt) and then press Enter. (This command copies all three files that have the extension SAM to the root directory and changes their extension to DUP.) DOS displays a message as it copies each file and then displays the message `3 file(s) copied`.

4 Type **cd ** and press Enter to return to the root directory.

5 Type **dir** and press Enter to see a list of the files, including the files you copied.

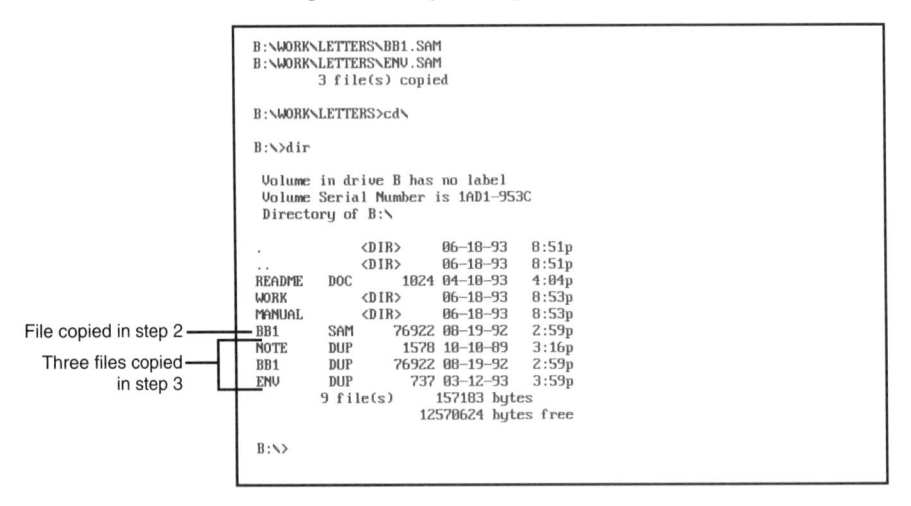

```
B:\WORK\LETTERS\BB1.SAM
B:\WORK\LETTERS\ENV.SAM
        3 file(s) copied

B:\WORK\LETTERS>cd\

B:\>dir

 Volume in drive B has no label
 Volume Serial Number is 1AD1-953C
 Directory of B:\

.            <DIR>      06-18-93   8:51p
..           <DIR>      06-18-93   8:51p
README   DOC      1024  04-10-93   4:04p
WORK         <DIR>      06-18-93   8:53p
MANUAL       <DIR>      06-18-93   8:53p
BB1      SAM     76922  08-19-92   2:59p
NOTE     DUP      1578  10-10-89   3:16p
BB1      DUP     76922  08-19-92   2:59p
ENV      DUP       737  03-12-93   3:59p
        9 file(s)     157183 bytes
                    12570624 bytes free

B:\>
```

File copied in step 2 — BB1 SAM
Three files copied in step 3 — NOTE DUP, BB1 DUP, ENV DUP

Copying Files and Directories

The XCOPY command copies all the files in a source directory, including files that are stored in a subdirectory (except for hidden files). XCOPY re-creates the directory structure on the destination path as it copies the files. This command is typed at the DOS prompt because the DOS Shell has no menu option for XCOPY. The syntax of the command is

xcopy source target /s

■ **Note:** In older versions of DOS, the XCOPY command also copied hidden files.

You type the drive and path name you are copying as the *source* and the drive and path you want to copy the file to as the *target*.

If you want to copy all the files from a disk like the one that accompanies this book, the task would be difficult without the XCOPY command. You would have to create the tree structure on the target destination by using the MD command (Make Directory) and then copy the files from each source directory to the corresponding target directory. By using the XCOPY command, however, you can accomplish the task with one command.

■ **Tip:** The /S part of the XCOPY command causes the command to copy the subdirectories, but it will not copy a subdirectory if it is empty. To force XCOPY to copy a directory even if it has no files, use /S /E.

▶ Your Turn

In this exercise, you create a directory on the hard drive and copy all the files from the SureSteps disk to that directory. All the commands are issued at the DOS prompt. Make sure that the disk is inserted in the floppy drive.

1 From the DOS prompt, change to drive C if your computer does not show a C prompt.

2 Type **cd ** and then press Enter to make certain that you are in the root directory.

3 Type **md surestep** and then press Enter.

4 If the SureSteps disk is in drive A, type **xcopy a:\ c:\surestep /s /e** and then press Enter. If the disk is in drive B, type **xcopy b:\ c:\surestep /s /e** and then press Enter.

```
A:\WORK\QUOTES\RETAIL\LEO.SSF
A:\WORK\QUOTES\RETAIL\BID2.WK1
A:\WORK\QUOTES\RETAIL\BID3.WK1
A:\WORK\QUOTES\RETAIL\BID1.WK1
A:\WORK\QUOTES\WHOLESL\PRICES.WK1
A:\WORK\QUOTES\WHOLESL\BID1.WK1
A:\WORK\LETTERS\PPIHIST.DOC
A:\WORK\LETTERS\DISCLOSE
A:\WORK\LETTERS\Q&A.ASC
A:\WORK\LETTERS\NOTE.SAM
A:\WORK\LETTERS\BB1.SAM
A:\WORK\LETTERS\ENV.SAM
A:\WORK\LETTERS\PPIHIST2.DOC
A:\WORK\CLIENTS\CLIENT.DBF
A:\MANUAL\CHAP2.ASC
A:\MANUAL\CHAP3.ASC
A:\MANUAL\EMPSEP.STY
A:\MANUAL\EMPSEP.CHP
A:\MANUAL\EMPSEP.CIF
A:\MANUAL\EMPSEP.ASC
A:\MANUAL\CHAP20.ASC
A:\MANUAL\CHAP1.ASC
        28 File(s) copied

A:\>
```

Commands that Deal with Files: *Copying Files and Directories*

5 To see the structure of the SURESTEP directory, type **tree c:\surestep /f |more** and then press Enter.

```
Directory PATH listing
Volume Serial Number is 1AD1-953C
C:\SURESTEP
    │   README.DOC
    │   BB1.SAM
    │   NOTE.DUP
    │   BB1.DUP
    │   ENV.DUP
    │
    ├───WORK
    │       BUDGET.SSF
    │
    ├───QUOTES
    │   ├───RETAIL
    │   │       LEO.SSF
    │   │       BID2.WK1
    │   │       BID3.WK1
    │   │       BID1.WK1
    │   │
    │   └───WHOLESL
    │           PRICES.WK1
    │           BID1.WK1
    │
 — More —
```

6 Press any key repeatedly to scroll the display until the DOS prompt is returned.

7 To delete the SURESTEP directory on your hard drive, type **deltree c:\surestep** and then press Enter.

8 Press **Y** for Yes and then press Enter.

9 Return to the DOS Shell by typing **exit** and then pressing Enter.

Moving Files

When a file is copied, it resides in both the original location and the new location. In contrast, when a file is moved, it resides only in the new location. To move selected files rather than copy them, follow these steps:

1 Pull down the File menu and choose Move or select the file and use the keyboard shortcut F7. A dialog box similar to the Copy File dialog box is then displayed.

2 To move a file to a new path, retaining the same file name, simply type the new path in the To box and choose OK.

To rename the file when it is moved, include the new file name with the path.

▶ **Your Turn**

Follow these steps to move a file from one directory to another.

1. Display the root directory of the SureSteps disk by selecting its icon drive.

2. Select the file PRICES.WK1 from the WHOLESL directory. (Expand the list by using Ctrl+*, if necessary.)

3. Pull down the File menu and choose **Move**.

4. Press the right arrow once. The highlighting in the To box is removed.

5. Press Backspace until you erase WHOLESL.

6. Type **retail**.

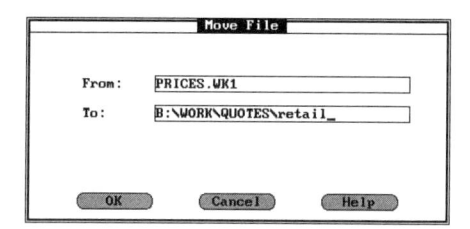

```
                    Move File
     From:   PRICES.WK1
     To:     B:\WORK\QUOTES\retail_


       ( OK )      ( Cancel )      ( Help )
```

7. Choose OK.

8. Select the RETAIL directory (if it is not already selected) to see that the file has moved.

▶ **On Your Own**

If you want to practice moving files, try moving the file back to its original directory.

If you have a mouse, you can use it to drag (or move) a file, much like dragging to copy a file. The only difference is that you do *not* press Ctrl while dragging. Try dragging (or moving) the file BID2.WK1 from the RETAIL directory to WHOLESL and back again.

Commands that Deal with Files: *Moving Files*

Replacing Files

If you have made copies of files in a directory for backup purposes, you probably will want to update the copied files when the originals change. The REPLACE command replaces the files in a directory with files of the same name from a source directory. The command also can be used to add uniquely named files to the destination directory. The REPLACE command can only be used at the DOS prompt.

To use the REPLACE command, follow these steps:

1 Change directories so that you are in the directory with the source file (the file that is replacing another file). The prompt should reflect the name of the directory.

2 Type **replace** *name path* and then press Enter. In the command, *name* is the name of the file you are replacing, and *path* is the drive and directory with the file to be replaced.

If the REPLACE command had no other options, it would be an unnecessary command because you could simply copy the updated file, but the REPLACE command has several useful variations.

- The parameter /U after *path* replaces only those files on the destination directory that have older dates than the source files.

- The parameter /S after *path* searches all subdirectories of the destination directory and replaces matching file names.

- The parameter /A after *path* adds new files to the destination directory and does not replace any existing files.

▶ Your Turn

In this exercise, you use the command line from the DOS Shell to replace a file that you copied in an earlier exercise.

1 Select the LETTERS directory.

2 Select the Main group in the Program List if it is not already selected.

3 Choose Command Prompt. You temporarily exit the DOS Shell, and the DOS prompt is displayed.

4 Type **replace ppihist2.doc c:** and press Enter. DOS displays the message `Replacing c:\ppihist2.doc` and then returns to the DOS prompt.

```
Microsoft(R) MS-DOS(R) Version 6
         (C)Copyright Microsoft Corp 1981-1993.

B:\WORK\LETTERS>replace ppihist2.doc c:\

Replacing C:\PPIHIST2.DOC

1 file(s) replaced

B:\WORK\LETTERS>
```

If you have problems... If you see the message `No files replaced`, the file was not in the c:\ directory, so it could not be replaced. This happens if you did not copy the file as instructed in the "Your Turn" in the section "Copying Files in the DOS Shell" in this lesson.

5 Type **exit** and then press Enter to return to the DOS Shell.

▶ On Your Own

Display the list of files for a directory that contains some of the files that you have created with one of your application programs (a spreadsheet or word processing program, for example). Select one of the files and copy it to another directory or drive. Exit the DOS Shell. Using the program that created the file, revise the original file, make a minor change, and save the file. From the DOS prompt, use the REPLACE command to replace the copied file with the revised original. Reboot your application program and revise the file that was updated to see that it now contains the minor change made

Commands that Deal with Files: Replacing Files

in the original file. When you are finished, close the file and the application program. Return to the DOS Shell and display the expanded view of drive B.

Deleting Files

■ **Tip:** If you have many old files that you rarely use but don't want to lose, see Lesson 8, "Backing Up and Restoring Files," to back them up before deleting them.

From time to time, you may find files on your disk that you don't need any longer. You may have several copies of the same file with different names and only want the newest one, or you may be running out of space on a disk and need more space for new files. To remove unwanted files from a disk, use the DOS DELETE command.

To delete a file or group of files, follow these steps:

1 Mark the desired file or files.

■ **Tip:** You can use the keyboard shortcut Del rather than step 2 to save time.

2 Pull down the File menu and choose Delete. If a group of files is selected, a dialog box displaying the options OK, Cancel, and Help appears. If only one file is selected for deletion, a dialog box displaying the options Yes, No, and Cancel appears.

3 Choose OK to delete a group of files. Alternatively, you can choose Yes to delete the single file.

If you do not want to delete the group of files, choose Cancel. If you do not want to delete the single file, choose No.

■ **Tip:** As a general rule, it is safer to confirm a deletion; however, if you are deleting 100 files, it's a nuisance to confirm the deletion of each file. You can disable this feature, however, by pulling down the **O**ptions menu, selecting **C**onfirmation, and deselecting Confirm on Delete.

4 If you are deleting a group of files, another dialog box displaying the first file name appears, and you must choose Yes to delete it. DOS displays a confirmation dialog box for each file; you must choose Yes to delete each one. Of course, you can choose No if you decide not to delete a file.

▶ **Your Turn**

Follow these steps to delete a group of files you copied earlier:

1 Select the root directory of the drive in which the SureSteps disk is inserted.

2 Select all files except README.DOC.

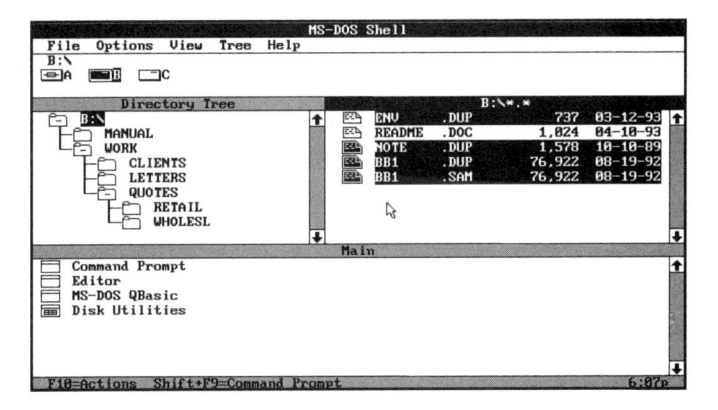

```
                          MS-DOS Shell
 File  Options  View  Tree  Help
 B:\
 ⊂A   ⊂B   ⊂C
                Directory Tree                    B:\*.*
   B:\                              ↑   ENV      .DUP      737   03-12-93
      MANUAL                            README   .DOC    1,024   04-10-93
      WORK                               NOTE    .DUP    1,578   10-10-89
         CLIENTS                         BB1     .DUP   76,922   08-19-92
         LETTERS                         BB1     .SAM   76,922   08-19-92
         QUOTES
            RETAIL
            WHOLESL
                                  Main
   Command Prompt
   Editor
   MS-DOS QBasic
   Disk Utilities


 F10=Actions  Shift+F9=Command Prompt                           6:07p
```

3 Pull down the File menu and choose **Delete**. This dialog box displays:

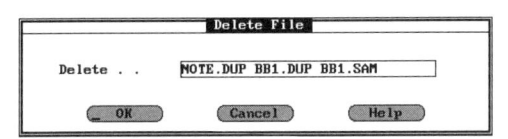

```
            Delete File
 Delete . .   NOTE.DUP BB1.DUP BB1.SAM

   ( OK )    ( Cancel )    ( Help )
```

4 Choose OK. This dialog box appears:

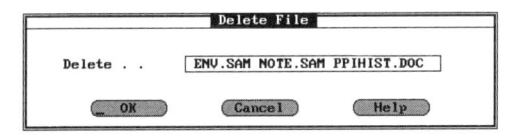

```
            Delete File
 Delete . .   ENV.SAM NOTE.SAM PPIHIST.DOC

   ( OK )    ( Cancel )    ( Help )
```

5 Choose OK and then choose Yes each time this confirmation box is displayed:

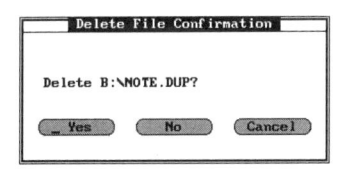

```
       Delete File Confirmation

  Delete B:\NOTE.DUP?

   ( Yes )   ( No )   ( Cancel )
```

■ **Tip:** If you want to delete files in multiple locations, pull down the **O**ptions menu and choose Select **A**cross Directories before selecting the files.

▶ On Your Own

Activate the Select Across Directories option in the Options pull-down menu. Display the files in the various directories

Commands that Deal with Files: *Deleting Files* **115**

that you have on your hard drive, and select the files that should be deleted. If you are not sure of a file's contents, view the file before selecting it for deletion. After deleting the files, deselect the Select Across Directories option and return to the expanded view of drive B.

Undeleting Files

When a file is deleted on a disk, it is not physically erased from the disk. The space that the file takes up is simply marked as usable space; therefore, if no new file has been written in the space, DOS can undelete the file. If you are using the special DOS program called Delete Sentry, DOS can restore a file even if its original space on the disk has been used.

It usually doesn't take long in a user's career before the day comes when a very important file is accidentally deleted, causing a sick feeling—especially if there is no backup for the file. Fortunately, the DOS UNDELETE command can save the day. You cannot find the UNDELETE command on the File pull-down menu as you can the DELETE command. Because this command is more like a utility, it is located in the Disk Utilities menu in the Program List at the bottom of the screen.

The capability of DOS to undelete a file depends on the level of deletion protection that is in force. DOS has three levels of deletion protection—Delete Sentry, Delete Tracker, and Standard. Both Delete Sentry and Delete Tracker require 13.5K of memory to run, and Delete Sentry requires approximately 7 percent of your hard disk for storing information about deleted files.

By default, DOS uses the Standard method of deletion protection unless you specifically issue a command from the DOS prompt to load the Delete Sentry protection or the Delete Tracker protection. Although the Standard method provides the least amount of protection for accidental deletion, it is sufficient if used in time—that is, if you undelete a file immediately after it has been accidentally deleted. If you do not undelete immediately, some or all of the file may be unrecoverable.

Delete Sentry is activated by entering **undelete /s** at the DOS prompt. When the Delete Sentry method is first activated, DOS creates a hidden directory called SENTRY. All deleted files are actually moved to this hidden directory. When files are undeleted, they are moved back to their original locations.

DOS Tracker keeps a record of a file's original location before it was deleted. Remember that a deleted file is not really erased from the disk. Its space is simply freed for use. When a file that has been tracked by DOS Tracker is undeleted, DOS tries to restore the file's original location if no other file has been stored in that space. If another file has been stored in the original file's space, it may not be possible to recover all or any of the file.

To activate DOS Tracker, enter **undelete /t** at the DOS prompt. To protect a specified drive only, enter the drive letter at the end of the command. To activate Delete Tracker for drive C only, for example, type **undelete /tc**.

To undelete files without the help of Delete Sentry or Delete Tracker, follow these steps:

1 Select the desired drive and directory in the DOS Shell.

2 Choose Undelete from the Disk Utilities menu in the Program List. A dialog box appears.

3 Choose OK in the Undelete dialog box. A list of the deleted files is then displayed, but the first letter of the original file name has been replaced by a question mark.

4 Press any key to return to the DOS Shell.

5 Choose Undelete again.

✖ **Warning:** DOS purges the SENTRY directory of the oldest files if the directory increases in size to more than 7 percent of the hard disk space. This means that older files cannot be undeleted.

■ **Tip:** It is best to automatically run Sentry or Tracker every time your computer starts. To do this, you can add the command to your AUTOEXEC.BAT file. See Lesson 7 for directions on how to add commands to AUTOEXEC.BAT.

Commands that Deal with Files: *Undeleting Files*

6 In the Parameters prompt, type the name of the file that you wish to undelete or type *.* to undelete all the deleted files.

7 Choose OK. DOS then asks if you want to undelete the specified file (or the first deleted file in the group you have selected). If you respond affirmatively, DOS instructs you to type the first letter of the file name. The file is undeleted, and the process is repeated (if there are other files to be undeleted). When all files have been undeleted, you are prompted to press any key to return to the DOS Shell.

▶ Your Turn

Follow these steps to undelete files that were deleted in a preceding exercise.

1 Select the root directory of the drive in which the SureSteps disk is inserted.

2 Choose Disk Utilities if the Main group is displayed in the Program List. Otherwise, skip to step 3.

3 Choose Undelete. The Undelete dialog box with a warning appears.

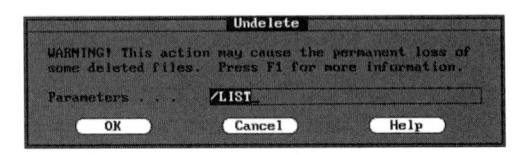

```
┌──────────────── Undelete ────────────────┐
│ WARNING! This action may cause the permanent loss of
│ some deleted files. Press F1 for more information.
│
│ Parameters . . .  /LIST
│         OK        Cancel        Help
└──────────────────────────────────────────┘
```

4 Choose OK. This screen appears:

```
UNDELETE - A delete protection facility
Copyright (C) 1987-1993 Central Point Software, Inc.
All rights reserved.

Directory: A:\
File Specifications: *.*

    Delete Sentry control file not found.

    Deletion-tracking file not found.

    MS-DOS directory contains    4 deleted files.
    Of those,    4 files may be recovered.

Using the MS-DOS directory method.

       ?B1      SAM     76922  8-19-92  2:59p   ...A
       ?OTE     DUP      1578 10-10-89  3:16p   ...A
       ?B1      DUP     76922  8-19-92  2:59p   ...A
       ?MV      DUP       737  3-12-93  3:59p   ...A


Press any key to return to MS-DOS Shell....
```

5 After reading the screen, press any key. You then return to the DOS Shell.

6 Choose Undelete again from the Program List. The Undelete dialog box appears.

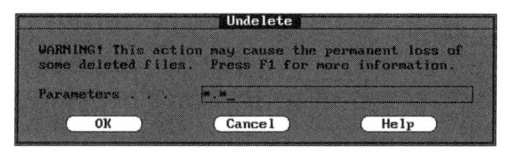

```
                    Undelete
  WARNING! This action may cause the permanent loss of
  some deleted files. Press F1 for more information.
  Parameters . . .   *.*
       OK            Cancel           Help
```

7 Type *.*.

8 Choose OK. A screen appears.

9 Type y.

10 Type the first letter of the file name. The original file names are BB1.DUP, ENV.SAM, BB1.SAM, and NOTE.SAM.

11 Repeat steps 9 and 10 until all files have been undeleted.

12 Press any key as prompted to return to the DOS Shell.

13 Select the drive in which the SureSteps disk is inserted so that the disk will be reread. The undeleted files should be visible in the list box on the right.

■ **Note:** If you do not know the first letter of the original file name, you can type any letter and DOS will still recover the file. You can then rename the file when you find out what the correct name is.

Commands that Deal with Files: *Undeleting Files*

▶ On Your Own

Decide which level of deletion protection you want to use on your system. If you want to use Delete Sentry or Delete Tracker, read more about these utility programs in DOS Help and in the DOS manual. After Lesson 7, when you should be more comfortable with editing the AUTOEXEC.BAT file, add the command line for the desired utility if you want the deletion protection to be activated each time you start your computer.

Renaming Files

Sometimes you may want to rename a file simply because you do not like the original name you gave it. You also may want to rename a file if the contents of the file no longer reflect the name. Perhaps you named your files in a random way and would like to name the files in a way that would enable you to use wild cards or group the files.

Suppose that you have three letters to Mr. Smith called INTRO.DOC, FOLLOWUP.DOC, and SALE.DOC, and you would like to rename them SMITH1.DOC, SMITH2.DOC, and SMITH3.DOC. By changing the names, the files will be listed together in the DOS Shell if the files are ordered alphabetically by name.

To rename a file or a group of files, follow these steps:

1 Select the file or files.

2 Pull down the File menu and choose Rename. If you have selected more than one file to rename, the dialog box lists the first file to be renamed.

3 Type the new name and choose OK.

If you select more than one file, the next file to be renamed is displayed. The dialog box is repeated until the last file to be renamed has been listed. Then all the files are renamed, and the DOS Shell displays the new names in the box on the right.

▶ Your Turn

Practice renaming files by following these steps:

1 Display the files in the RETAIL directory. (Use Ctrl+* to expand the directory tree, if necessary.)

2 Select all the files, except LEO.SSF.

3 Pull down the File menu and choose Rename.

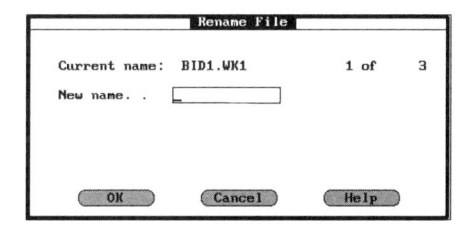

```
               Rename File
  Current name: BID1.WK1      1 of   3
  New name. .  [          ]


       ( OK )    ( Cancel )   ( Help )
```

4 As DOS prompts you for the new names, enter these names for the specified files: BIDA.WK1 for BID1.WK1, BIDB.WK1 for BID2.WK1, and BIDC.WK1 for BID3.WK1.

If you have problems... If you have problems renaming the files and you see a dialog box with the message Access denied, this usually indicates that you have made a mistake when entering the new file name. You may have chosen a name that already exists, a name that is too long, or a name that has illegal characters. Try again, making sure that you enter the new name correctly.

▶ On Your Own

Take inventory of the file names in the directories on your hard disk. Change the names of files that need a better name. View the contents of the files if you do not recognize the file.

Commands that Deal with Files: Renaming Files

Lesson Summary

To	Do this
Search for a file	Select the drive. Pull down the File menu. Choose Search. Type the file name. Choose OK.
Copy a file	Select the file and press F8. Type the destination. Choose OK.
XCOPY files	At the DOS prompt, type **xcopy source target**. To copy files in subdirectories, add the /S parameter. To copy subdirectories that are empty, use the /S/E parameters together.
Move a file	Select the file and press F7. Type the destination. Choose OK.
Replace a file	Use the command line with the proper syntax. Examples: 　　**replace *.* b:\/a** 　　**replace *.doc b:\/u** 　　**replace bid1.wk1 c:\/s**
Delete a file	Select the file and press Del. Choose Yes.
Undelete a file	Select the directory. Choose Undelete from the Disk Utilities menu. Type the file name. Choose OK. Type **y**. Type the original first letter of the file.
Rename a file	Select the file. Pull down the File menu. Choose Rename. Type the new name. Choose OK.

If You Want to Stop Now

If you want to stop now, return to the DOS prompt if it is not displayed. Then turn off your computer.

From Here

Now that you have a good grasp of handling files, you should learn how to handle disks. Lesson 6 discusses these disk topics: formatting and unformatting; checking a disk for errors and fixing fragmentation; duplicating and comparing disks; and naming a disk.

6

SURESTEPS LESSON 6

Commands that Deal with a Disk

The commands in this lesson help you prepare, monitor, and maintain your hard and floppy disks. Because the disk is the basic storage unit for data, knowing how to use the commands that deal with a disk is very important.

In this lesson, you learn how to do the following:

- Check a disk
- Defragment a disk
- Copy a disk
- Compare two disks
- Format a disk
- Unformat a disk
- Name a disk
- Display a disk's name

Lesson time:
45–60 minutes

Checking a Disk

The CHKDSK command checks the disk for errors in file storage and displays its findings in a status report. The command is unable to verify the readability of a file or identify bad sectors on the disk, although it reports any bad sectors that were found and set aside when the disk was first formatted. (For more information on bad sectors, see "Formatting a Disk" in this lesson.) The CHKDSK command should be performed periodically on a hard disk to monitor the disk for errors.

If DOS checks the disk and finds fragments of files on the disk that need to be converted to files, it displays a message above the status report that alerts you to the amount of space that is used. The report not only lists the total space and the available space on the disk, but also the total amount of memory and the available amount of memory.

▶ Your Turn

To practice using the CHKDSK command, go to the DOS prompt and follow these steps:

1 Make sure the DOS prompt reflects the hard drive. If your hard drive is C:, make sure that the DOS prompt is a C prompt (by typing **c:** and pressing Enter, if necessary).

2 Type **chkdsk** and press Enter. A status report appears that looks something like this figure:

■ **Note:** Because the files on your hard drive are different, your screen will not look exactly like the figure.

```
C:\>chkdsk
Volume Serial Number is 1AD1-AE59

   42661888 bytes total disk space
      79872 bytes in 2 hidden files
      61440 bytes in 25 directories
   18139136 bytes in 547 user files
   24381440 bytes available on disk

       2048 bytes in each allocation unit
      20831 total allocation units on disk
      11905 available allocation units on disk

     655360 total bytes memory
     494544 bytes free

C:\>
```

3 If the lost chains message is displayed, type **y** or **n**. (It doesn't matter whether you type Y or N because CHKDSK does not convert the lost chains unless you use the /F parameter that is discussed in the next section.)

■ **Note:** Lost clusters are usually created when you turn the PC off or reboot the PC when you are working on a file.

4 Insert a floppy disk in drive A or B to check the disk.

5 Type **chkdsk a:** or **chkdsk b:** (whichever is appropriate) and press Enter.

6 If the lost chains message is displayed, type **y** or **n**.

Using Parameters with CHKDSK

Parameters are additional conditions or tasks that can be added to a command. The following parameters are available with the CHKDSK command:

[PATH]FILENAME

/F

/V

Adding the path and file names causes DOS to check the specified files for fragmentation. You can use wild cards in the file name to specify multiple files. If DOS finds fragmentation, the status report on the disk is followed by information on each file that is fragmented. If no fragmentation is found, DOS reports that specified files are contiguous.

The CHKDSK command cannot fix fragmentation—DOS 6 provides the DEFRAG command for this problem. Defragmenting a disk is the next topic in this lesson.

✻Warning: Do not use the /F option if you have performed the CHKDSK command from Windows or from MS-DOS TaskSwapper or if you have a file open. Data could be lost.

The /F parameter fixes lost clusters on the disk by giving them a file name. These files can then be deleted to make more room on the disk. If fragments are found, DOS displays a message asking if you want to convert lost chains to files.

If you choose to convert the fragments to files, DOS uses the names FILE0001.CHK, FILE0002.CHK, FILE0003.CHK, and so on. These files are stored in the root directory.

The /V parameter displays the names of the files stored in each directory as the disk is checked.

▶ Your Turn

1 Insert the DOS SureSteps disk into the correct drive.

2 Type **chkdsk a:\manual*.asc** or **chkdsk b:\manual*.asc** (depending on which drive the SureSteps disk is in) and then press Enter. You should see the following screen:

```
C:\>chkdsk a:\manual\*.asc
Volume Serial Number is 2929-1CE6

    1213952 bytes total disk space
       5120 bytes in 10 directories
     200192 bytes in 23 user files
    1008640 bytes available on disk

        512 bytes in each allocation unit
       2371 total allocation units on disk
       1970 available allocation units on disk

     655360 total bytes memory
     494544 bytes free

All specified file(s) are contiguous

C:\>
```

3 Type **chkdsk a: /v** or **chkdsk b: /v** (depending on which drive the SureSteps disk is in) and press Enter. DOS displays a list of all the files as it checks the disk.

▶ On Your Own

Use the CHKDSK command on several of your disks to see if you have any lost chains. If you get the lost chains message, use the CHKDSK /F command to fix the lost chains. Then view the files listed in the root directory and delete the files called FILE0001.CHK, FILE0002.CHK, FILE0003.CHK, and so on. (These files are not usable files.)

Defragmenting a Disk

Fragmentation of a disk occurs naturally because files are written to the first available unused area on the disk. This placement causes files to be broken into pieces so that they fit in unused areas of the disk, and it creates small areas of unused disk space between existing files. The PC cannot read or write to a fragmented disk as quickly as it can to a defragmented disk.

Until the DEFRAG command was introduced with DOS 6, you had to use a program like Norton's Utilities to remedy the problem of fragmentation on a hard drive, but you could eliminate fragmentation on a floppy disk by copying the files to a newly formatted disk. With the DEFRAG command, however, you can optimize disk space on both a hard and a floppy disk.

To use the DEFRAG command, follow these steps:

1 Type **defrag** at the DOS prompt and press Enter.

2 When the dialog box appears, move the cursor to the drive that you want to defragment by using the up or down arrow and then press Enter.

DOS then analyzes the data on the disk and recommends a defragmentation procedure.

3 Start the recommended procedure by pressing Enter. While the defragmentation is taking place, DOS displays a screen that is a map of the sectors on the disk. DOS reads blocks of data (pieces of files) and moves them from the top of the screen to other places where they will fit. When all the data has been relocated to other places, DOS begins reading the data—whole files at a time—and writing the data in contiguous sectors at the top of the screen, leaving no unused spaces between files. The activity on-screen is very similar to the Nintendo game Tetris.

When the procedure is finished, DOS displays a dialog box that tells you the process is finished.

4 Choose OK. Another dialog box displays and you can elect to defragment another drive, reconfigure optimization for the current drive, or exit the defragmentation process.

5 To exit, choose Exit DEFRAG.

▶ Your Turn

✖Warning: Do not use the DEFRAG command when you are running Windows.

Defragmenting a large disk could take quite a while. You should not perform the operation when you have other pressing work to do. Select a time when the computer can be free. Before using the DEFRAG command, you should free up as much space on the disk as possible. To free space, delete all unnecessary files and perform the CHKDSK /F command to convert lost chains to files. Then delete the converted files. After getting the disk ready, take these steps to defragment the disk.

1 From the DOS prompt, type **defrag** and press Enter. This dialog box appears:

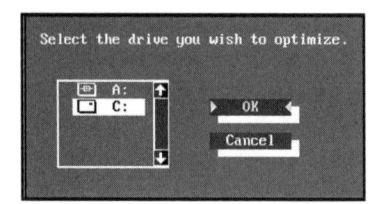

130 *DOS 6 SureSteps*

2 Choose drive C. The Recommendation dialog box appears:

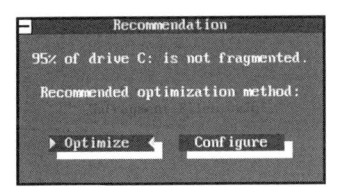

■ Tip: You can combine steps 1 and 2 by typing **defrag** followed by the designation of the drive to check and then pressing Enter. DOS does not ask you to select a drive when the Defrag program starts. It analyzes the specified disk immediately.

3 When DOS recommends a defragmentation method, press Enter to begin the process. This dialog box appears:

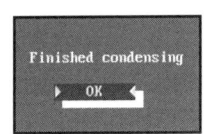

4 When the process is finished, choose OK. This dialog box appears:

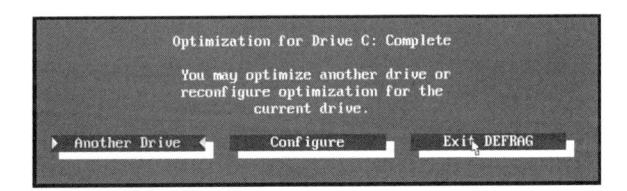

Reminder: Because the files on your hard drive are different, your screen will not look exactly like this.

5 Choose Exit DEFRAG.

Making an Exact Copy of a Disk

You can use the DISKCOPY command to make an exact copy of a disk. This command copies only floppy disks; it cannot be used to copy to or from a hard drive. The source disk (the disk being copied) and source drive must be identical in size and capacity to the target disk (the disk that is copied to) and drive. You cannot use the DISKCOPY command to copy a 3 1/2-inch disk to a 5 1/4-inch disk, for example.

The target disk does not have to be a formatted disk. The DISKCOPY command formats a disk while copying if it needs to do so. For more information about formatted disks, see the section "Formatting a Disk" in this lesson.

■ Note: If you try to use a hard drive as either the source or target disk, DOS displays an invalid drive error message.

✱Warning: All data on the target disk will be destroyed by the DISKCOPY command. Use a blank disk or one that has data that you do not want anymore.

Commands that Deal with a Disk: *Making an Exact Copy of a Disk*

■ **Tip:** It is easy to get the source and target disk mixed up if you do not pay close attention to the messages that prompt you to switch the disks. Before the disk copy procedure, write-protect the source disk by sliding open the plastic tab on a 3 1/2-inch disk or adding a write-protect tape to a 5 1/4-inch disk. After the copy is complete, you can close the plastic tab or remove the write-protect tape.

Reminder: A drive designation is the letter of the drive followed by a colon (A:, for example).

If you do not have a PC with two identical drives, you still can use the DISKCOPY command because DOS can copy from and to the same drive. If the source disk contains more information than the available memory can hold, DOS reads from the source disk, prompts you to insert the target disk, writes to the target disk, and then prompts you to insert the source disk again. This process continues until the entire source disk is copied.

To make an exact copy of a disk, follow these steps from the DOS Shell:

1 Select the source drive icon.

2 Display the Disk Utilities group in the Program List area if it is not displayed.

3 Choose Disk Copy.

4 Type the drive designations in this order: source and then target. If the source and target drives are the same, type only one designation.

5 Choose OK.

DOS temporarily leaves the DOS Shell and displays a message telling you to insert the source and target disks if you specified two drives or to insert the source disk if you specified one drive.

6 Insert the disk or disks and press any key to continue.

7 Follow the instructions on-screen to switch disks if you are copying to and from the same drive. When the copy is complete, DOS asks if you want to copy another disk.

8 Type **y** to make another copy of the same disk or to copy a different disk. Type **n** if you do not want to copy another disk.

If you type y for Yes, you are prompted to insert the disks and the process begins again.

9 When you have answered No to the message `Copy another diskette (Y/N)`, press any key to return to the DOS Shell.

▶ Your Turn

In this exercise, you make a copy of the SureSteps disk. Locate a blank disk or a disk that contains data that you do not need. After making the copy, save the disk. It will be used in later exercises. Now go to the DOS Shell and follow these steps:

1. Select the drive icon for the disk drive that you will use (a: or b:).

2. Display the Disk Utilities group.

3. Choose Disk Copy. This dialog box appears:

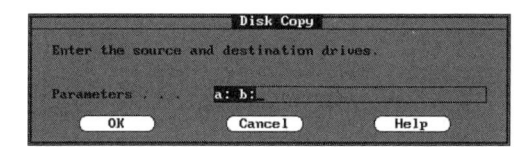

```
                    Disk Copy
    Enter the source and destination drives.

    Parameters . . .  a: b:
         OK           Cancel          Help
```

4. Type the appropriate drive designations and choose OK. If you are using only one drive, for example, type the appropriate drive specification, a: or b:. If you have two identical drives, type both drive specifications, separated by a space—a: b:, for example. DOS prompts for the disk to be copied.

```
Insert SOURCE diskette in drive A:
Press any key to continue . . .
Copying 80 tracks
15 sectors per track, 2 side(s)
Insert TARGET diskette in drive A:
Press any key to continue . . .
```

5. Follow the on-screen messages, inserting the disk or disks.

6. Press any key after you have inserted the source and target disks.

Commands that Deal with a Disk: *Making an Exact Copy of a Disk*

If you have problems... If you attempt to copy a disk of one capacity or size to a disk of a different capacity or size, DOS displays an error message. Remember that if you do not have two identical disk drives, you can copy to and from the same drive.

7 If you must switch the disks, continue to do so as prompted.

8 Type **n** in response to the prompt.

9 Press any key to return to the DOS Shell.

Comparing Two Disks

■ **Note:** If the source disk is fragmented, the target disk also will be fragmented because the DISKCOPY command makes an exact copy. To avoid fragmentation, use the COPY command to copy all the files on a disk or the XCOPY command to copy all the directories and files. You also can defragment the source disk before copying it.

The DISKCOMP command performs a track-by-track comparison of two floppy disks. You might use this command after performing the DISKCOPY command. The command cannot be used for hard disks or floppy disks of different sizes or capacities.

To compare two disks, follow these steps:

1 Go to the DOS prompt.

2 Type **diskcomp**, followed by the designation of the first drive and the designation of the second drive, and then press Enter. If you are using the same drive, change to that drive, type **diskcomp** followed by one drive designation, and press Enter. To compare a disk in drive A with a disk in drive B, for example, type **diskcomp a: b:**. To compare two disks in drive A, change to the A prompt and type **diskcomp a:**.

3 Follow the on-screen instructions to insert the disk or disks.

4 Press any key to begin the comparison.

If DOS finds inconsistencies in the disks during the comparison, a compare error message is displayed.

If no inconsistencies are found when the comparison process is complete, a Compare OK message is displayed and DOS asks if you want to compare another disk.

5 If you type **y** for Yes, DOS prompts you to insert the first disk, and the procedure begins again. If you type **n** for No, you return to the DOS prompt.

■ **Note:** If you use the same drive to compare the disks, DOS may have to prompt you to switch the disks several times.

▶ Your Turn

Use the SureSteps disk and the copy that you made of the disk and compare them by following these steps:

1 Go to the DOS prompt.

2 Change to the drive that you will be using (a: or b:).

3 Type the appropriate command (**diskcomp a: b:** or **diskcomp a:** or **diskcomp b:**) and press Enter.

4 Follow the on-screen instructions to insert the first disk.

5 Press any key as prompted.

6 Switch disks when prompted and press any key.

7 When DOS asks if you want to compare another disk, type **n** for No.

■ **Note:** When comparing disks, you can use either the copy or the original as the first disk. The order does not matter.

```
Step 3 ── A:\>diskcomp a:
Step 4 ── Insert FIRST diskette in drive A:
Step 5 ── Press any key to continue . . .
         Comparing 80 tracks
         15 sectors per track, 2 side(s)
         Insert SECOND diskette in drive A:
         Press any key to continue . . .
Step 6 ── Insert FIRST diskette in drive A:
         Press any key to continue . . .
         Insert SECOND diskette in drive A:
         Press any key to continue . . .
         Compare OK
Step 7 ── Compare another diskette (Y/N) ?
```

Commands that Deal with a Disk: *Comparing Two Disks*

Understanding Disks and Formatting

The FORMAT command prepares a new disk for use or reformats a previously formatted disk. Most disks sold today are unformatted, although for a higher price you can buy formatted disks. The Disk Utilities group displays two format commands—FORMAT and QUICK FORMAT. The FORMAT command is used for new or previously formatted disks. The QUICK FORMAT command is used only for previously formatted disks that are in good condition.

When preparing a new disk for use, DOS creates tracks and sectors on both sides of the disk. A 360K disk has 40 tracks and 9 sectors on each side. Each track and sector is numbered so that DOS can determine the address of any data that is written to the disk. (Because the disk in the drive is spinning like a record, the data is written to the disk in the first available space. Pieces of a file can be written in many different tracks and sectors.)

When formatting a new disk, DOS also creates the root directory and the File Allocation Table (FAT), used to store the file addresses. During the formatting, DOS checks each sector on the disk to ensure that the sector can properly store data. If a defective sector is found, DOS marks that sector to prevent it from being used. The QUICK FORMAT command does not check the disk for defects and should be used only with previously formatted disks that are known to have no defects.

If you format a previously used disk, DOS performs a safe format. It clears the File Allocation Table (FAT) and root directory of the disk, but it does not delete any files that are stored on the disk. You then can use the UNFORMAT command to recover the disk if you did not intend to format the disk.

The FORMAT command assumes that you want to format the disk to match the capacity of the drive that you are using. If you insert a disk in a 360K disk drive, for example, DOS assumes that you want to format the disk to 360K capacity even if the disk is a 1.2M disk. A drive cannot format a disk with a higher capacity than the drive's default capacity, but it can format a disk with a lower capacity. If you are using a 1.2M drive, for example, you can format a disk to a 360K capacity. If you are using a 360K drive, you cannot format a disk to a 1.2M capacity. You learn how to specify formatting capacity later in this section.

Formatting a Disk

You can use the DOS Shell to format a disk. Follow these steps:

1. Select the Disk Utilities group if it is not displayed in the Program List area.

2. Choose Format.

3. Type the drive designation in the Parameters prompt. DOS temporarily exits the DOS Shell and displays a message telling you to insert the disk and press Enter when ready.

4. Choose OK.

5. If you do not want to name the disk, press Enter. If you do want to, type a name for the disk when DOS asks you for the Volume Label. The name can be a maximum of 11 characters. Unlike a file name, the volume name can have spaces in its name.

    Regardless of whether you name the disk or not, DOS assigns a serial number to the disk.

6. When the formatting is complete, MS-DOS displays some technical information about the disk and then asks if you want to format another disk. If you have a new box of disks, you might want to format them all at the same time. You can type **y** and press Enter to format the next disk and then continue formatting all disks until you are finished.

7. When the last disk is formatted, you can type **n** and press Enter when DOS asks you if you want to format another one.

■ **Note:** You should not format a floppy disk with a different capacity than the disk is designed to hold; the disk will be unreliable.

Commands that Deal with a Disk: Understanding Disks and Formatting **137**

▶ Your Turn

In this exercise, you format the disk that you made when you copied the SureSteps disk. Insert the copy in the disk drive and take these steps to format the disk:

1. Go to the DOS Shell.

2. Display the Disk Utilities group.

3. Choose Format.

4. Type **a:** or **b:** (whichever is correct for your system).

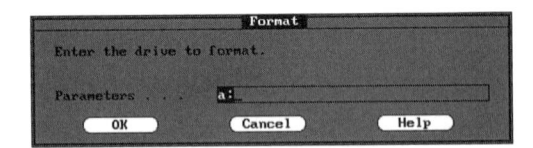

```
                    Format
Enter the drive to format.

Parameters . . .  a:
     OK           Cancel         Help
```

5. Choose OK.

6. Insert the disk in the appropriate drive, as instructed by DOS, and then press Enter.

7. When the last disk is formatted, you can type **n** and press Enter when DOS asks you if you want to format another one.

> **If you have problems...** If DOS begins the formatting process and reports that the existing format differs from that specified and the disk cannot be unformatted, you are probably trying to format a disk that does not have the capacity to be formatted in the drive. DOS asks whether you want to proceed. If you do proceed, DOS may or may not be able to format the disk. If DOS terminates the format, the disk will be rendered unreadable, but you will be able to format the disk with the correct capacity.

8. When prompted for the disk label, type your first name and press Enter. DOS then displays some information about the disk as shown in this figure:

```
Insert new diskette for drive A:
and press ENTER when ready...

Checking existing disk format.
Saving UNFORMAT information.
Verifying 1.2M
Format complete.

Volume label (11 characters, ENTER for none)? yvonne

    1213952 bytes total disk space
    1213952 bytes available on disk

        512 bytes in each allocation unit.
       2371 allocation units available on disk.

Volume Serial Number is 281C-1DDA

Format another (Y/N)?
```

9 Type **n** and press Enter.

10 Press any key to return to the DOS Shell.

Using Other Formatting Options

You can add a number of parameters to the FORMAT command to implement different options. This section covers the most common and useful ones.

/S	Copies the hidden files (IO.SYS and MSDOS.SYS) and COMMAND.COM from the PC's startup drive to a newly formatted disk. The new disk is then capable of starting the PC.
/Q	Specifies a quick format of a disk. You can select the QUICK FORMAT command rather than use this parameter. This command does not check the disk for bad areas.
/U	Destroys all existing data on a disk. This parameter speeds up the formatting process, but it prevents you from later unformatting the disk. Use this parameter if you have received read and write errors while using a disk.

✹ **Warning:** The FORMAT command can also be used to format a hard disk, but this is rarely done after the initial formatting of the disk when it is new. If you enter the command to format the hard disk, DOS displays this message:

WARNING: ALL DATA ON NON-REMOVABLE DISK DRIVE x: WILL BE LOST!

Proceed with Format (Y/N)?_

If you really want to format the hard disk, type **y**; if you do not want to format the disk, type **n**. Then press Enter.

Commands that Deal with a Disk: Understanding Disks and Formatting

✖ **Warning:** Some 360K drives will not be able to read disks that have been formatted by high-density drives.

■ **Note:** Quadruple-density is also called high density.

/F:size   Specifies the capacity of the floppy disk to format, where size is one of the following:

160 for a single-sided, double-density, 5 1/4-inch disk

180 for a single-sided, double-density, 5 1/4-inch disk

320 for a double-sided, double-density, 5 1/4-inch disk

360 for a double-sided, double-density, 5 1/4-inch disk

720 for a double-sided, double-density, 3 1/2-inch disk

1200 for a 1.2M double-sided, quadruple-density, 5 1/4-inch disk

1440 for a 1.44M double-sided, quadruple-density, 3 1/2-inch disk

2880 for a 2.88M double-sided, extra-high-density, 3 1/2-inch disk

With the FORMAT command, you can use several parameters together if you want. You can speed up the formatting process considerably if you use both the /Q and /U parameters. Remember though, if you use /U, the disk cannot be unformatted later. When you use multiple parameters, separate them by a space.

▶ Your Turn

The following steps walk you through three of the parameters available for the FORMAT command. If you want to get familiar with any others, you can try them on your own.

1 Go to the DOS Shell.

2 Display the Disk Utilities group.

3 Choose Format.

4 Type **a:** /s or **b:** /s (whichever is correct for your system). This formats a disk and includes the system files.

5 Choose OK.

6 Insert the disk in the appropriate drive, as instructed by DOS, and then press Enter.

> **If you have problems...** If DOS begins the formatting process and reports that the existing format differs from that specified and the disk cannot be unformatted, you are probably trying to format a disk that does not have the capacity to be formatted in the drive. DOS asks whether you want to proceed. If you do proceed, DOS may or may not be able to format the disk. If DOS terminates the format, the disk will be rendered unreadable, but you will be able to format the disk with the correct capacity.

7 When prompted for the disk label, type your first name and press Enter. DOS displays information about the disk.

8 Type **n** and press Enter.

9 Press any key as prompted to return to the DOS Shell.

10 Choose Format.

11 If you are using a 5 1/4-inch disk, type one of the following commands:

a: /f:360 /v:work /u

or

b: /f:360 /v:work /u

(whichever is correct for your system) and then press Enter. This formats a disk as a 360K disk, destroys all previous information on the disk, and names the disk WORK.

If you are using a 3 1/2-inch disk, type one of the following commands:

a: /f:720 /v:work /u

or

b: /f:720 /v:work /u

(whichever is correct for your system) and then press Enter. This formats a disk as a 720K disk, destroys all previous information on the disk, and names the disk WORK.

12 Insert a different disk or the disk you formatted in the preceding exercise and then press any key.

✱ **Warning:** All the data on this disk will be destroyed.

13 Follow the directions on-screen, typing **n** when asked if you want to format another, and then return to the DOS Shell.

▶ On Your Own

Try booting your computer from the disk you formatted with the system. Then reboot the computer as you normally would. Use CHKDSK to see the vital information about the disk or disks you formatted. Note that the system disk has additional information about hidden files in the CHKDSK report. These are the system files.

■ **Note:** If the formatted disk has already had data written to it, the new data will be lost when the disk is unformatted.

Unformatting a Disk

By using information in the root directory and the FAT, the UNFORMAT command can restore the directories and files on a disk that has been formatted with the safe format. If the disk was formatted with the /U parameter, it cannot be restored.

If DOS finds a file that it cannot completely recover because of fragmentation, you can choose to recover part of the file or delete the file. DOS cannot always tell that a file is partially unrecoverable, however. After a disk is unformatted, you may have a file that is incomplete. If the file contains a program, the program will not work, of course.

To unformat a disk, follow these steps:

1 Go to the DOS prompt.

2 Type **unformat**, followed by the drive designation and press Enter. For example, type:

unformat a:

3 Insert the disk and press Enter.

4 When DOS displays the following message, type **y**:

```
Are you sure you want to update the system area of
your drive x (Y/N)?
```

DOS then searches for the necessary information to restore the disk.

■ **Note:** If the /L parameter is not used, the UNFORMAT command lists only the files and directories that are fragmented.

These parameters are available for the UNFORMAT command:

/L   Lists every file and subdirectory found. To halt the scrolling of the list, press CTRL+S. Press any key to continue.

/TEST   Shows how DOS would restore the information on the disk but does not actually unformat the disk. You can use this parameter to see if any files will be unrecoverable because of fragmentation.

/P   Sends output messages to the printer connected to the printer port LPT1.

▶ Your Turn

To practice using the UNFORMAT command, use the disk that began as a disk copy and was formatted in the last exercise. From the DOS prompt, follow these steps:

1 Type **unformat a:** or **unformat b:** and press Enter.

2 Insert the disk and press Enter. DOS displays information about the disk and asks you to confirm the update.

Commands that Deal with a Disk: *Unformatting a Disk*   **143**

```
                (C)Copyright Microsoft Corp 1981-1993.

A:\>unformat a:

Insert disk to rebuild in drive A:
and press ENTER when ready.

Restores the system area of your disk by using the image file created
by the MIRROR command.

        WARNING !!      WARNING !!

This command should be used only to recover from the inadvertent use of
the FORMAT command or the RECOVER command.  Any other use of the UNFORMAT
command may cause you to lose data!  Files modified since the MIRROR image
file was created may be lost.

Searching disk for MIRROR image.

The last time the MIRROR or FORMAT command was used was at 22:16 on 06-18-93.

The MIRROR image file has been validated.

Are you sure you want to update the system area of your drive A (Y/N)?
```

3 Type y.

▶ On Your Own

Find a disk that you know contained data and then was formatted. Use the UNFORMAT command with the /TEST parameter to see what was previously on the disk. If you cannot find such a disk, format a disk that has data and then test the UNFORMAT command.

The UNFORMAT command is a great safety net for catastrophic events like the accidental formatting of the hard disk. If, by some stroke of bad fortune, you do accidentally format the hard disk, you can breathe a sigh of relief knowing that the UNFORMAT command can unformat the disk and hopefully recover a large majority of the disk.

You will have just one small problem when you try to unformat the hard disk, however. The UNFORMAT command will not be there because it, like all the other files, will have been erased by the FORMAT command. It may be starting to dawn on you that with all the files erased, you will not be able to perform any commands and when you turn the computer off, you will not be able to boot it either.

Before you get to this sad state of affairs, take this precaution. Make a bootable disk by formatting a disk with the /S parameter. Remember that this parameter copies the system files (IO.SYS and MSDOS.SYS) and COMMAND.COM to the disk.

Then copy the UNFORMAT.COM file to the disk. Keep this disk in a safe place. If you ever format the hard drive, you can start the computer with this disk and then unformat the hard drive with it.

Naming a Disk and Displaying the Name

The LABEL command can name a disk, rename a disk, or remove a disk name. The name can be a maximum length of 11 characters, and spaces can be included in the name. Because the DOS Shell doesn't have a LABEL command, the command must be issued from the DOS prompt.

You can type the LABEL command in several different ways to name a disk.

- You can change to the drive, type **label**, and then press Enter. DOS then prompts you for the name.

- Without changing to the drive, you can type **label**, followed by the drive designation, and then press Enter. DOS then prompts you for the name.

- You can change to the drive and type **label**, followed by the desired name and then press Enter.

If a disk already has a name, you can use the same command that you use to name a disk with no name. To delete a disk name, use the same command, but when you are prompted for the name, press Enter. Then type **y** for yes when prompted.

The VOL command displays the disk label. Like the LABEL command, the VOL command must be issued from the DOS prompt. To display a label, change to the desired drive, type **vol**, and then press Enter or you can type **vol**, followed by the drive designation, and press Enter.

Commands that Deal with a Disk: Naming a Disk

▶ **Your Turn**

Use the following steps to rename one of the floppy disks you formatted earlier:

1. Insert the disk in the floppy drive.
2. Type **a:** or **b:** and press Enter.
3. Type **label** and press Enter.
4. Type **mary** and press Enter.
5. Type **vol** and press Enter.
6. Type **c:** and press Enter.

```
C:\>a:

A:\>label
Volume in drive A is YVONNE
Volume Serial Number is 2B1C-1DDA
Volume label (11 characters, ENTER for none)? mary

A:\>vol

 Volume in drive A is MARY
 Volume Serial Number is 2B1C-1DDA

A:\>
```

7. Type **label a:** or **label b:** and then press Enter to give the disk a new name.
8. Type a friend's first name and then press Enter.
9. Type **vol a:** or **vol b:** and then press Enter.

Lesson Summary

To	Do this
Check the disk	At the DOS prompt, type **chkdsk** and press Enter.
Defragment a disk	Type **defrag** at the DOS prompt and press Enter. Select the disk. Wait for DOS to recommend a defragmentation method. Press Enter. When the process is complete, choose OK. To exit, choose Exit DEFRAG.

To	Do this
Copy a disk	From the DOS Shell, display the Disk Utilities and choose Disk Copy. Type the drive designation of the source disk followed by a space and then type the drive designation of the target disk. Choose OK. (If you use the same drive for the source and the target disks, select the icon for the source drive, display the Disk Utilities, choose Disk Copy, type the single drive designation, and choose OK.)
Compare two disks	At the DOS prompt, type **diskcomp**, followed by the drive designation of the source disk and the drive designation of the comparison disk. Press Enter. (If you use the same drive for the source and the comparison disk, change to the source drive and type **diskcomp** followed by the single drive designation.)
Format a disk	From the DOS Shell, select Disk Utilities and select Format or Quick Format. Type the drive to be formatted and choose OK. When prompted, type the desired name of the disk and press Enter or press Enter to bypass naming the disk. When prompted, type **y** to format another disk or **n** to stop formatting disks.
Unformat a disk	At the DOS prompt, type **unformat** followed by the drive designation. Press Enter. Type **y** to confirm the update.
Name a disk	At the DOS prompt, type **label**, followed by the drive designation. Type the desired name for the disk and press Enter.
Display a disk name	At the DOS prompt, type **vol**, followed by the drive designation. Press Enter.

Commands that Deal with a Disk: Lesson Summary

If You Want to Stop Now

To stop now, return to the DOS prompt if you are in the DOS Shell and turn off your system.

From Here

In this lesson, you learned the basic commands for working with the hard disk and floppy disks. You can continue acquiring a basic knowledge of DOS by completing the next lesson. This lesson covers commands and files that deal with your PC system itself. The discussion of the AUTOEXEC.BAT and the CONFIG.SYS files is an important topic that you should not overlook.

Section Three

Customizing and Enhancing Your System

3

7. Commands and Files that Deal with the System
8. Backing Up and Restoring Files
9. Protecting the PC from Viruses
10. Increasing Your Disk Space with DoubleSpace
11. Optimizing Memory and Speed

7
SURESTEPS LESSON 7

Commands and Files that Deal with the System

In this lesson, you learn how to do the following:

- Display the version of DOS that is operating your PC
- Set the date
- Set the time
- Set the path
- Set the prompt
- Create an AUTOEXEC.BAT file
- Create other batch files
- Revise the CONFIG.SYS file

This lesson presents commands and two special files that affect the way your PC is set up and the way it operates. These commands are explained in terms of the DOS prompt because they are not included in the DOS Shell.

The setup commands can be typed by the user every time the computer is booted, or the commands can be stored in a special file. When the PC boots, any commands contained in this special file are read into memory. After you have learned the purpose and the syntax of the setup commands, you learn how to add them to this file.

Lesson time:
25–35 minutes

Displaying the Version of DOS

The command to display the version of DOS that is operating the computer is VER. When you issue this command at the DOS prompt, the type of DOS and the version number are displayed.

■ **Note:** Because Microsoft makes minor improvements and adds them to the program version as a new release, you sometimes need to know the exact release of a version (such as 6.0, 6.1, and so forth).

You may think this command is a rather insignificant one, but after you have been using your computer for a while, you may forget what version of DOS you have installed. The version of DOS that you are using can be a significant piece of information if you are troubleshooting. If you have a problem with a particular program and you call the support line for that program, for example, the technician may ask you what version of DOS you are using.

If you are working in an environment with many PCs, the version of DOS that is installed on each PC can become a critical issue because different versions have different capabilities. You may need to use the XCOPY command to copy files from a disk that has hidden files, for example. If you use a PC with DOS 6, the XCOPY command does not copy the hidden files. If you use a PC with an earlier version of DOS, you can copy the hidden files.

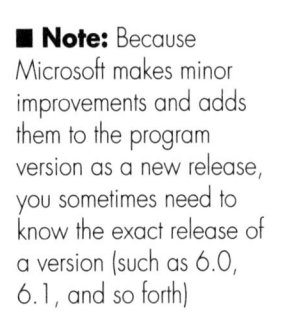

▶ Your Turn

Verify that you are using MS-DOS 6 by following these steps:

1. Go to the DOS prompt.
2. Type **ver** and press Enter. Your screen should display this message:

   ```
   MS-DOS Version 6.00
   ```

3. Insert a floppy disk in the disk drive.
4. Type **a:** or **b:** (whichever is appropriate) and press Enter.
5. Type **ver** and press Enter.

The same DOS message should be displayed. Even though you changed to a drive where DOS is not stored, DOS can still display the version because the version number is held in memory.

▶ On Your Own

If you have several PCs at your disposal, use the VER command to see what versions of DOS are installed on each PC.

Setting the Date

Almost all computers have an internal calendar and clock that are battery-powered so that they keep the correct date and time even when the PC is not running. DOS *date-stamps* every file with the date that is logged in the computer at the time it saves the file to disk.

The command to set the date is DATE. When you issue the command, DOS displays the date that is currently logged in the computer and a prompt that allows you to type a different date. If you enter a different date, the calendar is reset to that date.

Although the DATE command is seldom needed, it can be very useful in some situations. In 1992, a computer virus called Michelangelo infected many computers across the nation, for example. The virus was set to do its dirty work on Michelangelo's birthday. As a preventative, the day before Michelangelo's birthday, computer users set the dates on their computers two days ahead to avoid the date that would trigger the virus.

▶ Your Turn

Find out the day of the week on which your next birthday falls by following these steps to reset the date in your computer:

1 Type **date** and press Enter.

```
C:\>date
Current date is Sat 06-19-1993
Enter new date (mm-dd-yy):
```

2 Type the date of your next birthday (including the year) and press Enter. (Use the mm-dd-yy format as indicated.)

3 Type **date** and press Enter. Observe the day of the week.

4 Type the current date to reset the calendar and press Enter.

▶ On Your Own

Find out what day Christmas falls on next year. Then change the date back to the current date.

Setting the Time

■ **Note:** Some computers can automatically change the time when Daylight Savings Time goes into effect.

When DOS date-stamps files, it also time-stamps them with the time that is logged in the computer. The command to set the time is TIME. When you issue the command, DOS displays the current time in hours, minutes, seconds, and hundredths of seconds. It also displays a prompt that allows you to enter a different time. You will find this command useful in the spring and fall of the year if you set the clocks up an hour or back an hour.

When you set a new time in the computer, you don't have to type the seconds and hundredths of seconds. You can type the hour and minutes in a 24-hour format (military time) or a 12-hour format. If you use the 12-hour format, be sure to include *a* for a.m. or *p* for p.m. If you do not type an *a* or *p*, DOS assumes that the time is a.m.

▶ **Your Turn**

Practice using the TIME command by following these steps:

1 Type **time** and press Enter.

2 Type **22:00** and press Enter to set the time to 10:00 p.m.

> **If you have problems...** If you get a message Invalid time, type the time again, making sure that you use a colon between the hour and minutes. When using *a* or *p* to designate a.m. or p.m., don't leave a space between the time and the letter.

3 Type **time** and press Enter. The display should show a few seconds after 10:00 p.m.

4 Type **11:15p** and press Enter to set the time to 11:15 p.m.

5 Type **time** and press Enter.

6 Finally, type the current time and press Enter.

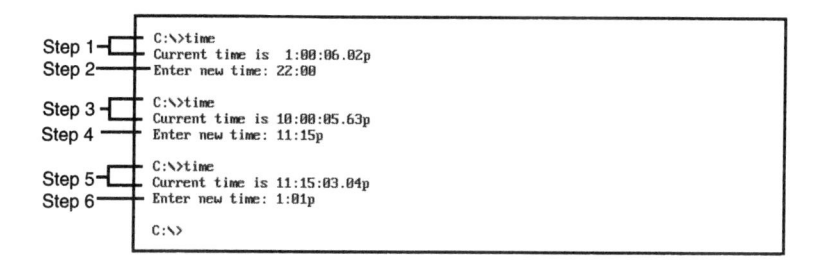

```
Step 1  C:\>time
Step 2  Current time is  1:00:06.02p
        Enter new time: 22:00

Step 3  C:\>time
Step 4  Current time is 10:00:05.63p
        Enter new time: 11:15p

Step 5  C:\>time
Step 6  Current time is 11:15:03.04p
        Enter new time: 1:01p

        C:\>
```

Setting the Path

The PATH command instructs DOS where to look for executable files when the executable file name is typed at the DOS prompt. Typing the file name of an executable file at the DOS prompt is like typing a DOS command. In fact, executable file names are really considered commands.

Reminder: In Lesson 3, you learned that executable files have extensions of COM, EXE, or BAT, and they contain programs or commands that are executed when the file name is typed.

Commands and Files that Deal with the System: *Setting the Path*   **155**

■ **Tip:** Don't forget to include the root directory (c:\) in the path if you want to execute commands in the root directory from other directories.

■ **Tip:** To speed up the DOS search process, list frequently used directories at the beginning of the path statement.

■ **Note:** AUTOEXEC.BAT files are covered later in this lesson.

If DOS does not have a path to follow and a command is typed at the DOS prompt, DOS looks for the executable file in the current directory. If the file is not in the current directory, DOS cannot execute the file.

The PATH command lists multiple directories separated by semicolons, as in the following command:

> path=c:\;c:\dos;c:\wp51

The command cannot exceed 127 characters in length. When a command is issued, DOS always searches in the current directory first and then searches the directories listed in the path, in the order in which they are listed.

If you have executable files in the same directory with the same file name but different extensions, DOS executes the files in this order: COM files first, then EXE files, and finally BAT files. To specify which file you want to run, type the file name and extension. If you have two or more files with the same name and extension but stored in different directories, DOS executes the file in the directory listed first in the search path.

Your PC probably has an AUTOEXEC.BAT file that contains a PATH command. If so, you can display the path by typing **path** and pressing Enter. DOS then displays the path statement or the message No path if no path is set. To clear the path setting, type **path** ; (semicolon). If you clear all path settings, DOS looks only in the current directory for executable files. To set the path, type **path=**, followed by the desired directory names (separated by semicolons), and then press Enter.

▶ **Your Turn**

Try these steps to experiment with using the PATH command:

   1 Type **path** and press Enter. If DOS displays the message No path, skip to step 6.

   2 Type **path** ; and press Enter.

---

156 DOS 6 SureSteps

This step clears the path. Now DOS cannot execute a command unless the command file is in the current directory.

3 Type **path** and press Enter. This verifies that there is no path set now.

4 Change to drive C if you have an A prompt or a B prompt and type **cd ** and press Enter.

5 Type **chkdsk** and press Enter. DOS should respond to your command with the message `Bad command or file name`.

6 Type **path=c:\dos** and press Enter. (This command assumes that you are using drive C and the DOS program is installed in a directory called DOS. If DOS is installed on a different drive or in a different directory, use the appropriate designation.)

7 Type **chkdsk** and press Enter. DOS should be able to execute the command this time because you have provided the path where the executable file (CHKDSK.COM) can be found.

8 Type **autoexec** and press Enter.

Step 8 should restore the path that is set in your AUTOEXEC.BAT file. If you do not have an AUTOEXEC.BAT file, DOS responds with the message `Bad command or file name`.

9 Type **path** and press Enter.

The same path or message that displayed after step 1 should be displayed now.

■ **Note:** Step 4 is included to ensure that the root is the current directory. If you were already in the root, the step has no effect. The root must be the current directory because you are about to perform steps that demonstrate that DOS cannot execute a command because the executable file is stored in the DOS directory and not the root.

■ **Note:** If your computer starts Windows or runs an application at startup, you need to exit to DOS to continue with the following steps.

▶ On Your Own

Look at the path that your PC uses. Should you add any other directories? When you learn how to revise the AUTOEXEC.BAT file later in this lesson, add these directories to the path statement and rearrange the order of directories so that the directories used most often are listed first.

Setting the Prompt

■ **Note:** Even though Microsoft refers to C> as the default prompt, it does not use it as the default. If no prompt is specified, DOS uses a prompt that displays the drive, the current directory, and the greater-than sign. The default prompt can be specified only by issuing the Prompt command with no parameters.

■ **Note:** AUTOEXEC.BAT and CONFIG.SYS files are covered later in this lesson.

The PROMPT command controls the appearance of the DOS prompt. The default DOS prompt is the disk drive letter followed by the greater-than sign (>). If you are working from drive C, for example, the default DOS prompt is C>.

You can customize the DOS prompt to display text or useful information such as the date, time, or the name of the current path. The DOS prompt seen on most computers displays the current path, followed by the greater-than sign. This is the most useful information you can display in the DOS prompt. Knowing exactly where you are at all times can prevent you from making some disastrous mistakes. If your DOS prompt displays something other than the current path, for example, you could be in the root directory but think you were in another directory. You could issue the command to erase all the files in the directory, and you would erase all the files in the root, including COMMAND.COM, AUTOEXEC.BAT, and CONFIG.SYS—rendering your computer incapable of booting.

To set the DOS prompt to the default, type **prompt** and press Enter. To customize the DOS prompt, type **prompt** followed by the desired text. The most commonly used codes to include special information or characters in the prompt are shown below.

Code	Meaning
$T	Current time
$D	Current date
$P	Current drive and path
$N	Current drive
$G	> (greater-than sign)
$_	Makes the text or codes that follow display on the next line
$H	Backspace (to delete a character that has been written to the prompt command line)

▶ Your Turn

Follow these steps to practice using the PROMPT command:

1 Type **prompt** and press Enter.

2 Type **prompt Your wish is my command $g** and then press Enter.

3 Type **prompt t_pg** and then press Enter. This command produces a time display on the line preceding the C:\> prompt.

4 Type **prompt thhh$_$p$g** and then press Enter. This command erases the decimal and the hundreths-of-seconds positions from the time display.

5 Type **prompt pg** and then press Enter. This command restores the prompt to the C:\> form. The following figure shows this exercise:

■ **Tip:** This prompt is fun, but really too long for practical use. It could cause commands to wrap to the next line, which is confusing.

```
Step 1 — C:\>prompt
Step 2 — C>prompt Your wish is my command $g
Step 3 — Your wish is my command >prompt $t$_$p$g
         13:22:40.15
Step 4 — C:\>prompt $t$h$h$h$_$p$g
         13:23:02
Step 5 — C:\>prompt $p$g
         C:\>
```

▶ On Your Own

There are other less-used options for the prompt. Use the DOS built-in Help to see what they are. Then see if you can change the prompt to the following specifications:

Prompt	Specifications	Example
1	The date is date Current path>	The date is 04-24-93 C:\>
2	Command =	Command =
3	DOS Version Current path>	MS-DOS Version 6.00 C:\>

Commands and Files that Deal with the System: Setting the Prompt   **159**

The answers are at the end of this lesson. Change the prompt back to its original appearance, using pg.

Using an AUTOEXEC.BAT File

In Lesson 3, you learned that a BAT file, called a batch file, contains a series of DOS commands that are executed when you type the file name of the batch file at the DOS prompt. The AUTOEXEC.BAT file fits this definition, but it has one quality that no other batch file has. Not only will the file be executed if you type **autoexec** at the DOS prompt, it also is automatically executed every time the PC is booted if AUTOEXEC.BAT is in the root directory.

To remember the string of events that are responsible for executing the AUTOEXEC.BAT file, you may need to review what happens when you turn on your computer. First, the computer checks the hardware to see that everything is in working order; this is called the Power On Self Test (POST). Then the Bootstrap Loader program looks on drive A for the two hidden files, IO.SYS and MSDOS.SYS. If the hidden files are not found on drive A (and they won't be unless you have a DOS disk in drive A), the Bootstrap Loader looks on drive C. The IO.SYS file initializes any hardware devices attached to the system, loads the MSDOS.SYS program in memory, opens the CONFIG.SYS file and follows the instructions in it, and finally loads the DOS file called COMMAND.COM. The COMMAND.COM file reads the AUTOEXEC.BAT file (if there is one) and follows the instructions in it.

The AUTOEXEC.BAT file contains DOS commands. You have learned many of the DOS commands that are commonly stored in the AUTOEXEC.BAT file in this lesson. At the beginning of this lesson, you learned that the commands can be typed every time the computer is booted or the commands can be stored in the AUTOEXEC.BAT file. Storing the commands in the AUTOEXEC.BAT file is preferable, however, to typing the setup commands every time you turn the computer on or warm-boot the computer.

You can create an AUTOEXEC.BAT file that contains the commands that you have learned in this lesson. Before attempting to create an AUTOEXEC.BAT file, however, you need some practice creating a file if you do not know how to use the MS-DOS Editor.

Creating a File

To create a file without the help of the MS-DOS Editor, you use the COPY command from the DOS prompt. The COPY command can copy the contents of another file, as you learned in Lesson 5, but it also can copy from the screen. To instruct DOS to copy from the screen, you use this form of the COPY command:

    copy con filename

Con means console and *filename* is the name of the file created to store the data that is copied from the console. When you use this method to create a file, you enter the data in the file, line by line. Each line must be correct before you type the next line because you cannot go back to a line that you have already entered. If you make a mistake while the cursor is still on the line, however, you can backspace and retype the line. The file that is created by COPY CON is an ASCII file—the only file format that can be used for batch files.

▶ Your Turn

In this exercise, you create a simple file that contains information about your system. From the DOS prompt, follow these steps:

1 Type **copy con readme.txt** and press Enter.

2 Type **My PC is made by** _____ and then press Enter. (Fill in the blank with the name of the PC manufacturer—IBM, Compact, or Epson, for example.)

> **If you have problems...** If you fail to correct a mistake on a line before you press Enter, end the file by pressing F6 and then pressing Enter. Start the exercise again at step 1.

---

3 Type **My CPU is an** _____ and then press Enter. (Fill in the blank with 8088, 8086, 80286, 80386, or 80486, for example. If you do not know what CPU your system has, fill in the blank with **unknown chip**.)

4 Type **My printer is made by** _____ and then press Enter. (Fill in the blank with the name of the manufacturer, such as Epson, Hewlett-Packard, NEC.)

5 Type **I am using the** _____ **version of DOS** and then press Enter. (Fill in the blank with 6.0. If you are using any other version, you aren't getting much out of this book!)

6 Press F6 and then press Enter.

The function key F6 adds the end-of-file character to the file. The only way to end a file created with COPY CON is to press F6, and then press Enter. Because the end-of-file character precedes Enter, DOS knows that you are finished with the file and ready to copy it. DOS copies the contents of the screen to the file called README.TXT and responds with the message `1 file(s) copied`.

7 Type **type readme.txt** and then press Enter to review what you have typed in the file.

You can view the contents of an ASCII file at any time, by using the TYPE command or by booting the DOS Shell, and choosing File, View File Contents. If you use the TYPE command from the DOS prompt, however, you must specify the path of the file if it is not in the current directory. If you have the file stored in the root of drive C and your DOS prompt is an A prompt, for example, you must type **type c:\readme.txt** to see the file contents.

Creating Your Own AUTOEXEC.BAT File

Now you are ready to create a new AUTOEXEC.BAT file. Because you probably have an AUTOEXEC.BAT file on your PC already, you should protect it by renaming the file AUTOEXEC.1 or copying it to a floppy disk (or both). After you have experimented with an AUTOEXEC.BAT file of your own making, you can delete that file and restore the old one so that your system works the way it did originally.

✖ **Caution:** Always keep a backup copy of your original AUTOEXEC.BAT file. If something goes wrong in editing AUTOEXEC.BAT, you may need this backup to restore the original file.

▶ Your Turn

To create your own AUTOEXEC.BAT file with the COPY CON command, follow these steps:

1. Make sure that the DOS prompt for your hard drive is displayed. (It must be the drive where DOS is installed.) If your DOS prompt is A:\>, for example, and DOS is installed on drive C, type **c:** and press Enter to change to the correct drive.

2. Type **cd ** and press Enter. This step is very important because the AUTOEXEC.BAT must be stored in the root directory of the drive where DOS is installed.

3. Use the DIR command to see if you have an AUTOEXEC.BAT file in the root of your hard drive. If you do, copy the file to a floppy disk and then rename the file on the hard disk to AUTOEXEC.1.

4. Type **copy con autoexec.bat** and then press Enter.

5. Type **date** and then press Enter. This step causes DOS to prompt you for the date after you have booted.

6. Type **time** and press Enter, causing DOS to prompt you for the time after you have booted.

7. Type **prompt pg$g** and press Enter. This changes the default DOS prompt to display the current directory, followed by two greater-than signs.

■ **Tip:** If you know how to use the MS-DOS Editor, start the Editor and begin with step 5. Follow the rest of the steps, but rather than completing step 12, save the file and exit to the DOS prompt. Then continue with the remaining steps.

Commands and Files: Using an AUTOEXEC.BAT File　**163**

8 Type **path=c:\;c:\dos** and then press Enter. (If you are working from a different drive letter, substituted your drive letter for "c." If DOS is installed in a directory by a different name, substitute that name for "dos.")

This step establishes the path that DOS searches when an executable file name is entered at the DOS prompt.

9 Type **chkdsk** and press Enter to check the disk and to display a status report.

10 Type **pause** and press Enter. In this step, the PAUSE command, used only in batch files, causes DOS to display the following message:

```
Press any key to continue...
```

DOS waits to process the next command in the batch file until a key is pressed. You must use the PAUSE command in this batch file because the CHKDSK command displays a report and you need time to read it before the next command in the file is executed.

11 Type **dosshell** or (if you have a monochrome monitor) **dosshell/b** and press Enter. This step takes you from the DOS prompt to the DOS Shell.

12 Press F6 and then press Enter to end the file and copy it to disk.

13 Press Ctrl+Alt+Del to warm-boot the PC.

14 When prompted, type the date or go to the next step if the correct date is displayed. Notice that the DATE command is displayed on-screen above the prompt.

15 Press Enter.

16 Type the time or go to the next step if the correct time is displayed. Notice that the TIME command is displayed on-screen above the Time prompt.

17 Press Enter. Notice that the CHKDSK command is displayed before the disk is analyzed and the report is displayed.

18 After DOS prompts you and you have read the disk report, press any key. Notice that the PAUSE command is displayed above the DOS message.

You should be in the DOS Shell. Your AUTOEXEC.BAT file has performed all the commands that you stored in the file. To exit the DOS Shell, you must use keyboard commands because your AUTOEXEC.BAT did not include a command to boot a mouse program. To exit the DOS Shell, press Alt, **f**, **x**.

✖ **Warning:** If you don't want to complete the next On Your Own exercise, you **must** restore your original AUTOEXEC.BAT file by following the steps in the last paragraph of that exercise.

If you have problems...

If none of the commands in your AUTOEXEC.BAT file were executed, you probably made a typing error when you named the file in step 4. Use the DIR command or go back into the DOS Shell to see what you named the file. Rename the file correctly and begin again at step 13.

If some of the commands in the AUTOEXEC.BAT were carried out correctly and others were not, you probably made typing errors on the lines that did not execute properly. Use the TYPE command or go to the DOS Shell and then view the contents of the file to see whether you made a typing error. If you find a typing error, revise the file and correct the mistake by using MS-DOS Editor or a word processing program that is capable of reading and writing ASCII files. If you are using a word processing program, be sure to save the file in ASCII format. (MS-DOS Editor saves in ASCII format automatically.) If you are not familiar with a word processing program and you have no previous experience with MS-DOS Editor, you can begin the exercise again from step 1. (The MS-DOS Editor is discussed in detail in Lesson 12.)

▶ **On Your Own**

In this exercise, you add more commands to the AUTOEXEC.BAT file that you have been creating. If you do not want to perform these steps, skip to the last paragraph in this exercise and follow the instructions to restore your original AUTOEXEC.BAT to the disk.

✖ Warning: Be very careful that you do not change anything in the AUTOEXEC.BAT file that you do not understand. Some commands that are contained in the AUTOEXEC.BAT file are added by other programs during installation routines. The lines may be essential to the proper working of that program. Do not delete or change any lines in the file that begin with ***mode***, ***set***, ***doskey***, ***vsafe***, or ***smartdrv***.

If you followed the instructions in the preceding Your Turn section carefully, you probably noticed that each command stored in the AUTOEXEC.BAT was displayed on-screen before the action of the command was performed. This is called *echoing to the screen*. If you do not want to see each command before it is performed, you can turn off the echo with the ECHO OFF command. Normally, this is the first command in a batch file. To keep the ECHO OFF command itself from echoing to the screen, the *at* symbol (@) must precede the command like this:

```
@echo off
```

Using a word processing program, MS-DOS Editor, or the COPY CON command, add the @ECHO OFF command to the AUTOEXEC.BAT file as the first line of the file. Warm-boot the PC. Notice that the commands are performed, but the commands themselves are not echoed (displayed) to the screen.

If you would like to experiment with other DOS commands in the AUTOEXEC.BAT file, add those commands when you add the @ECHO OFF command.

Look at the contents of your old AUTOEXEC.BAT file, now named AUTOEXEC.1 (or AUTOEXEC.BAT on your floppy back up). Are there any commands that you would like to add to the file? If so, add the commands, using the method that is most convenient for you.

When you have revised the AUTOEXEC.1 file so that it contains all the commands that you want, delete the AUTOEXEC.BAT file and rename AUTOEXEC.1 to AUTOEXEC.BAT. Warm-boot your PC to make sure that everything is working correctly.

If there is a problem and you do not know how to correct it, locate the AUTOEXEC.BAT file that you copied to a floppy disk at the beginning of this part of the lesson. Copy that file to the root of your hard disk.

Creating Other Batch Files

Now that you have learned about the most important batch file, the AUTOEXEC.BAT, you might want to create other batch files that will be useful to you. You might want to create a batch file that starts a program in another directory, for example.

▶ Your Turn

Use these steps to create a batch file that starts the DOS Shell:

1. Change directories to the root of the hard drive.
2. Type **copy con ds.bat** and press Enter.
3. Type **@echo off** and press Enter.
4. Type **cd \dos** and press Enter. (If your DOS files are in a different directory, substitute that for **dos** here.) This step ensures the correct execution of the batch file if there is no path statement in memory or if there is a path statement in memory that does not include the DOS directory.
5. Type **dosshell** and press enter. If you have a monochrome monitor, type *dosshell /b*.
6. Type **cd ** and press Enter. When the batch file runs, this command is not executed until after you exit the DOS Shell. After you exit, the batch file returns you to the root directory and then it is finished.
7. Press F6 and then press Enter.
8. Type **ds** and press Enter to run the batch file.
9. Press Alt+F4 or choose the File menu and then choose Exit. You are returned to the DOS prompt at the root directory.

■ **Note:** With this batch file, you can start the DOS Shell with only three keystrokes. Ordinarily, you use nine or more keystrokes to start the Shell when entering the commands yourself at the DOS prompt.

▶ On Your Own

Use COPY CON to create a simple batch file that starts one of your programs. If there are any parameters you use every time you start the program, include them in the batch file to save steps.

Batch File Commands

DOS provides a special set of commands that are used only in batch files. You have already used three of these commands—PAUSE, ECHO, and @. Other commands include CALL, CHOICE, FOR, GOTO, IF and REM. All the batch commands are summarized in Table 7.1.

■ **Note:** Use DOS Help to learn more about the batch file commands. Pay particular attention to the examples given for each command.

Table 7.1. Special Batch File Commands

Command	Definition
@	Suppresses the echo of the current line to the screen.
CALL	Executes a batch file that is nested in the current batch file. When execution of the second batch file is complete, DOS returns to the first batch file and executes the remaining commands in the file.
CHOICE	Prompts the user to make a choice during the execution of a command. The default choices are Y and N, but the user can specify different choices or add choices to Y and N.
ECHO	Echoes commands to the screen when set to ON. When set to OFF, ECHO suppresses the echo of commands to the screen. If the command is used with no parameter, it echoes the text of the current line to the screen. ECHO creates a blank line if it is used with a period (.).
FOR	Executes a command for a set of variables.
GOTO	Causes command execution to skip to a specific location specified by the GOTO command.
IF	Specifies a condition and a command that will be executed if the condition is true.

Command	Definition
PAUSE	Causes the batch file to pause until the user strikes any key.
REM	Designates a line as a remark and not a command. These remarks are echoed to the screen unless another command is used to suppress the remark.

▶ Your Turn

In this exercise, you create a menu using batch commands. The menu will look like this:

```
                DOS Commands


1. Recover and Delete Lost Clusters on Hard Disk
2. Format a Disk in the A Drive
3. View the Contents of AUTOEXEC.BAT and CONFIG.SYS




Type the number of your choice and press Enter.
```

Follow these steps to create and test the four files necessary to create the menu system. All files should be created in the root of drive C.

1 Use COPY CON or the MS-DOS Editor to create a file called MENU.BAT. The file should have the following lines in it:

```
@echo off
cls
echo.
echo                 DOS Commands
echo.
echo     1. Recover and Delete Lost Clusters on Hard Disk
echo     2. Format a Disk in the A Drive
```

Commands and Files: *Creating Other Batch Files*

```
    echo      3. View the Contents of AUTOEXEC.BAT and
                 CONFIG.SYS
```

    echo.

    echo.

```
    echo      Type the number of your choice and press
                 Enter.
```

The CLS command in the second line of the file, clears the screen.

2 Use COPY CON or the MS-DOS Editor to create a file called 1.BAT. The file should have these lines in it:

    @echo off

    cls

    cd \dos

    chkdsk /f

    pause

    del *.chk

    cd \

    menu

The MENU command on the last line of the file runs the batch file MENU.BAT which recalls the menu to the screen.

3 Use COPY CON or the MS-DOS Editor to create a file called 2.BAT. The file should have these lines in it:

    @echo off

    cls

    cd \dos

    format a:

    cd \

    menu

4 Use COPY CON or MS-DOS Editor to create a file called 3.BAT. The file should have these lines in it:

```
@echo off

cls

echo This is the AUTOEXEC.BAT file:

type \autoexec.bat

pause

echo This is the CONFIG.SYS file:

type \config.sys

pause

menu
```

5 At the DOS prompt, type **MENU** and press Enter.

If you have problems... If the menu does not display, make sure that you are in the root directory when you type the MENU command. If the menu still does not display, make sure that you stored the MENU.BAT file in the root.

6 Press **1** and then press Enter. The CHKDSK /F command in the batch file executes. When you press any key, the DEL command in the batch file executes and the menu redisplays.

7 Press **3** and then press Enter. The AUTOEXEC.BAT file displays. When you press any key, the CONFIG.SYS file displays, and then the menu redisplays.

8 If you have a disk to format, press **2** and then press Enter.

▶ On Your Own

Add the command that calls the MENU.BAT as the last command in the AUTOEXEC.BAT file. Reboot the system so that the menu displays after DOS loads.

Commands and Files: Creating Other Batch Files

Understanding the CONFIG.SYS File

The CONFIG.SYS file stores instructions that affect (or *configure*) the PC's hardware and memory. You may have a special piece of hardware that requires its own program to operate. The command that tells DOS to use this program must be stored in the CONFIG.SYS file.

Following are some common commands you might see in your CONFIG.SYS file:

Command	Function
FILES	Specifies the number of files DOS can access at one time. The maximum is 255. A range of 20 to 40 is the normal. Don't set this range too high because it wastes memory.
BUFFERS	Sets the number of data buffers DOS uses when reading and writing disks. A setting of 20 or 30 is good for DOS programs. If you are using SMARTDRV, you can reduce this to 3.
DEVICE	Loads device drivers—special programs that let DOS communicate with non-standard devices such as a fax board or a mouse. DOS comes with several drivers, and others are provided with special hardware. Several of the DOS drivers are discussed later in this book. The DoubleSpace driver is discussed in more detail in Lesson 10; memory drivers, in Lesson 11; and the InterInk and Power drivers, in Lesson 13.
STACKS	Creates a memory area that DOS uses to store information when it is interrupted by other hardware or software. If DOS runs out of stacks, the computer locks up. Keep the number and size of stacks small to conserve memory.
INSTALL	Loads some terminate-and-stay-resident (TSR) programs into memory.

Command	Function
REM	Places remarks (comments) in CONFIG.SYS.

If you are intimidated by these commands, don't worry. Most hardware and software that you might add to your system automatically update this file if you let them when you run the installation programs. Unless you become a "power user," you may never need to bother with this file.

▶ On Your Own

If you have a CONFIG.SYS file, examine each of the statements in the file by viewing the file through the DOS Shell or by using the TYPE command at the DOS prompt.

Try to determine what each statement does for your system. If you see statements that look incorrect, like `Buffers=90`, try to determine if any of the programs installed on your PC require these statements. If not, make adjustments to the statements and see if your system runs more efficiently.

▶ On Your Own

Use MS-DOS Help at the DOS prompt to display information about other system configuration statements like DEVICE, DEVICEHIGH, and LASTDRIVE. To learn about the DEVICEHIGH statement, for example, type **help devicehigh** and press Enter. All the commands used in the CONFIG.SYS file are listed in Appendix A of the DOS *User's Guide*.

Troubleshooting the CONFIG.SYS File

The statements in the CONFIG.SYS file can be executed or bypassed one at a time during the booting process. This process is described for you in detail in Lesson 1. Go back and

Reminder: If you have a CONFIG.SYS, it is located in the root directory of the startup drive (usually C).

■ **Tip:** Before making any changes to the CONFIG.SYS file, make a copy of the file so that you can restore it to the hard disk if you make a change that causes a problem. Remember that you can bypass the commands in the CONFIG.SYS file by pressing F5 during the boot process.

review that procedure now if you would like to test the need or validity of the statements in the CONFIG.SYS file.

Lesson Summary

To	Do this
Display the version of DOS	Type **ver** and press Enter.
Set the date	Type **date** and press Enter. Type the desired date and press Enter.
Set the time	Type **time** and press Enter. Type the desired time and press Enter.
Set the path	Type **path=** and follow it by the list of directories separated by semicolons. Press Enter.
Set the prompt	Type **prompt** and follow it by the desired text or codes and then press Enter.
Create an AUTOEXEC.BAT file	Use COPY CON or MS-DOS Editor. If you use a word processing program, be sure to save the file in ASCII format. Include the desired DOS commands in the file.
Create a CONFIG.SYS file	Use COPY CON or MS-DOS Editor. If you use a word processing program, be sure to save the file in ASCII format. Include all the desired statements in the file.

If You Want to Stop Now

If you are in the DOS Shell, return to the DOS prompt. At the DOS prompt, turn off your system.

From Here

In this lesson, you used commands that set up and configure the system, and you learned the basic facts about the AUTOEXEC.BAT and CONFIG.SYS files. To extend your knowledge of disk commands, complete Lesson 8, "Backing Up and Restoring Files."

On Your Own Answers

Answers for Setting Prompt Specifications:

Prompt Specifications	Syntax
1. The date is date Current path>	prompt The date is d_pg
2. Command =	prompt Command $q
3. DOS Version Current path>	prompt v_pg

Backing Up and Restoring Files

SURESTEPS LESSON 8

In this lesson, you learn how to do the following:

- Back up data
- Compare backed-up data with the original data
- Restore backed-up data
- Run Microsoft Backup from Windows

Lesson time: 35–45 minutes

Backing up important files is not just a wise habit to cultivate—it should be considered mandatory. As wonderful as computers are and as easy as they can make our lives, they are not perfect; and users, as you know, are far from perfect. Hard disks crash, floppy disks get coffee spilled on them, and users have been known to erase data accidentally (and on purpose) and even, yes, even to format a hard disk.

If you feel that you do not have time to back up your work, remember that you will have to *make* time to reenter it if something happens to the data. Microsoft estimates that it takes about 2,000 hours of work (that's a year of 40-hour workweeks!) to replace the data on the average hard disk.

Understanding Microsoft Backup

DOS has always had a fairly sophisticated BACKUP command, but the DOS 6 includes a completely new and powerful system of backing up data.

Microsoft Backup has five basic functions: Backup, Compare, Restore, Configure, and Quit. Each of these functions is summarized in Table 8.1.

Table 8.1. Functions of Microsoft Backup

Function	Description
Backup	Creates a backup file for specified drives, directories, and files. Note: The backup file does not contain individual, usable files. The backup file must be restored in order to use the files it contains.
Compare	Compares the files in a backup set to the original files to verify that the backups are accurate. You should use the COMPARE command after performing each backup to ensure the reliability of the backup set.
Restore	Copies backup files to the original or a new location.
Configure	Enables you to select default settings for the BACKUP command.
Quit	Exits Microsoft Backup.

DOS includes two backup programs—one for DOS and one for Windows. During the installation of DOS 6, you have the option of installing one, both, or none of these programs on your system. If you choose to install the Windows version, DOS creates a Tools group in the Program Manager, complete with icon.

Configuring Microsoft Backup

The first time you use the BACKUP command on your computer, DOS prompts you through a procedure that configures the BACKUP command to your system. DOS also runs a compatibility test to ensure that the BACKUP command is configured correctly. The compatibility test performs a small backup to the disk drive of your choice and requires two disks.

■ **Tip:** Before using the BACKUP command the first time, make sure that you have two usable disks that are blank or do not contain important data.

▶ Your Turn

To use Microsoft Backup for the first time, exit any programs that are running, remove all floppy disks, and follow these steps:

1 From the DOS prompt of the hard drive, type **msbackup** and then press Enter. The Alert dialog box shown below appears:

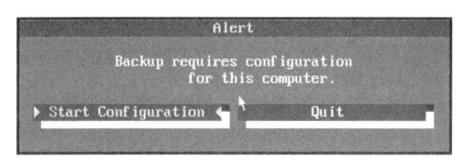

```
                    Alert
         Backup requires configuration
              for this computer.
     ▶ Start Configuration ◀        Quit
```

If you have problems... If you get the message Bad command or file name, change to the DOS directory and repeat step 1.

2 Choose Start Configuration. A screen showing the video and mouse configuration appears:

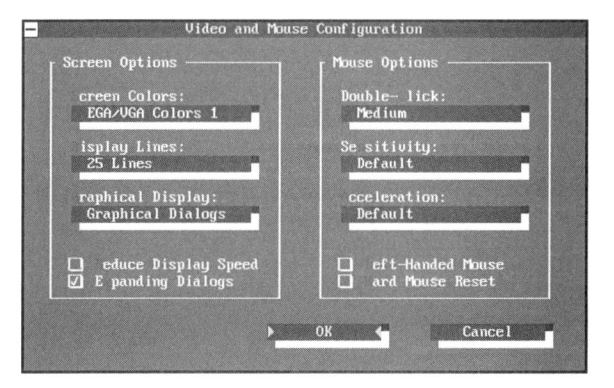

```
              Video and Mouse Configuration
   ┌ Screen Options ──────┐  ┌ Mouse Options ──────┐
      creen Colors:             Double- lick:
      EGA/VGA Colors 1          Medium

      isplay Lines:             Se sitivity:
      25 Lines                  Default

      raphical Display:         cceleration:
      Graphical Dialogs         Default

      □ educe Display Speed     □ eft-Handed Mouse
      ☑ E panding Dialogs       □ ard Mouse Reset

              OK                     Cancel
```

Backing Up and Restoring Files: *Configuring Microsoft Backup*

3 The options displayed are generally acceptable because DOS reads the configuration of the hardware. If you don't want the default options, select the ones that you want.

4 When you have set all options, choose OK. A screen announcing the floppy drive change line test appears.

5 Select **S**tart Test. When the test is finished, the results are shown.

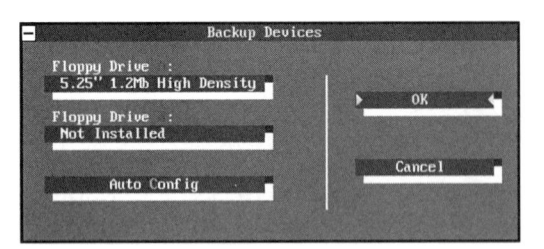

```
┌─                   Backup Devices                    ─┐
 Floppy Drive  :
  5.25" 1.2Mb High Density
                                      ►    OK    ◄
 Floppy Drive  :
  Not Installed
                                        Cancel
        Auto Config
```

6 Choose OK. DOS then checks the processor speed and the hard disk speed and displays a screen announcing the floppy disk compatibility test.

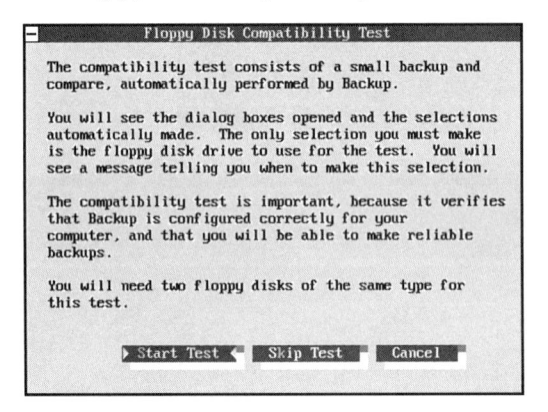

```
┌─            Floppy Disk Compatibility Test            ─┐
 The compatibility test consists of a small backup and
 compare, automatically performed by Backup.

 You will see the dialog boxes opened and the selections
 automatically made. The only selection you must make
 is the floppy disk drive to use for the test. You will
 see a message telling you when to make this selection.

 The compatibility test is important, because it verifies
 that Backup is configured correctly for your
 computer, and that you will be able to make reliable
 backups.

 You will need two floppy disks of the same type for
 this test.

           ► Start Test ◄   Skip Test    Cancel
```

You can skip the test. If you perform the test, however, you must have two floppy disks of the same size for the test. These disks are used as backups and any data on the disks will be destroyed. Be sure to select disks that are empty or have data that you can afford to lose.

7 Choose Start Test. DOS displays several menus, makes choices in the menus automatically, and then displays this Alert message:

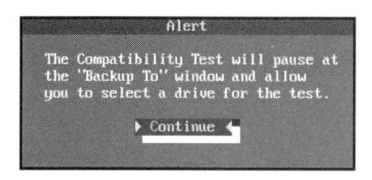

> *Alert*
>
> The Compatibility Test will pause at the "Backup To" window and allow you to select a drive for the test.
>
> ▶ Continue ◀

8 Choose Continue. The types of disk drives are displayed.

9 Select the drive that corresponds to the one you intend to use with the two disks. (If you are using a mouse, simply click the drive selection. If you are using the keyboard, move the cursor to the drive selection and press the space bar to select it.)

10 Choose OK. This Alert message appears:

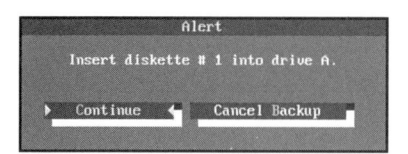

> *Alert*
>
> Insert diskette # 1 into drive A.
>
> ▶ Continue ◀   Cancel Backup

11 Insert the first disk and choose Continue. If the disk that you are using contains data, DOS displays this screen:

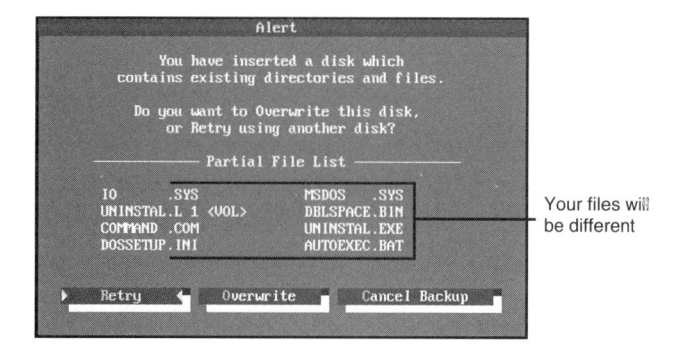

> *Alert*
>
> You have inserted a disk which contains existing directories and files.
>
> Do you want to Overwrite this disk, or Retry using another disk?
>
> ——— Partial File List ———
>
> | IO   .SYS | MSDOS   .SYS |
> | UNINSTAL.L 1 <VOL> | DBLSPACE.BIN |
> | COMMAND .COM | UNINSTAL.EXE |
> | DOSSETUP.INI | AUTOEXEC.BAT |
>
> ▶ Retry ◀   Overwrite   Cancel Backup

Your files will be different

Because you were instructed in this lesson to select a disk that did not contain important information, you can select Overwrite to continue.

When the backup process starts, DOS displays this screen, which shows the progress of the backup:

Backing Up and Restoring Files: Configuring Microsoft Backup   **181**

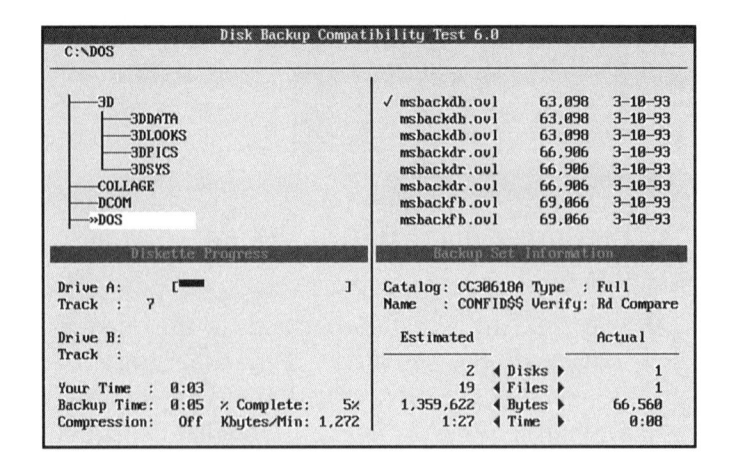

```
         ┌─────────── Disk Backup Compatibility Test 6.0 ───────────┐
         │ C:\DOS                                                    │
         ├──────────────────────────┬────────────────────────────────┤
         │  ┌─3D                    │ √ msbackdb.ovl  63,098  3-10-93│
         │      ├─3DDATA            │   msbackdb.ovl  63,098  3-10-93│
         │      ├─3DLOOKS           │   msbackdb.ovl  63,098  3-10-93│
         │      ├─3DPICS            │   msbackdr.ovl  66,906  3-10-93│
         │      └─3DSYS             │   msbackdr.ovl  66,906  3-10-93│
         │  ├─COLLAGE               │   msbackdr.ovl  66,906  3-10-93│
         │  ├─DCOM                  │   msbackfb.ovl  69,066  3-10-93│
         │  └»DOS                   │   msbackfb.ovl  69,066  3-10-93│
         ├──── Diskette Progress ───┼──── Backup Set Information ────┤
         │ Drive A:   [▬▬▬       ]  │ Catalog: CC30618A Type  : Full │
         │ Track  :  7              │ Name   : CONFID$$ Verify: Rd Compare │
         │ Drive B:                 │      Estimated          Actual │
         │ Track  :                 │            2  ◄ Disks ►      1 │
         │ Your Time  : 0:03        │           19  ◄ Files ►      1 │
         │ Backup Time: 0:05  % Complete:  5%│ 1,359,622  ◄ Bytes ► 66,560 │
         │ Compression: Off  Kbytes/Min: 1,272│     1:27  ◄ Time  ►   0:08 │
         └──────────────────────────┴────────────────────────────────┘
```

The box in the upper left corner shows the directory that DOS is backing up. The box in the upper right corner shows the files that are being backed up. The box in the lower left corner shows the Diskette Progress and displays a message when it is time to insert the next disk. The lower right box shows the Backup Set Information.

When DOS is ready for the next disk, it displays a message in the lower left box. If you do not respond to the message immediately, DOS displays a dialog box instructing you to insert the second disk.

12 Insert the disk and choose Continue. If the second disk also contains data, you must select **Overwrite** to continue.

When the backup is complete, this information is displayed:

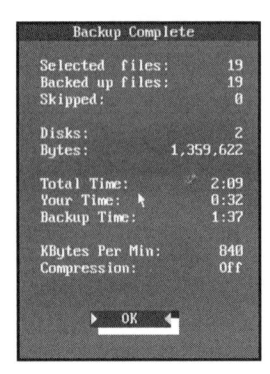

```
┌──── Backup Complete ────┐
│  Selected files:     19 │
│  Backed up files:    19 │
│  Skipped:             0 │
│                         │
│  Disks:               2 │
│  Bytes:       1,359,622 │
│                         │
│  Total Time:       2:09 │
│  Your Time:        0:32 │
│  Backup Time:      1:37 │
│                         │
│  KBytes Per Min:    840 │
│  Compression:       Off │
│                         │
│       ►  OK  ◄          │
└─────────────────────────┘
```

13 Choose OK. DOS compares the backup disks to the original files and prompts you to insert the first disk.

14 Insert Disk 1 and choose Continue.

15 When prompted for the next disk, insert it and choose Continue. When the comparison is complete, DOS displays this information:

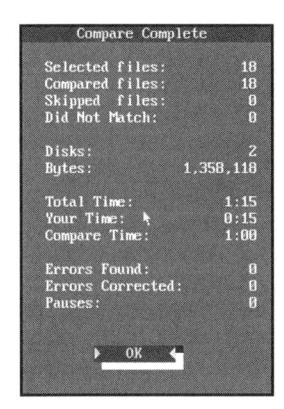

```
       Compare Complete
   Selected files:         18
   Compared files:         18
   Skipped files:           0
   Did Not Match:           0

   Disks:                   2
   Bytes:           1,358,118

   Total Time:           1:15
   Your Time:            0:15
   Compare Time:         1:00

   Errors Found:            0
   Errors Corrected:        0
   Pauses:                  0

            OK
```

16 Choose OK. A report then displays on the results of the compatibility test.

17 Choose OK. A dialog box showing the final configuration displays:

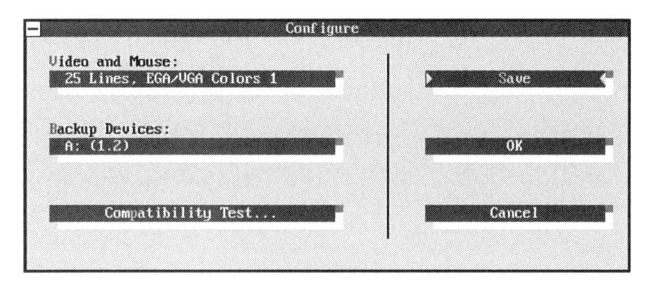

```
                    Configure
   Video and Mouse:
   | 25 Lines, EGA/VGA Colors 1 |        |    Save    |

   Backup Devices:
   | A: (1.2)                   |        |     OK     |


   |   Compatibility Test...    |        |   Cancel   |
```

18 Choose Save. DOS saves the settings in a file called DEFAULT.SET.

DOS then displays the Backup menu, and you can perform a backup or restoration. You also can change the configuration or perform another compatibility test.

Backing Up and Restoring Files: Configuring Microsoft Backup **183**

Performing a Backup

Although you can back up data to any DOS-supported drive or device, you must start Microsoft Backup from a hard disk.

To perform a complete backup after you have configured Microsoft Backup (the directions are given in the preceding section), follow these steps:

1 At the DOS prompt, type **msbackup** and press Enter.

2 Select Backup. The backup options are displayed.

3 Select the Backup From location. Select all the files on the drive by using the space bar or the right mouse button.

4 Select the Backup To location.

5 Choose Options, select the option settings you want, and then choose OK. You can choose from the following options.

■ **Tip:** The first time you run Microsoft Backup, back up all of your files by selecting Full as the Backup Type.

■ **Note:** Choose Select Files and select the specific directories and files if you do not want to back up all the files on a drive. Then choose OK.

Option	Description
Verify Backup Data	Forces Microsoft Backup to read the files from the backup disk after it is written and compare them to the original files to ensure that the backup is safe and accurate. This option adds a great deal of time to the backup process.
Compress Backup Data	Causes the program to compress the data before writing it, resulting in the use of fewer disks. This option also causes the backup procedure to operate faster.
Password Protect Backup Sets	Enables you to enter a password, which will be required to access the backup data when restoring or comparing it. The password is case-sensitive.

Option	Description
Prompt Before Overwriting Used Diskettes	Causes the program to display a warning before writing backup data on a disk that contains data and displays a partial list of files.
Always Format Diskettes	Forces the program to format every backup disk before writing to it whether the disk is formatted or not. DOS normally formats an unformatted disk automatically during the backup procedure.
Use Error Correction on	Adds special coding to each Diskettes backup disk to make recovering the data easier if the backup disks become damaged or worn out. Always use this option if you do not use the Verify Backup Data option.
Keep Old Backup Catalogs	Prevents the program from erasing the catalogs in the current master catalog when you perform a full backup.
Audible Prompts (Beep)	Causes the computer to beep every time the user is prompted to take some action.
Quit After Backup	Automatically exits Microsoft Backup when the backup procedure is complete.

6 Pull down the File menu and choose Save Setup As if you want to retain the settings on the Backup menu. Type the name and choose Save. (Setup files are discussed in more detail later in this lesson.)

7 Select Start Backup. The program begins by creating a backup catalog listing the files to be backed up and the options chosen.

■ **Note:** Label each disk in the backup (for example, #1, #2). You will have to refer to these numbers if you need to restore files.

■ **Tip:** Before you start this exercise, check to see how much space is used on the hard disk. Divide this number by the capacity of the floppy disk you will be using. For example, divide by 360 or 1200. The quotient is the number of disks required; however, fewer disks are required if you compress the backup data.

8 When prompted, insert disk #1 into the specified drive.

9 Continue inserting disks when prompted until the backup is complete.

▶ Your Turn

To back up all files on your hard disk, obtain a sufficient number of floppy disks and follow these steps:

1 At the DOS prompt of the hard disk, type **msbackup** and press Enter. The Backup options are displayed:

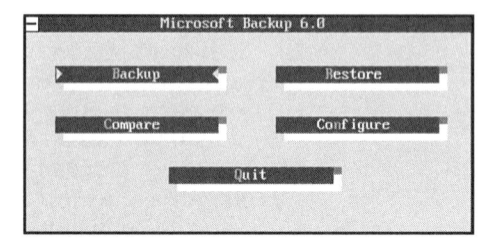

```
         Microsoft Backup 6.0
    ▶  Backup              Restore

       Compare             Configure

                   Quit
```

If you have problems... If you get the message Bad command or file name, change to the DOS directory and repeat step 1.

2 Select Backup.

3 From Backup From, make sure that the cursor is on the drive in which DOS is stored and then press the space bar. This selects all the files on the drive.

4 From Backup To, select the floppy drive that you intend to use.

5 Select Options. The dialog box is displayed.

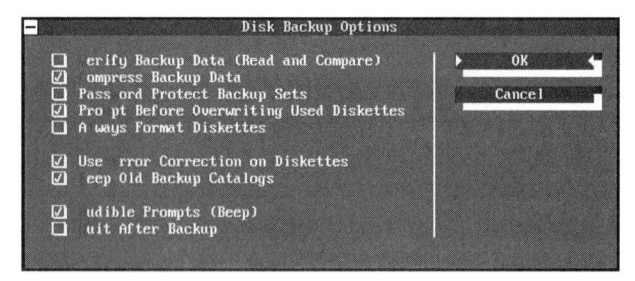

```
                Disk Backup Options
    ☐  erify Backup Data (Read and Compare)      ▶   OK
    ☑  ompress Backup Data
    ☐  Pass ord Protect Backup Sets                  Cancel
    ☑  Pro pt Before Overwriting Used Diskettes
    ☐  A ways Format Diskettes

    ☑  Use rror Correction on Diskettes
    ☑  eep Old Backup Catalogs

    ☑  udible Prompts (Beep)
    ☐  uit After Backup
```

DOS 6 SureSteps

6 Verify that the following options are checked: Compress Backup Data, Prompt Before Overwriting Used Diskettes, Use Error Protection on Diskettes, Keep Old Backup Catalogs, and Audible Prompts (Beep).

7 Choose OK.

8 Pull down the File menu and select Save Setup As.

9 Type **dos**.

10 Choose Save.

11 Choose Start Backup.

12 When DOS indicates, insert the first disk and choose Continue. If the disk contains data, DOS prompts you to Retry Overwrite or Cancel Backup. Select Overwrite to continue if the disk does not contain important data. Keep on inserting disks and choosing Continue when prompted.

13 Choose OK when the Backup Complete screen is displayed. The Backup Options on the main menu will be displayed.

▶ On Your Own

Make another backup and choose Select Files. From the dialog box, select Special. Explore how files can be backed up according to dates. Use the Help feature to learn more about special backup options.

Comparing Backup Copies with Originals

The Compare option of the BACKUP command verifies that a backup set contains exact copies of the original files. By comparing the files, you ensure a successful restoration.

■ **Tip:** After you complete a backup, you should used the Compare option.

To compare the original data and the backed-up data just after it has been backed up, follow these steps.

1 Select Compare from the Backup menu. The Compare dialog appears.

2 If you have more than one catalog and the desired catalog is not selected, select Backup Set Catalog.

3 Select the desired catalog from the list.

4 Select Load.

5 Select the Compare From location.

6 Select the Compare To location.

7 Choose Select Files if you want to select individual files for comparison.

8 Select Options if you want to change either of these two options: Audible Prompts (Beep) or Quit After Compare.

9 Select Start Compare.

If DOS detects a problem, it attempts to correct it. The number of corrections are reported at the end of the process.

▶ Your Turn

To compare the files that you backed up in the preceding exercise, follow these steps:

1 Select Compare from the Backup menu. The Compare dialog box appears:

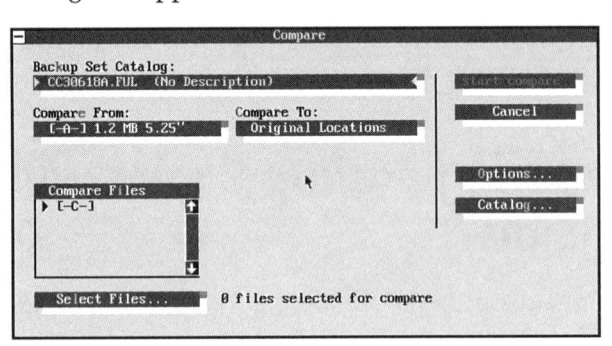

```
┌─────────────────────── Compare ───────────────────────┐
│ Backup Set Catalog:                                   │
│ ▶ CC30618A.FUL  (No Description)        Start compare │
│ Compare From:      Compare To:                        │
│ [-A-] 1.2 MB 5.25" Original Locations      Cancel     │
│                                                       │
│                                          Options...   │
│ ┌Compare Files─┐                                      │
│ │ ▶ [-C-]     ↑│                          Catalog...  │
│ │             ↓│                                      │
│ └──────────────┘                                      │
│  Select Files...   0 files selected for compare       │
└───────────────────────────────────────────────────────┘
```

■ **Note:** Your catalog name will not match the figure.

The Backup Set Catalog box displays the name of the catalog for the backup you just made.

188 DOS 6 SureSteps

2 In the Compare Files box, select all files on the hard drive you backed up by pressing the space bar when the cursor is on the drive letter or by clicking the right mouse button on the drive letter.

3 Select **S**tart Compare.

4 Insert the first disk in the set and choose Continue. Keep on inserting disks in order and choosing Continue as prompted.

5 Choose OK when the Compare Complete information is displayed.

Restoring Files

Restoring files that have been backed up with the BACKUP command is easy. When you restore files, they are transferred from the backup set to the original location or one that you specify. If your hard disk gets erased accidentally, for example, you can restore the files to their original locations. If you want to move files from one computer to another, you can back up the files on the first computer and restore them to the second computer.

Restoring a Backup Set

To restore a backup set, follow these steps:

1 At the DOS prompt, type **msbackup** and press Enter.

2 Select **R**estore. The Restore dialog box appears.

3 If the desired catalog is not selected, select Backup Set Catalog.

4 Select the desired catalog from the list.

5 Select **L**oad.

6 Select the Resto**r**e From location.

7 Select the **R**estore To location.

8 Select the files that you want to restore if you do not want to restore all the files.

Backing Up and Restoring Files: *Restoring Files*

9 Select Options if you want to change any of the following options:

Option	Description
Verify Restore Data (Read and Compare)	Forces DOS to verify the accuracy of the data transfer after the restore process is complete. This option makes the restoration process considerably slower.
Prompt Before Creating Directories	Causes DOS to alert you before creating any new directories during the restoration process. After you are alerted, you have the option not to create the directory.
Prompt Before Creating Files	Causes DOS to alert you before creating any new files during the restoration process. After you are alerted, you have the option not to create the new files.
Prompt Before Overwriting Existing Files	Causes DOS to alert you before overwriting any existing files during the restoration process. You can choose to overwrite or skip the file.
Restore Empty Directories	Enables you to restore the complete directory structure on your disk as it is backed up (including directories that do not contain files).
Audible Prompts (Beep)	Causes the computer to beep every time the user is prompted to take some action.
Quit After Restore	Automatically exits Microsoft Backup when the restore procedure is complete.

10 Select Start Restore. The Backup procedure displays status information while it restores the files.

▶ Your Turn

To restore some of the files that you backed up in the first exercise, follow these steps:

1 At the DOS prompt, type **msbackup** and press Enter.

> **If you have problems...** If you get the message Bad command or file name, change to the DOS directory and repeat step 1.

2 Select Restore from the Backup menu. The Restore dialog box displays:

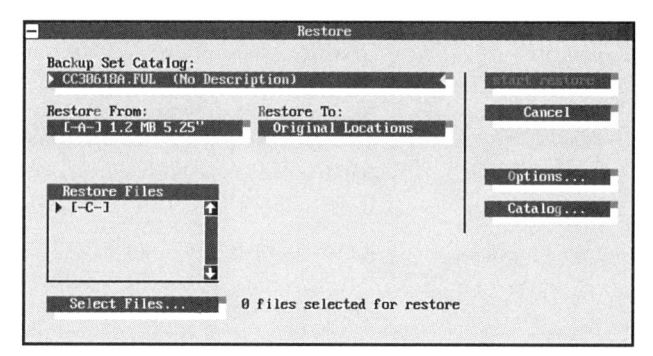

```
┌─────────────────────── Restore ───────────────────────┐
│ Backup Set Catalog:                                    │
│ ▶ CC30618A.FUL  (No Description)        ┌───────────┐ │
│                                         │Start restore│ │
│ Restore From:        Restore To:        └───────────┘ │
│ [-A-] 1.2 MB 5.25"   Original Locations  ┌─────────┐  │
│                                          │ Cancel  │  │
│                                          └─────────┘  │
│                                          ┌─────────┐  │
│  ┌─Restore Files─┐                       │Options..│  │
│  │ ▶ [-C-]    ↑  │                       └─────────┘  │
│  │            │  │                       ┌─────────┐  │
│  │            ↓  │                       │Catalog..│  │
│  └───────────────┘                       └─────────┘  │
│  ┌─Select Files..┐ 0 files selected for restore       │
│  └───────────────┘                                    │
└───────────────────────────────────────────────────────┘
```

3 Choose Select Files.

4 Use the space bar or right mouse button on the DOS directory file name to select all files in the DOS directory.

5 Choose OK.

6 Select Start Restore.

7 Insert the designated disk and choose Continue.

8 Repeat step 7 each time you are prompted.

9 Choose OK when the Restore Complete information is displayed.

10 Choose Quit to exit Microsoft Backup.

Making Subsequent Backups

Remember that the first time you back up your data, you should use the Full method. After you have a full backup, you can select one of the other types of backups for subsequent backups. The types of backups and backup strategies are discussed in the next two sections.

Selecting the Right Type of Backup

DOS performs three different types of backups, summarized in Table 8.2.

Table 8.2. Types of Backup Procedures

Type	Description
Full Backup	Used for backing up large amounts of data. It can back up all the files on a hard disk, all files that match a particular wild card pattern, all files on a particular drive, or all files in one or more directories.
Incremental Backup	Backs up only new files or files that have changed since the last full or incremental backup was made.
Differential Backup	Backs up any new files or files that have changed since the last full backup. To restore data from this type of backup, the last full backup disks and the last differential backup disks are required.

Establishing a Backup Strategy

It is essential that you establish a backup strategy and follow it faithfully. Two strategies are suggested in this section. Decide which strategy is best for you and then establish your own timetable for implementing it.

If you work with the same files each day, you may want to begin your backup procedure by performing first a full backup and then a differential backup each day (or periodically as the need dictates). You should use two sets of disks for the differential backups—that is, perform one differential backup on one set of disks and the next differential backup on a second set of disks. Then reuse the first and second sets alternately as you make subsequent backups. This regimen uses disks efficiently, minimizing the number of disks that must be retained in order to perform a complete restoration of data. If any problem arises with the most recent set of incremental backups, you can use the second set. Of course, you will lose any changes that were made between the first and second incremental backup.

If you work with different files each day, you may want to begin your backup procedure with a full backup and perform incremental backups as the need dictates. Because the incremental backup backs up only files that have changed since the last full or incremental backup, this procedure requires less time than a differential backup, but it requires more disks. You must save the full backup set of disks and each set of incremental backup disks to perform a complete restoration of data. This method also is useful if you need to keep older versions of your files because you can select the version of a file that you want to restore.

Using Setup Files

Setup files make your work easier. By storing the settings that you use to perform a backup in a setup file, you can perform the same backup without making the same selections again. The setup file contains a list of the files that you back up and the options you use to perform the backup.

To create a setup file, follow these steps:

1 Make all your selections from the **Backup** menu.

2 Pull down the **File** menu and select **Save Setup As**.

3 Give the file a name and select **Save**.

When you want to use the setup file to perform the backup, select it from the list of setup files that is displayed when you select the **Setup** File option.

✘ **Caution:** With incremental or differential backups, new files are not included unless the drive or directory is included in the setup file or referenced by an INCLUDE statement. In a directory where individual files have been selected, new files are not included.

▶ Your Turn

In this exercise, you make an incremental backup of the hard disk. If you have been following the exercises in this lesson without interruption, you do not have any new files that have been stored on the hard disk since you backed it up. You will copy a file so that there is a new file on the disk to back up. Follow these steps from the DOS prompt of the hard drive:

1 Type **cd ** and press Enter.

2 Type **copy autoexec.bat newfile.txt** and press Enter.

3 Type **msbackup** and press Enter.

| **If you have problems...** | If you get the message Bad command or file name, change to the DOS directory and repeat step 1. |

4 Choose Backup.

5 Select all files on the hard drive (in the Backup From box).

6 Select Backup Type. This dialog box displays:

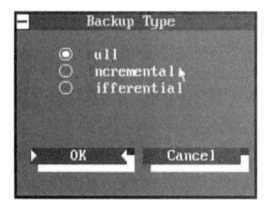

```
┌─ Backup Type ─┐
│ ● all         │
│ ○ ncremental  │
│ ○ ifferential │
│               │
│ ▶ OK  Cancel  │
└───────────────┘
```

7 Select Incremental and choose OK. Your screen should look like this:

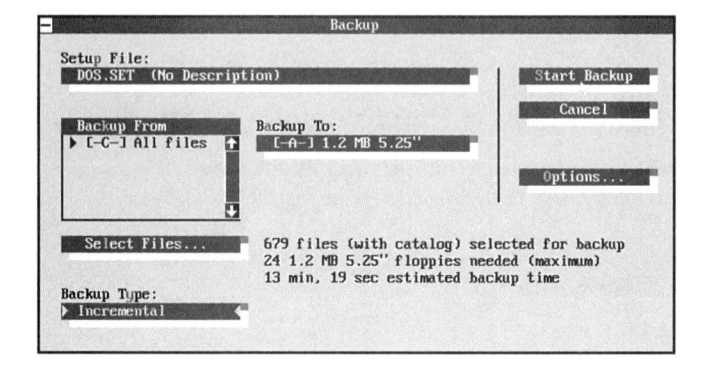

```
┌──────────────────── Backup ────────────────────┐
│ Setup File:                                    │
│ DOS.SET  (No Description)       Start Backup   │
│                                                │
│                                 Cancel         │
│ Backup From     Backup To:                     │
│ ▶[-C-] All files  [-A-] 1.2 MB 5.25"           │
│                                                │
│                                 Options...     │
│                                                │
│                                                │
│ Select Files...  679 files (with catalog) selected for backup │
│                  24 1.2 MB 5.25" floppies needed (maximum)   │
│                  13 min, 19 sec estimated backup time        │
│ Backup Type:                                   │
│ ▶ Incremental                                  │
└────────────────────────────────────────────────┘
```

194 DOS 6 SureSteps

8 Select the floppy drive in Backup To.

9 Pull down the File menu and select Save Setup As.

10 Type **hdinc** for the file name and then press Enter. Your screen should look like this:

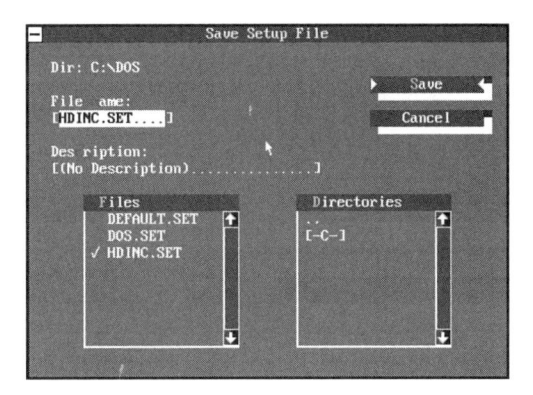

11 Choose Start Backup.

12 Insert the disk and choose Continue.

13 Choose OK when the backup information is displayed.

Using Catalogs

When DOS performs a backup, it creates a backup catalog that contains information about the directories and files you back up. The information includes the directory structure; names, size, and attributes of the directories and files; the total number of files backed up; the total size of the backup; the name of the setup file that was used; and the date of the backup.

DOS places one copy of the backup catalog on the hard disk and another copy on the disk or network drive that contains the actual backup.

The catalog file has a unique name that is coded to help you identify the backup. Each character in the name of the catalog file has a code assigned to it, as described in table 8.3.

Table 8.3. Codes Used in the Backup Catalog Names

Character Position	Code
1	The letter of the first drive backed up.
2	The letter of the last drive backed up.
3	The last digit of the year in which the backup was made.
4 and 5	The month in which the backup was made.
6 and 7	The day on which the backup was made.
8	The position in the sequence of backups. If more than one backup of the same drive or drives is performed on the same day, this letter can have a value from A to Z. If the option Keep Old Backup Catalogs is set to OFF, this letter alternates between A and B.
Extension	The extension can be FUL, INC, or DIF indicating the type of backup (full, incremental, or differential).

▶ Your Turn

In this exercise, you look at the Backup Catalogs on your system. Follow these steps from the Microsoft Backup main menu:

1 Choose Restore.

2 Choose Backup Set Catalog. A dialog box similar to this is displayed.

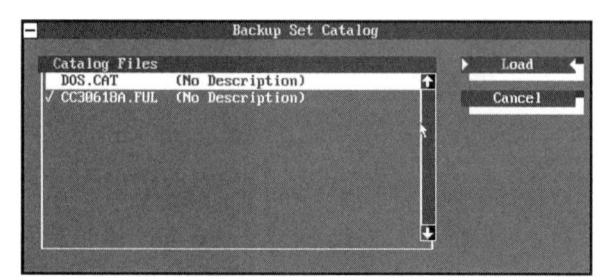

```
┌─────────────────── Backup Set Catalog ───────────────────┐
│ Catalog Files                                   ┌ Load  ┐│
│   DOS.CAT      (No Description)     ↑           └───────┘│
│ √ CC30618A.FUL (No Description)                 ┌ Cancel┐│
│                                                 └───────┘│
│                                                          │
│                                                 ↓        │
└──────────────────────────────────────────────────────────┘
```

3 Refer to table 8.3 to decipher the name of the CC30618A.FUL catalog in the figure.

  4 Decipher the names of the catalogs on your own system.

  5 Choose Cancel to exit the dialog box.

  6 Choose Cancel to exit the **Restore** menu.

  7 Choose **Q**uit to exit Microsoft Backup.

Using Master Catalogs

The master catalog is created by DOS to include the catalogs in a backup cycle. DOS creates the master catalog each time you perform a full backup using a specific setup file.

Use the master catalog when you need to restore a complete backup cycle. When you load the master catalog, DOS automatically merges all the catalogs of all the backups that were created during the backup cycle. This makes it easier for you to restore the latest version of each backed-up file, but you can still choose to restore an earlier version if you wish.

Reminder: You can keep all of the old catalogs or only the current catalogs on your hard disk.

Using Microsoft Backup from Windows

If you have Windows on your computer and you installed a Windows version of Microsoft Backup, you can use this version of the program rather than the DOS version. This program works much like the DOS version and has the same options. This section, a brief overview of how to use Microsoft Backup from Windows, assumes that you know how to start Windows and that you understand the menus and using the mouse in Windows.

  1 From the Windows Program Manager, choose File **R**un and type **c:\dos\mwbackup** and click OK, or double-click on the Backup icon in the Microsoft Tools group.

  2 Configure Microsoft Backup. Like the DOS version, the Windows version of Microsoft Backup must be

■ **Note:** If you did not install the Windows Microsoft Backup version, you can install it now by inserting the DOS 6.0 Upgrade Disk 1 in the floppy drive, typing **a:setup /u /e** or **b:setup /u /e**, and then pressing Enter. When the Welcome screen is displayed, follow the steps in Appendix A of this book to install Microsoft Backup for Windows.

configured before it can be used. The process is similar to what you have already done in DOS. Windows prompts you through the process. When Microsoft Backup is configured, you are ready to use the program.

3 Select the desired drive from Backup From.

4 Select the desired drive in Backup To and insert a disk in the floppy drive if selected.

5 Select specific files from Select Files or select all files on a drive by using the right mouse button to click the drive letter icon.

6 Select the desired Backup Type.

7 Select Options if desired.

8 Select Start Backup.

9 Insert additional disks as prompted.

10 Choose OK when the Backup is finished.

▶ Your Turn

1 Start Windows.

2 Start Microsoft Backup. This dialog box appears:

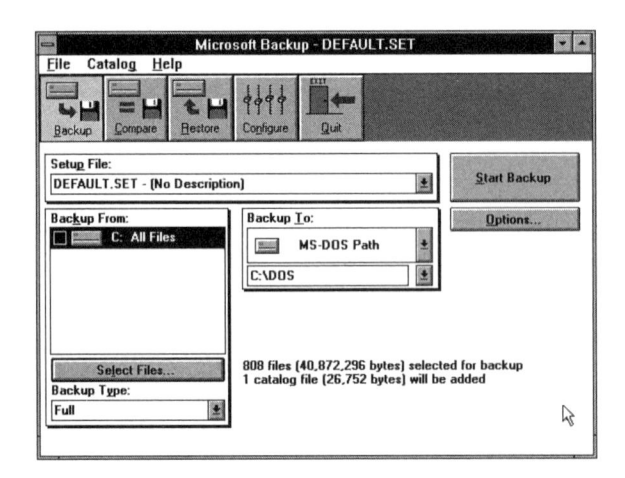

3 Select the hard drive in Backup From.

198   DOS 6 SureSteps

4 Select the floppy drive in Backup To and insert a disk.

5 Select Select Files.

6 Select all files in the DOS directory and choose OK.

7 Make sure that Full is selected in Backup Type. Your screen should look similar to this:

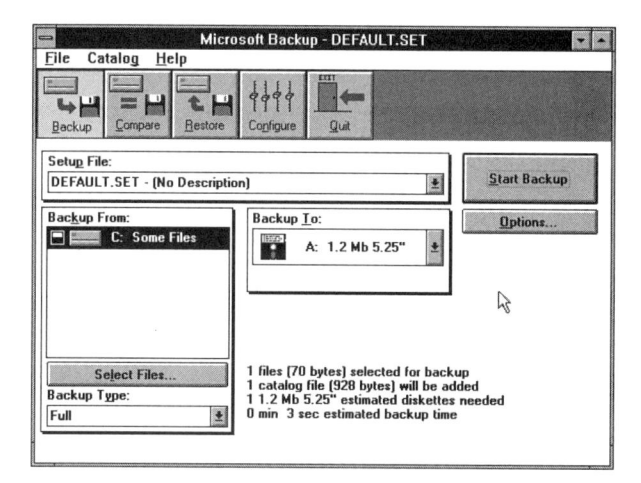

8 Select Start Backup.

9 Insert additional disks as prompted.

10 Choose OK when the backup is complete.

▶ On Your Own

If you have another hard drive, back it up, too.

Lesson Summary

To	Do this
Backup data	At the DOS prompt (from the hard disk), type **msbackup** and press Enter. Select Backup. Select all desired options. Select Start Backu

> continues

Backing Up and Restoring Files: *Lesson Summary*

> **continued**

To	Do this
Compare backed-up data	At the DOS prompt (from the hard disk), type **msbackup** and press Enter. Select Compare. Select all desired options. Select Start Compare.
Restore backed-up data	At the DOS prompt (from the hard disk), type **msbackup** and press Enter. Select Restore. Select all the desired options. Select Start Restore.

If You Want to Stop Now

If you want to stop now, exit all programs and turn off your system.

From Here

You have now covered most of the basics of DOS 6. From this point on, you can select the remaining lessons that interest you the most. The order of selection is not important. Remaining lessons cover these features: Anti-Virus, DoubleSpace, MemMaker, MS-DOS Editor, and InterInk.

9
SURESTEPS LESSON 9

Protecting the PC from Viruses

In this lesson, you learn how to do the following:

- Create a bootable emergency disk
- Prevent viruses
- Use Anti-Virus to detect and remove viruses
- Use VSafe
- Use Anti-Virus in Windows

Lesson time:
20–30 minutes

Designed by capricious or malicious individuals, computer viruses are programs that reproduce themselves and spread. Capricious viruses may do nothing more than reproduce and spread, but they can be a nuisance because they take up disk space. Other frivolous viruses may display unexpected screen messages or cause random sounds. The malicious strains of viruses destroy files or format the hard disk.

Viruses are contracted by using floppy disks and downloading files by telecommunications. Viruses are so rampant that even a reputable software manufacturer unknowingly released its program with infected disks. When the problem was detected, the programs were recalled, of course, but programs that were sold before the recall enabled the virus to spread.

Preventing Viruses

Unless you never use a disk given to you by another person and you never download files from any source, you will have difficulty avoiding a computer virus. Even if you meet both conditions, you still have to buy programs that you load on your computer, and even a legitimate program can have a virus.

You can significantly decrease the chances of your computer getting a virus if you do not use pirated copies of software (which is illegal, anyway), you do not download programs and files from sources unless you know they check all their files for viruses before making them available, and you use an anti-virus program to scan all disks from other sources for viruses.

Unfortunately, there is one glaring flaw in all methods of preventing viruses. The anti-virus programs can never be current. Someone is always inventing a new virus that circumvents detection. This means that every computer user should prepare for the worst by keeping a bootable disk that can start the computer and keeping a current backup of all important data. (Be sure to read Lesson 8, "Backing Up and Restoring Files," if you have not done so already. Creating and maintaining backup files is easier than ever with DOS 6.)

▶ Your Turn

If you don't have a bootable disk, now is a good time to make one. The following steps walk you through this simple process.

■ **Note:** If you do not have a blank formatted disk, type **format a:/s** or **format b:/s** and press Enter. Then skip to step 4.

1 Insert a blank disk in the floppy drive.

2 At the DOS prompt, type **sys a:** or **sys b:** and press Enter.

3 Type **cd ** and press Enter.

4 Type **copy autoexec.bat a:** or **copy autoexec.bat b:** and press Enter.

5 Type **copy config.sys a:** or **copy config.sys b:** and press Enter.

6 If you are using a 5 1/4-inch disk, apply a write-protect tape to the notch in the disk. If you are using a 3 1/2-inch disk, slide the write-protect tab into the correct position. Store the disk in a safe place.

Classifying Viruses

Viruses are classified in three categories: boot sector, file infector, and Trojan horse. A *boot sector virus* replaces the system's original boot sector with its own and loads the virus into memory. (The boot sector controls how DOS starts when you turn on the computer.) After the virus is in memory, it spreads.

A *file infector virus* adds virus program code to files that run programs. When the program is booted, the virus is activated and it spreads to other program files.

The *Trojan horse virus* is hidden in a legitimate program. (Game programs are a favorite type of program for Trojan horse viruses.) When you use the program, the Trojan horse virus is activated. Most Trojan horse viruses destroy data or format the hard disk.

Using Anti-Virus

DOS has two methods to detect computer viruses—Anti-Virus and the memory-resident program VSafe. Anti-Virus can detect and remove over 800 known viruses plus more than 200 known variants, and you can purchase updates (for as little as $9.95) from Microsoft to keep the program current. A service plan for ongoing protection also is available from Microsoft. This section covers Anti-Virus. VSafe is covered later in this lesson.

The Anti-Virus program has the following options: **D**etect, **D**etect and Clean, **S**elect New Drive, **O**ptions, and **E**xit. If you use the **D**etect option, DOS scans for viruses, and, if it finds any, enables you to remove the virus, continue without removing the virus, or stop the scanning process. The Detect and Clean option scans for viruses and removes any that are found. The **Select New Drive** option enables you to select a different drive to scan. With **Options**, you can configure the Anti-Virus program. With **Exit**, you can exit Anti-Virus.

To use Anti-Virus to detect viruses, follow these steps:

1   At the DOS prompt, type **msav** and then press Enter.

2   Choose **Select New Drive**, and then choose the desired drive from the upper left corner of the screen.

■ **Tip:** Press F2 to select a different drive.

3   Choose **Detect and Clean**. DOS begins searching for viruses.

■ **Tip:** Use F5 to select Detect and Clean.

4   When DOS displays the Anti-Virus final report, choose OK.

5   Choose **Exit** to leave Anti-Virus.

■ **Tip:** If you want to run Anti-Virus each time the computer is booted, add the Anti-Virus command to your AUTOEXEC.BAT file. If the AUTOEXEC.BAT has several lines in it, add the Anti-Virus command near the top. Read the Help information on Anti-Virus to determine what parameters you should use with the command. The command MSAV /A /C scans all drives except A and B and cleans any viruses that are found.

▶ Your Turn

Check your hard disk and a floppy disk for viruses by following these steps:

1   Make the root directory of the hard disk the current directory.

2   Type **msav** and press Enter. This screen displays:

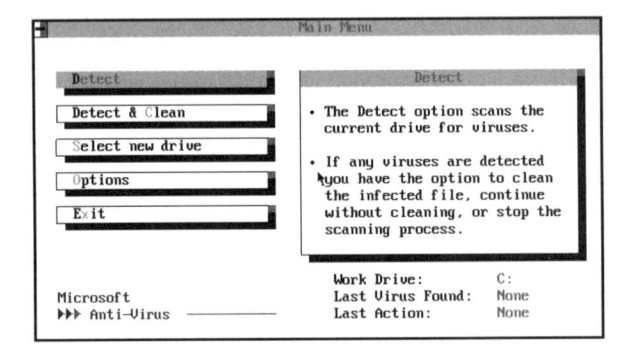

```
┌─────────────────────── Main Menu ───────────────────────┐
│                                                         │
│   ┌─ Detect ──────────┐    ┌─ Detect ──────────────┐   │
│   │ Detect & Clean    │    │ • The Detect option scans the │
│   │ Select new drive  │    │   current drive for viruses.  │
│   │ Options           │    │ • If any viruses are detected │
│   │ Exit              │    │   you have the option to clean│
│   └───────────────────┘    │   the infected file, continue │
│                            │   without cleaning, or stop the│
│                            │   scanning process.           │
│                            └───────────────────────────────┘
│                                                         │
│                            Work Drive:        C:        │
│   Microsoft                Last Virus Found:  None      │
│   ▶▶▶ Anti-Virus           Last Action:       None      │
└─────────────────────────────────────────────────────────┘
```

DOS 6 SureSteps

If you have problems...

If you get the message Bad command or file name, change to the DOS directory and repeat step 2. If you get the same message again, Anti-Virus is probably not installed. To install Anti-Virus, follow these steps:

1 Insert disk 1 of the DOS 6 Upgrade in the floppy drive.

2 Type **a:setup /u /e** or **b:setup /u /e** and press Enter.

3 Follow the steps in Appendix A to install the Windows version of Anti-Virus.

3 Select Detect and Clean. If DOS finds a virus, it displays the name of the virus in the lower right corner and cleans the disk.

4 When DOS displays the report, choose OK.

5 Insert a floppy disk in the disk drive to scan for viruses.

6 Choose **S**elect New Drive. The system drive icons are displayed in the upper left corner of the screen.

7 Select the appropriate drive.

8 Select Detect and Clean. Anti-Virus scans the disk.

9 When the report is displayed, choose OK. If a virus was found and cleaned, the report should look similar to this:

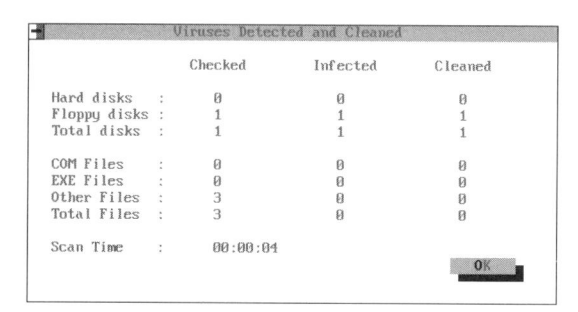

```
                 Viruses Detected and Cleaned

                  Checked      Infected      Cleaned

Hard disks   :       0            0             0
Floppy disks :       1            1             1
Total disks  :       1            1             1

COM Files    :       0            0             0
EXE Files    :       0            0             0
Other Files  :       3            0             0
Total Files  :       3            0             0

Scan Time    :    00:00:04
                                              [ OK ]
```

Reminder: You can use the function keys to select options from the Anti-Virus menu.

Protecting the PC from Viruses: Using Anti-Virus   **205**

10 Choose Exit and OK to leave Anti-Virus. You return to the DOS prompt.

11 If this message is displayed, choose **Reboot**.

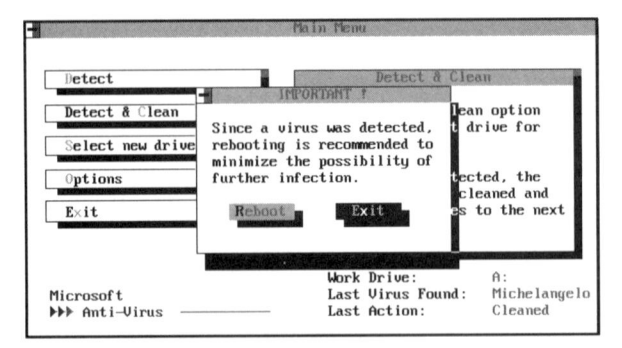

Configuring Anti-Virus

When DOS displays the Anti-Virus dialog box, you can select Options to configure the system. DOS provides the following options:

- *Verify Integrity.* This option detects changes that have been made to executable files. It can find file infector type viruses even if they are not known viruses.

- *Create New Checksums.* This option creates the file CHKLIST.MS for each directory that is scanned. It is a database of information about each executable file in the directory.

- *Create Checksums on Floppy.* This option creates the CHKLIST.MS file for each directory that is scanned on a floppy disk.

- *Disable Alarm Sound.* This option disables the alarm tone that is sounded with Anti-Virus messages.

- *Create Backup.* This option creates a backup of an infected file before the virus is removed from the original file. The still-infected backup file has the extension of VIR.

- *Create Report.* This option writes a report of the Anti-Virus findings to an ASCII file called MSAV.RPT.

- *Prompt While Detect.* If a virus is detected, this option displays a prompt that enables you to clean the file, continue the scan without cleaning the file, or stop the scan.

- *Anti-Stealth.* This option detects unknown viruses that infect executable files without making outward changes that can be detected by the Verify Integrity option.

- *Check All Files.* This option checks all files for viruses. If the option is turned off, only files with these extensions are checked: EXE, COM, OVL, OVR, SYS, BIN, APP, or CMD.

To change any of these options, follow these steps:

1 From the Anti-Virus main menu, choose Options.

2 Change any desired options.

3 Choose OK to return to the Main menu.

▶ Your Turn

In this exercise, you change the Anti-Virus options and scan the hard drive again. Follow these steps:

1 Start Anti-Virus. The Anti-Virus menu appears.

2 Select Options. This dialog box is displayed:

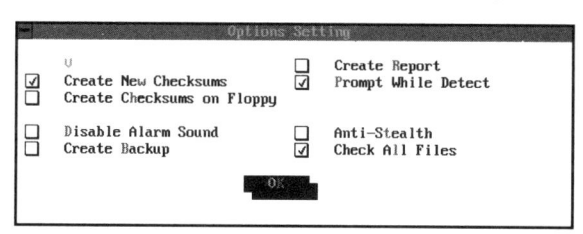

3 Verify that the default options are checked (Verify Integrity, Create New Checksums, Prompt While Detect, Check All Files).

4 Select Create Report.

5 Choose OK to accept the options selected in the dialog box.

Protecting the PC from Viruses: Using Anti-Virus

6 Choose Detect and Clean to scan the disk.

7 Choose OK when the report is displayed. The information in this report is saved in the MSAV.RPT file.

8 Choose Exit and then choose OK to return to the DOS prompt.

9 Type **type \msav.rpt** and press Enter. This command displays the contents of the MSAV.RPT file.

■ **Note:** The report is always called MSAV.RPT and is stored in the root directory of the scanned drive.

▶ On Your Own

If you want to change any options in Anti-Virus, change them now.

Displaying Information about Viruses

The Anti-Virus program has a list of all the viruses that it recognizes. To see the list, press F9 when the Anti-Virus menu is displayed. The Virus list shows the name of the virus, the type, the size, and the number of variants it has. Indented under the virus name are aliases used for the virus.

To get more information about a virus when the cursor is highlighting the name, press Enter or select Info. A brief description of the virus and its side effects is displayed. The list of viruses can be printed by selecting Print.

▶ Your Turn

Follow these steps to see how the Virus list is used:

1 Start Anti-Virus and press F9. This dialog box is displayed:

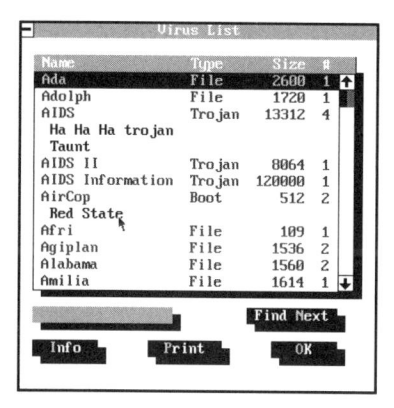

Name	Type	Size	#
Ada	File	2600	1
Adolph	File	1720	1
AIDS	Trojan	13312	4
Ha Ha Ha trojan			
Taunt			
AIDS II	Trojan	8064	1
AIDS Information	Trojan	120000	1
AirCop	Boot	512	2
Red State			
Afri	File	109	1
Agiplan	File	1536	2
Alabama	File	1560	2
Amilia	File	1614	1

2 Move the cursor to the virus called AirCop and press Enter. This screen is displayed:

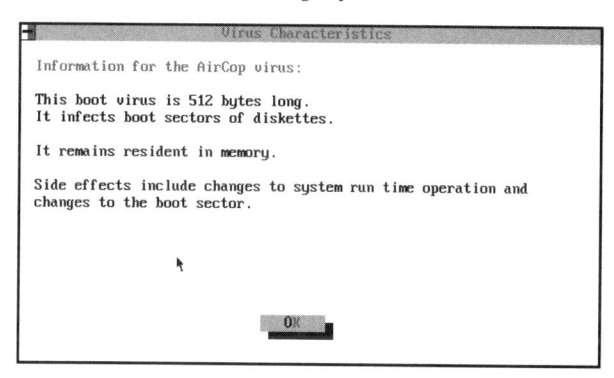

Information for the AirCop virus:

This boot virus is 512 bytes long.
It infects boot sectors of diskettes.

It remains resident in memory.

Side effects include changes to system run time operation and changes to the boot sector.

3 Choose OK to return to the Virus list.

4 Move the cursor to Beast and press Enter.

5 Choose OK to return to the Virus list.

6 Press Esc to return to the Anti-Virus menu.

7 Choose Exit and then choose OK to exit Anti-Virus.

Recognizing False Alarms

Some normal conditions on a system can trigger a virus alarm. When you upgrade a program and the executable file changes, for example, Anti-Virus reacts as if a virus has infected the file. Also, if you change the CONFIG.SYS file, an Anti-Virus alarm is triggered.

To avoid getting the Anti-Virus message when you upgrade software, follow these procedures:

1. Scan the original software disk with Anti-Virus.
2. Write-protect the installation disks.
3. Install the software.
4. Use Anti-Virus to scan the drive on which the software is installed. Anti-Virus automatically updates its files.

▶ Your Turn

In this exercise, you make a change in the CONFIG.SYS file and scan the hard disk for viruses. You should get an error message showing that a change has been made in the CONFIG.SYS file. Follow these steps:

1. Using MS-DOS Editor, edit the CONFIG.SYS file and add REM to the beginning of any line.
2. Save the file and exit MS-DOS Editor.
3. Start Anti-Virus.
4. Choose Detect and Clean. A dialog box similar to this should be displayed:

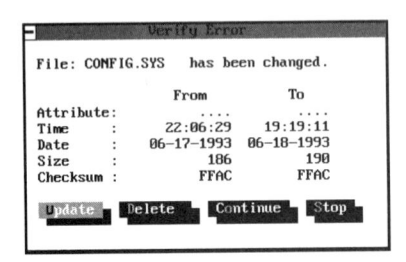

```
                    Verify Error
File: CONFIG.SYS    has been changed.
                    From            To
Attribute:          ....            ....
Time      :         22:06:29        19:19:11
Date      :         06-17-1993      06-18-1993
Size      :              186             190
Checksum  :             FFAC            FFAC
   Update    Delete    Continue    Stop
```

5. Choose Update.
6. When the report displays, choose OK.
7. Choose Exit and OK to leave Anti-Virus.
8. Remove the REM command from the CONFIG.SYS file and save the file.
9. Reboot the system.

Using VSafe

VSafe is a memory-resident program, requiring up to about 44K of memory, that continually monitors the system for suspicious activity indicative of a virus infection. To start the program, type **vsafe** at the DOS prompt. If you want VSafe to be used every time DOS is booted, add the VSAFE command to the AUTOEXEC.BAT file.

To unload VSafe from memory, at the DOS prompt press Alt+V and Alt+U.

The VSAFE command has several options that can be turned on or off. To display the options, press ALT+V at the DOS prompt after VSafe has been loaded in memory. Following are the VSAFE command options:

Option	Description
HD low-level format	Warns of formatting that could erase the hard disk.
Resident	Warns if a program tries to stay resident in memory. Does not necessarily indicate a virus.
General write protect	Prevents programs from writing to a disk.
Check executable files	Checks programs opened by DOS.
Boot sector viruses	Checks for boot sector viruses on all disks.
Protect HD boot sector	Warns of attempts to write to the hard disk boot sector or partition table.
Protect FD boot sector	Warns of attempts to write to the floppy disk boot sector.
Protect executable files	Warns of attempts to modify executable files.

▶ Your Turn

To experiment with using the VSAFE command, follow these steps:

1. At the DOS prompt, type **mem /c |more** and press Enter. Notice how much conventional memory is used.

2. Press any key to continue.

3. At the DOS prompt, type **vsafe** and then press Enter.

4. Type **mem /c |more** and then press Enter. Notice the amount of conventional memory now being used.

5. Press any key to continue. (If necessary, continue pressing any key until the DOS prompt appears.)

6. Press Alt+V. The VSafe Warnings Options dialog box appears.

7. Press Alt+U.

Using Anti-Virus with Windows

If you have Windows on your computer, the DOS setup program installs a Windows version of Anti-Virus. This program works much like the DOS version and has the same options. This section is a brief overview of how to use Anti-Virus from Windows. This section assumes you know how to start Windows and understand the menus and using the mouse in Windows.

1. From the Windows Program Manager, choose File Run and type **c:\dos\mwav** or double-click on the Anti-Virus icon in the Microsoft Tools Group.

2. Select a drive from the drive box to scan.

3. Choose Detect and Clean to begin scanning.

4. When the report is displayed, choose OK.

▶ Your Turn

Follow these steps to scan the hard drive with Windows Anti-Virus:

1. Start Windows.

2. Display the Microsoft Tools Window.

3. Double-click the Anti-Virus icon. This window is displayed:

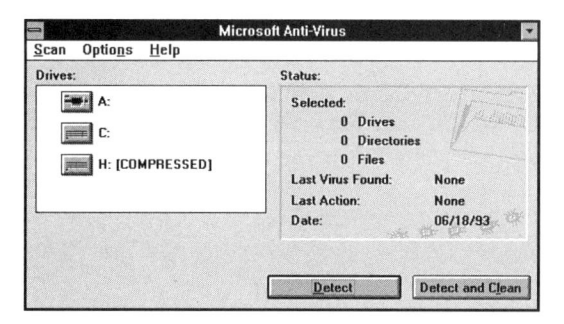

4. Select Drive C.

5. Choose Detect and Clean.

6. When this report displays, choose OK.

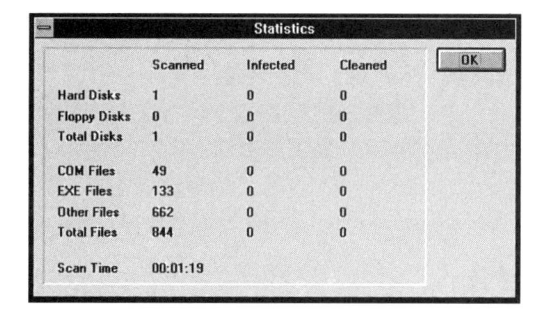

7. Close the Anti-Virus window.

8. Close Windows.

Protecting the PC from Viruses: *Using Anti-Virus with Windows*

▶ On Your Own

If you have another hard drive, run Anti-Virus on it, too. If you have any floppy disks you want to check, run Anti-Virus on them. Look at the different options. See "Configuring Anti-Virus" in this lesson for information about the various options that are available, and then make desired changes.

Lesson Summary

To	Do this
Scan for and remove viruses	At the DOS prompt, type **msav** and press Enter. Select the desired drive. Choose Detect and Clean. Choose OK when the report is displayed. Select Exit.
Continually monitor the system for viruses	At the DOS prompt, type **vsafe** and press Enter.
Unload VSafe from memory	At the DOS prompt, press Alt+V followed by Alt+U.

If You Want to Stop Now

If you want to stop now, exit all programs and turn off your system.

From Here

In this lesson, you learned to use Anti-Virus and VSafe. If you decide to use VSafe, you may want to read Lesson 11 on optimizing system memory; VSafe uses conventional memory.

Increasing Disk Space with DoubleSpace

SURESTEPS LESSON 10

In this lesson, you learn how to do the following:

- Determine whether to use DoubleSpace
- Install DoubleSpace
- Display information about a compressed drive
- Change the size of a compressed drive
- Change the compression ratio
- Defragment a compressed drive
- Format a compressed drive
- Delete a compressed drive
- Repair a damaged CVF

Lesson time: 30–45 minutes

As mentioned in Lesson 1, when the hard disk first came on the market, its size was very small compared to the sizes available today. Although today's average-sized hard disk—60 to 120M—may seem adequate at first, before long it often becomes inadequate. As the user creates more and more files and installs more and more programs, the disk space seems to evaporate.

Some users solve the problem of inadequate disk space by adding another hard disk. Others simply buy new PCs with larger hard disks. Both of these solutions involve hardware changes. A third solution uses compression software to make more space available. Several popular utility programs that compress data are currently sold, but with DOS 6 you don't need to buy an additional piece of software. You can use the DOS utility program, DoubleSpace, which can make 50 to 100 percent more space available on a disk.

Considering the Advantages and the Disadvantages

Compressing the data on a disk provides an obvious advantage, one that has almost irresistible allurement, but there also are some disadvantages attached to compressing a disk. First, you need to consider the loss of memory. DoubleSpace uses about 40K of memory. The type of memory that it uses is dependent on the other programs on your system and how they use memory. Normally, DoubleSpace is loaded into conventional memory (640K of RAM), but if there is room and no conflicts result, DoubleSpace can be loaded into upper memory, the 384K of memory above 640K. (To learn more about memory, refer to Lesson 11.) If your programs are already pushing the PC to its limit on memory, it may not be advisable for you to use DoubleSpace. On the other hand, it may be less expensive to install more memory and use DoubleSpace than to buy a new hard disk.

Slower processing speed is another disadvantage connected with using DoubleSpace. DOS must compress a file each time it is stored and then decompress it each time it is used. If you have a 386 or 486 processor, the difference in processing speed is unnoticeable for most files, but if you have a 286 or lower processor, the slowdown in processing time is noticeable. The question to consider is "Can I sacrifice a little time to gain more disk space?" The answer to this question usually is "yes."

Another disadvantage to consider is the fact that all the compressed files depend on one reference file (created by DoubleSpace) for their existence. If anything happens to this reference file, all the compressed data is lost. This disadvantage can be overcome, however, by making frequent backups.

■ **Note:** Windows permanent swap files must be located on an uncompressed disk.

The possibility that some of your programs may not work well with DoubleSpace is another disadvantage. Much testing of DoubleSpace and other compression programs has been done, however, and most popular programs do work well with compression software. If this is your only concern, back up the hard disk before you install DoubleSpace. Then install DoubleSpace and test all your software to be sure it loads properly and reads and writes files correctly. If you experience problems, remove DoubleSpace and restore the backup.

The last disadvantage of DoubleSpace is that after you run it you will not be able to use the Uninstall disks to restore your previous version of DOS to the PC. This disadvantage is probably the most insignificant. If you must restore your old version of DOS, you will probably realize it before you reach the point of considering the installation of DoubleSpace.

Installing DoubleSpace

You can install DoubleSpace by using Express Setup or Custom Setup. It is easier to use the Express Setup, but Custom Setup gives you more options and thus more control of the process.

■ **Note:** Express Setup compresses drive C. If you want to compress a different drive, you must use Custom Setup.

Whether you use Express or Custom Setup, the general results of compressing a disk are the same. DOS compresses the specified drive and creates a new, uncompressed drive to store files that cannot be compressed. This drive is called the *host* drive. DOS also stores the DoubleSpace reference file on the host drive. These files are DBLSPACE.BIN, DBLSPACE.INI, and the *Compressed Volume Files* (CVFs) DBLSPACE.000, DBLSPACE.001, and DBLSPACE.002. These files actually hold all the compressed data from the compressed drive, and, because these files also are compressed, they can store more data than the space they use.

■ **Note:** Because the DoubleSpace files on the uncompressed disk are so important, they are protected with the Read-Only, Hidden, and System attributes.

Compressing Your Hard Drive

Before installing DoubleSpace, back up your entire hard drive (see Lesson 8) and use the CHKDSK /F command (see Lesson 6). If any errors are found on the disk, convert the lost chains to files and then delete the files.

■ **Note:** If you do not perform this command first and if DoubleSpace finds errors on the disk, you will have to exit the installation process and perform the command anyway.

To install DoubleSpace using the Express Setup, follow these steps:

1 Exit all programs that are running, including Windows or the DOS Shell.

Increasing Disk Space with DoubleSpace: Installing DoubleSpace **217**

2 At the DOS prompt, type **dblspace** and press Enter. The Welcome Screen is displayed.

3 Press Enter to continue.

4 Choose Express Setup. A screen with the estimated time for compression is displayed.

5 Type **c**.

■ **Note:** The compression process is very safe. DOS double-checks the validity of the data as it compresses it. Even if there is a power failure during the process, no data will be lost.

The process of compressing the disk begins. As part of the process, DOS also defragments the disk. During the process, DOS restarts the PC twice. When the process is finished, a screen displays telling how long the process took and how much free space is available after the compression. The screen also gives information about a new drive that it has created to stores files that cannot be compressed.

6 To exit, press Enter.

▶ Your Turn

■ **Note:** If you do use the Express Setup, you will not be able to use the Custom Setup to install Doublespace.

If you have decided that you want to install and use DoubleSpace, follow the steps in this exercise to compress your drive C. If you still have not decided to compress drive C, skip this exercise and continue with the next section, "Using Custom Setup To Compress a Disk." In that section, you create a new compressed drive with space that is available on drive C.

1 Before you run DoubleSpace, make a full backup of your hard disk. Make a bootable disk and copy all the DOS backup programs to the disk. (These include MSBACKUP.EXE, MSBACKUP.OVL, MSBACKUP.INI, MSBACKDB.OVL, MSBACKDR.OVL, MSBACKFB.OVL, MSBACKFR.OVL, and MSBCONFG.OVL.)

2 Perform the CHKDSK /F command (see Lesson 6). If any errors are found on the disk, convert the lost chains to files and then delete the files.

3 Exit all programs that are running.

4 At the DOS prompt, type **dblspace** and press Enter. The Welcome Screen is displayed.

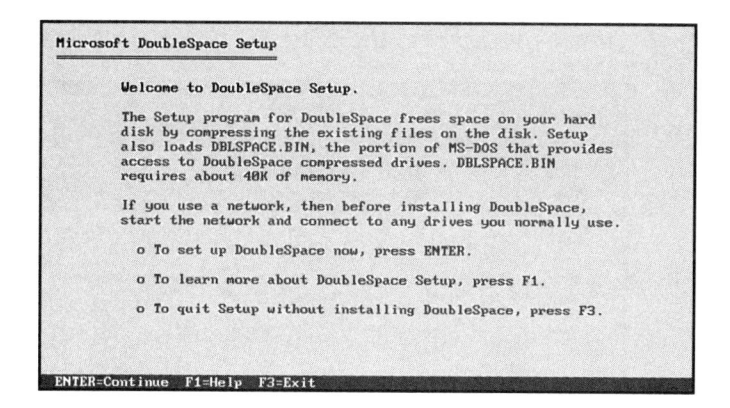

```
Microsoft DoubleSpace Setup

    Welcome to DoubleSpace Setup.

    The Setup program for DoubleSpace frees space on your hard
    disk by compressing the existing files on the disk. Setup
    also loads DBLSPACE.BIN, the portion of MS-DOS that provides
    access to DoubleSpace compressed drives. DBLSPACE.BIN
    requires about 40K of memory.

    If you use a network, then before installing DoubleSpace,
    start the network and connect to any drives you normally use.

       o To set up DoubleSpace now, press ENTER.

       o To learn more about DoubleSpace Setup, press F1.

       o To quit Setup without installing DoubleSpace, press F3.



ENTER=Continue  F1=Help  F3=Exit
```

5 Press Enter to continue.

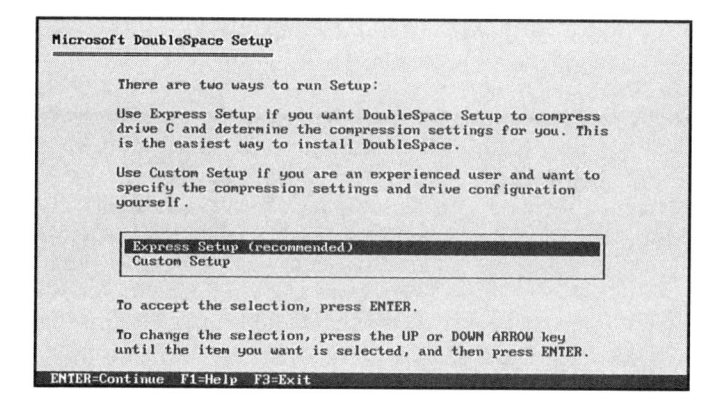

```
Microsoft DoubleSpace Setup

    There are two ways to run Setup:

    Use Express Setup if you want DoubleSpace Setup to compress
    drive C and determine the compression settings for you. This
    is the easiest way to install DoubleSpace.

    Use Custom Setup if you are an experienced user and want to
    specify the compression settings and drive configuration
    yourself.

       ┌─────────────────────────────────────┐
       │ Express Setup (recommended)         │
       │ Custom Setup                        │
       └─────────────────────────────────────┘

    To accept the selection, press ENTER.

    To change the selection, press the UP or DOWN ARROW key
    until the item you want is selected, and then press ENTER.

ENTER=Continue  F1=Help  F3=Exit
```

6 Choose Express Setup. DoubleSpace displays the time required for compression and then prompts you to press C to compress the drive.

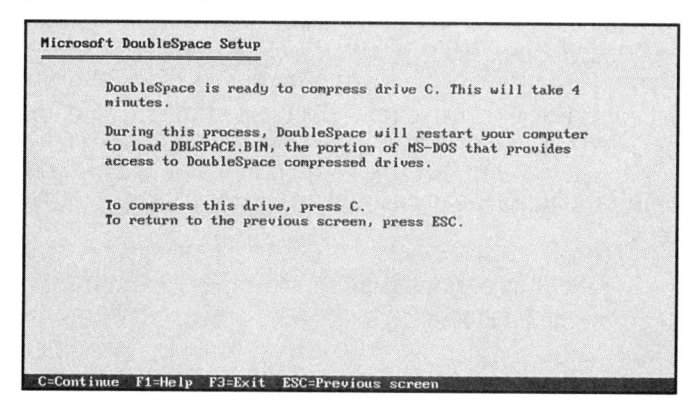

```
Microsoft DoubleSpace Setup

    DoubleSpace is ready to compress drive C. This will take 4
    minutes.

    During this process, DoubleSpace will restart your computer
    to load DBLSPACE.BIN, the portion of MS-DOS that provides
    access to DoubleSpace compressed drives.

    To compress this drive, press C.
    To return to the previous screen, press ESC.




C=Continue  F1=Help  F3=Exit  ESC=Previous screen
```

7 Press **c** to compress the drive.

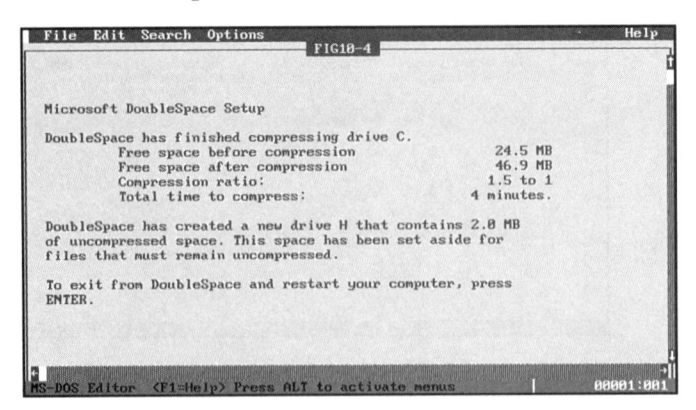

```
File  Edit  Search  Options                                    Help
                         FIG10-4

Microsoft DoubleSpace Setup

DoubleSpace has finished compressing drive C.
       Free space before compression            24.5 MB
       Free space after compression             46.9 MB
       Compression ratio:                       1.5 to 1
       Total time to compress:                  4 minutes.

DoubleSpace has created a new drive H that contains 2.0 MB
of uncompressed space. This space has been set aside for
files that must remain uncompressed.

To exit from DoubleSpace and restart your computer, press
ENTER.



MS-DOS Editor  <F1=Help> Press ALT to activate menus        00001:001
```

8 Press Enter to exit Doublespace and restart your computer.

| **If you have problems...** | If any of your programs do not work correctly, you will have to remove DoubleSpace. If your computer will not boot, use the bootable disk you created and then remove DoubleSpace. Remove DoubleSpace by following the steps in "Removing DoubleSpace" in this lesson. |

Using Custom Setup to Compress a Disk

■ **Note:** If you used the Express Setup to install DoubleSpace, you cannot use Custom Setup.

You can use Custom Setup to compress drive C or a hard drive other than drive C. You also can use it to create a new compressed drive from existing free space. This option does not compress existing data. This creates an empty compressed drive that can be used in the future.

To install DoubleSpace using the Custom Setup, follow these steps:

1 Exit all programs that are running, including Windows or the DOS Shell.

2 At the DOS prompt, type **dblspace** and then press Enter. The Welcome Screen is displayed.

3. Press Enter to continue.

4. Choose Custom Setup.

5. Choose Compress an Existing Drive if you want to compress one of your drives. Then select the desired drive.

   Alternatively, you can choose Create a New Empty Drive and select the drive.

6. Make changes to the compression settings if desired and press Enter.

7. Type **c** to continue.

8. When the process is finished, press Enter.

▶ Your Turn

In this exercise, you create an empty compressed drive from available space on drive C. You can perform this task without anxiety. No data will be jeopardized. Follow these steps:

1. Exit all programs that are running.

2. At the DOS prompt, type **dblspace** and press Enter. The Welcome Screen is displayed.

3. Press Enter to continue. This dialog box appears:

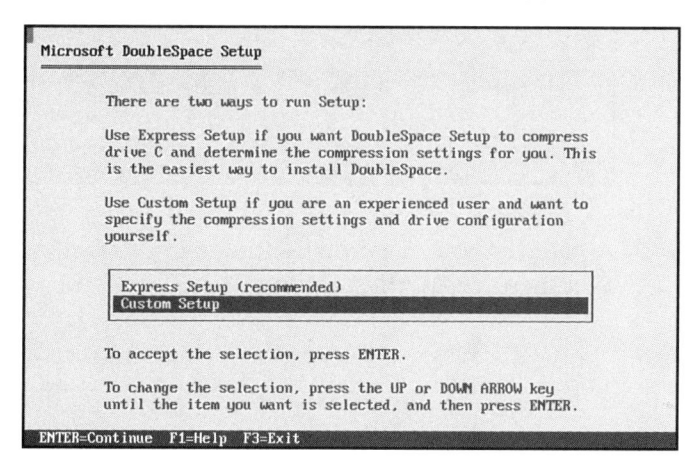

```
Microsoft DoubleSpace Setup

    There are two ways to run Setup:

    Use Express Setup if you want DoubleSpace Setup to compress
    drive C and determine the compression settings for you. This
    is the easiest way to install DoubleSpace.

    Use Custom Setup if you are an experienced user and want to
    specify the compression settings and drive configuration
    yourself.

       ┌─────────────────────────────────┐
       │ Express Setup (recommended)     │
       │ Custom Setup                    │
       └─────────────────────────────────┘

    To accept the selection, press ENTER.

    To change the selection, press the UP or DOWN ARROW key
    until the item you want is selected, and then press ENTER.

 ENTER=Continue   F1=Help   F3=Exit
```

Increasing Disk Space with DoubleSpace: *Installing DoubleSpace*

4 Choose Custom Setup.

5 Choose Create a New Empty Compressed Drive. This screen appears:

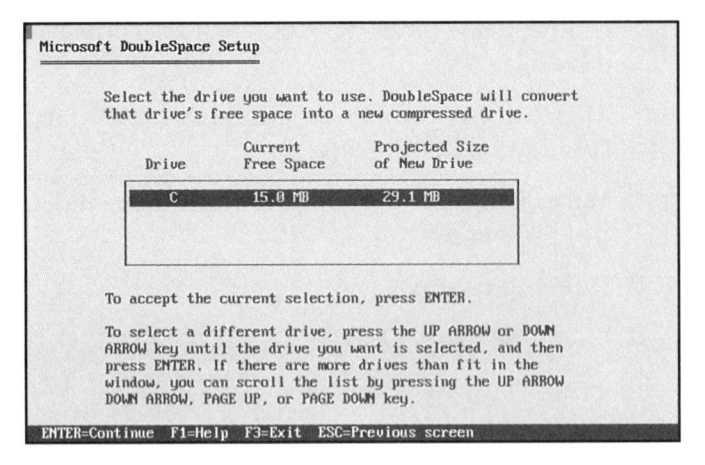

```
Microsoft DoubleSpace Setup

    Select the drive you want to use. DoubleSpace will convert
    that drive's free space into a new compressed drive.

                      Current         Projected Size
           Drive      Free Space      of New Drive

             C          15.0 MB          29.1 MB



    To accept the current selection, press ENTER.

    To select a different drive, press the UP ARROW or DOWN
    ARROW key until the drive you want is selected, and then
    press ENTER. If there are more drives than fit in the
    window, you can scroll the list by pressing the UP ARROW
    DOWN ARROW, PAGE UP, or PAGE DOWN key.

ENTER=Continue  F1=Help  F3=Exit  ESC=Previous screen
```

6 Select drive C. This screen appears:

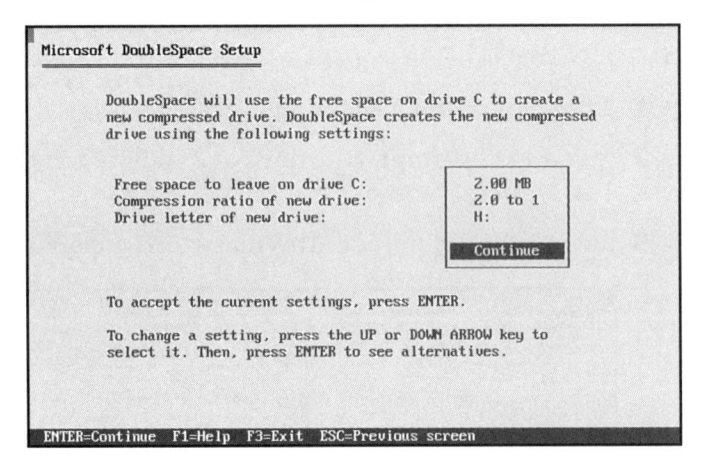

```
Microsoft DoubleSpace Setup

    DoubleSpace will use the free space on drive C to create a
    new compressed drive. DoubleSpace creates the new compressed
    drive using the following settings:

    Free space to leave on drive C:        2.00 MB
    Compression ratio of new drive:        2.0 to 1
    Drive letter of new drive:             H:

                                          [ Continue ]

    To accept the current settings, press ENTER.

    To change a setting, press the UP or DOWN ARROW key to
    select it. Then, press ENTER to see alternatives.

ENTER=Continue  F1=Help  F3=Exit  ESC=Previous screen
```

7 Accept the recommended setting by pressing Enter. You then see another screen.

222 *DOS 6 SureSteps*

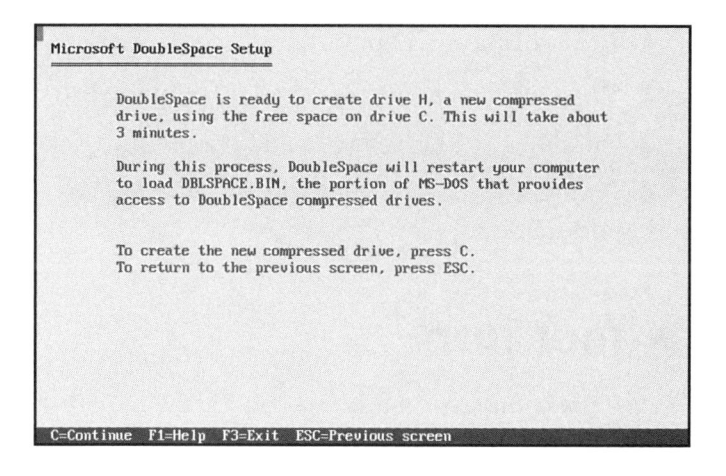

```
Microsoft DoubleSpace Setup

        DoubleSpace is ready to create drive H, a new compressed
        drive, using the free space on drive C. This will take about
        3 minutes.

        During this process, DoubleSpace will restart your computer
        to load DBLSPACE.BIN, the portion of MS-DOS that provides
        access to DoubleSpace compressed drives.


        To create the new compressed drive, press C.
        To return to the previous screen, press ESC.




 C=Continue   F1=Help   F3=Exit   ESC=Previous screen
```

8 Press **c** to begin the compression. DOS checks the disk for errors.

If no errors are found, the new compressed disk is created, and DOS reports the amount of space used, the free space on the new drive, and the time it took to compress.

9 Press Enter to restart the PC.

■ **Note:** Your compressed drive will probably be called H, but its name depends on the configuration of your system.

Maintaining Compressed Drives

Very little maintenance is required for compressed drives. They are really just like any other drive; however, you may want to change the size of the compressed drive, change the compression ratios, or simply get information about a compressed drive. The DoubleSpace program provides a menu system that performs these tasks and more.

After you have run the DoubleSpace program the first time, a menu system displays automatically when you enter the DOUBLESPACE command.

Displaying Information about a Compressed Drive

It is a good idea to monitor compressed drives as often as you monitor an uncompressed drive. To get information about a compressed drive, follow these steps:

1. Type **dblspace** and press Enter.
2. Move the cursor to the desired drive in the list.
3. Pull down the Drive menu and choose Info.
4. Choose OK when you are finished viewing the information.

▶ Your Turn

To view the compression information for the hard disk (if you have compressed it), follow these steps:

1. Type **dblspace** and press Enter.
2. Move the cursor to the appropriate drive in the list.

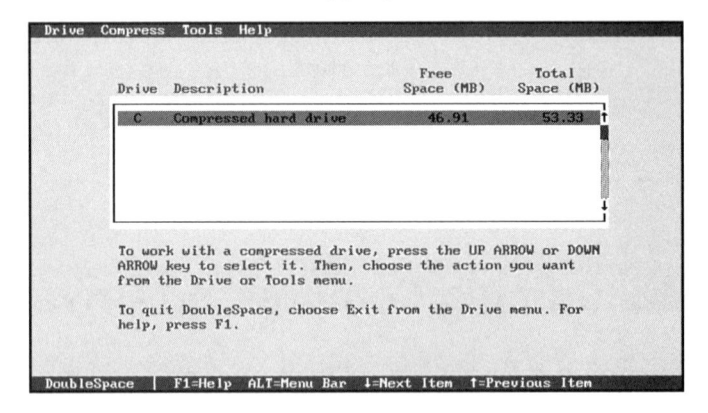

■ **Note:** The information for your drive will be different.

3. Pull down the Drive menu and choose Info. You then see this screen:

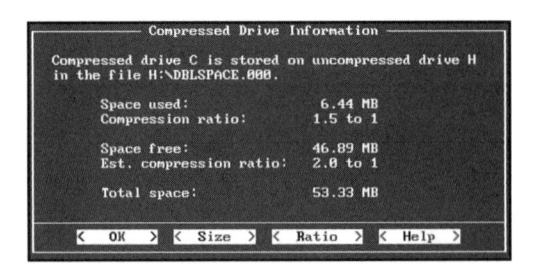

4. Choose OK.

224   DOS 6 SureSteps

▶ On Your Own

If you have more than one compressed drive, view the information for your other compressed drives.

Changing the Size of a Compressed Drive

After viewing information about a compressed drive, you may want to change the size of the drive. To increase or decrease the size of a compressed drive, follow these steps:

1 In the DoubleSpace Main menu, move the cursor to the desired drive in the list.

2 Pull down the **Drive** menu and choose Change **Si**ze. A dialog box appears.

3 Type the desired size for the host drive.

4 Choose OK.

If the host drive has extra room, you might want to increase the size of the compressed disk. Conversely, if you need more room on the host drive, you might want to decrease the size of the compressed disk.

▶ Your Turn

Follow these steps to decrease the size of the compressed drive you created in a preceding exercise:

1 In the Doublespace Main menu, move the cursor to the compressed drive.

2 Pull down the **Drive** menu and choose Change **Si**ze. You then see the Change Size dialog box.

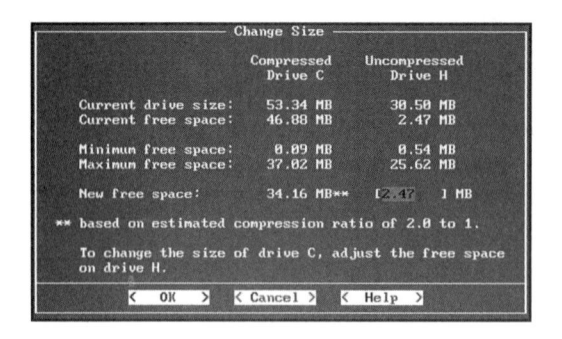

```
                     ─ Change Size ─
              Compressed      Uncompressed
              Drive C         Drive H
Current drive size:  53.34 MB      30.50 MB
Current free space:  46.88 MB       2.47 MB

Minimum free space:   0.09 MB       0.54 MB
Maximum free space:  37.02 MB      25.62 MB

New free space:      34.16 MB**   [2.47  ] MB

** based on estimated compression ratio of 2.0 to 1.

To change the size of drive C, adjust the free space
on drive H.

        <  OK  >   < Cancel >   < Help >
```

3 Type a larger number for the free space on the uncompressed drive.

4 Press Enter. DOS then displays the new size of the compressed drive in the Main menu.

Changing the Compression Ratio

■ **Tip:** To determine the compressibility that each type of file you may be working with has, store a sample of each file on the compressed disk and then see how much it has been compressed by using the DIR /C command. This command lists the files and their compression ratio. Its use is only valid on compressed drives.

Rather than enlarging the compressed disk to add more space, you can increase the estimated compression ratio. Changing the compression ratio does not affect how much a file is compressed; it changes the way DOS estimates how much a disk can hold. If you choose a higher compression ratio, then you know that you will be storing files that can be compressed more than others. Bit-mapped files can be compressed more than program files, for example.

To change the compression ratio of a compressed disk, start DoubleSpace and then follow these steps:

1 Move the cursor to the desired disk in the list.

2 Pull down the Drive menu and choose Change Ratio.

3 Type the desired ratio.

4 Choose OK.

▶ Your Turn

Follow these steps to change the compression ratio for the compressed drive you created earlier. You should still be in the DoubleSpace Main menu:

1. Move the cursor to the compressed drive created earlier. Notice the total space available.

2. Pull down the Drive menu and choose Change Ratio. This dialog box appears:

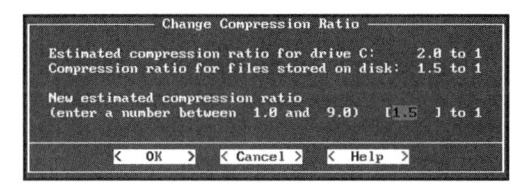

```
─────────── Change Compression Ratio ───────────
Estimated compression ratio for drive C:    2.0 to 1
Compression ratio for files stored on disk: 1.5 to 1

New estimated compression ratio
(enter a number between 1.0 and 9.0)   [1.5 ] to 1

         <   OK   >    < Cancel >    <  Help  >
```

■ **Note:** Selecting a compression ratio that is too high or too low can cause trouble. DOS either overestimates or underestimates the amount of available space on the disk. If the compression ratio is too high, you may get error messages indicating that the disk is full even when it appears that there is still free space on the disk.

3. Type a smaller number than the one displayed and press Enter. The DoubleSpace Main menu is redisplayed. Notice that there is less space available on the compressed disk.

Defragmenting a Compressed Drive

One other method of freeing space on a compressed drive is to defragment the drive. Although free space is consolidated, no decrease in processing time is realized as it is when you defragment a physical drive.

To defragment a compressed drive, start DoubleSpace and follow these steps:

1. Move the cursor to the desired drive in the list.

2. Pull down the Tools menu and choose **Defragment**.

3. Choose Yes.

■ **Note:** Use the Defragment command in DoubleSpace to defragment a compressed drive. Use the DEFRAG command at the DOS prompt to defragment an uncompressed drive.

▶ Your Turn

Because the compressed drive that you created earlier has no data written on it, it really does not need to be defragmented. To familiarize yourself with the procedure, however, follow these steps:

1. From the DoubleSpace Main menu, move the cursor to the compressed drive.

Increasing Disk Space with DoubleSpace: Maintaining Compressed Drives

2 Pull down the Tools menu and choose **Defragment**. You then see this dialog box:

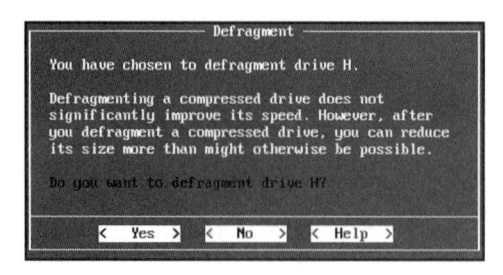

```
─────────────── Defragment ───────────────
You have chosen to defragment drive H.

Defragmenting a compressed drive does not
significantly improve its speed. However, after
you defragment a compressed drive, you can reduce
its size more than might otherwise be possible.

Do you want to defragment drive H?

        < Yes >   < No >   < Help >
```

3 Choose Yes. DOS defragments the drive and returns to the Main menu.

Formatting a Compressed Drive

The result of formatting a compressed drive is the same as formatting an uncompressed drive—all data is erased. Unlike an uncompressed drive, however, you cannot unformat a compressed drive.

✖ **Warning:** Do not format a compressed drive unless you have performed a full backup or you do not care about the data on the disk. You will lose the data on the disk.

To format a compressed drive, start DoubleSpace and follow these steps:

1 Move the cursor to the desired drive in the list.

2 Pull down the **D**rive menu and choose Format.

3 Choose OK to confirm.

4 Choose Yes to reconfirm.

✖ **Warning:** Make sure that you have selected a compressed drive that is empty. If you have more than one compressed drive and you are not sure that you have selected the correct one, do not continue the exercise. From the **D**rive menu, choose E**x**it.

▶ **Your Turn**

Because there is no data on the compressed drive created earlier, follow these steps to format the drive:

1 Within the DoubleSpace Main menu, move the cursor to the compressed drive.

2 Pull down the **D**rive menu and choose Format. This dialog box appears:

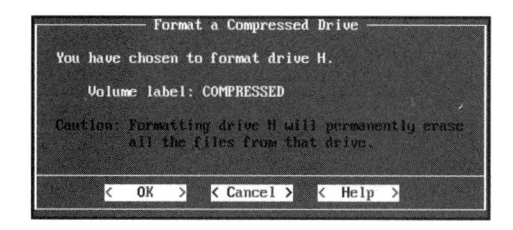

3 Choose OK. This Format Confirmation dialog box appears:

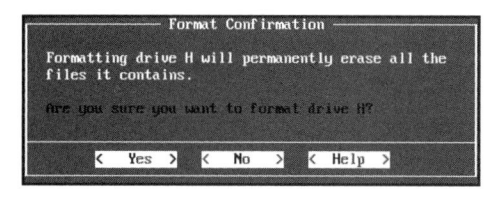

4 Choose Yes. DoubleSpace formats the drive and returns to the Main menu.

Deleting a Compressed Drive

Deleting a compressed drive deletes not only the selected drive but also the CVF associated with it. This deletion does not remove the DoubleSpace program itself. This topic is discussed in a following section.

To delete a compressed drive, start DoubleSpace and follow these steps:

1 Move the cursor to the desired drive in the list.

2 Pull down the Drive menu and choose Delete.

3 Choose OK to confirm.

4 Choose Yes to reconfirm.

▶ Your Turn

Follow these steps to delete the compressed drive you created earlier:

1 In the DoubleSpace Main menu, move the cursor to the compressed drive you created earlier (probably H).

✖ **Warning:** If you have other compressed drives, make sure that you do not delete the wrong drive. You will lose all the data. If you are unsure, do not continue the exercise. From the **D**rive menu, choose E**x**it.

2 Pull down the **Drive** menu and choose **Delete**. You then see this dialog box:

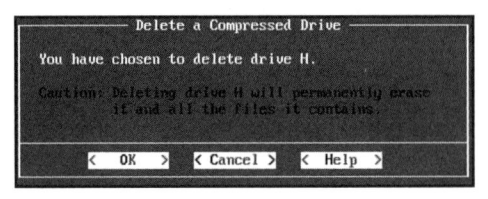

3 Choose OK. This Delete Confirmation dialog box appears:

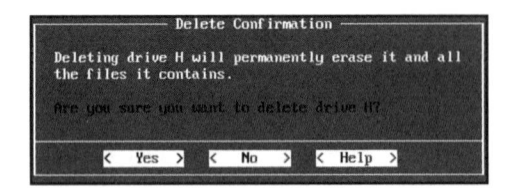

4 Choose Yes. If you have only one compressed drive, the DoubleSpace menu should look like this:

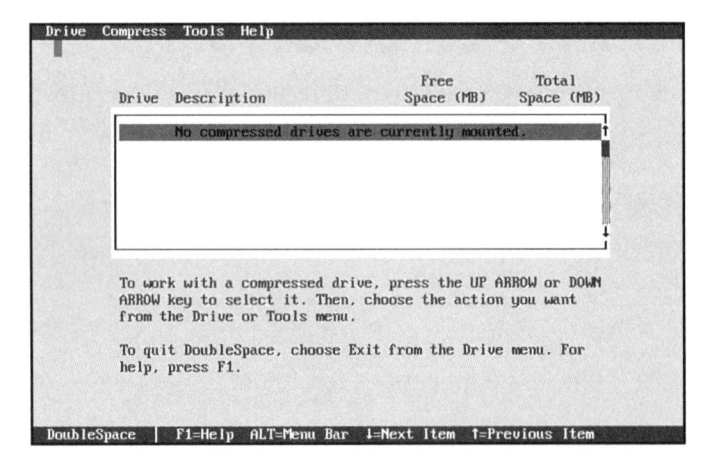

5 Exit DoubleSpace by pulling down the **Drive** menu and selecting **Exit**. You then return to the DOS prompt.

Compressing Floppy Disks

Floppy disks can be condensed just as hard disks can, but DOS has a few stipulations for floppy disks:

- The disk must have a minimum of .65M of free space.
- The disk must be formatted.
- The disk cannot be a 360K disk.

To compress a floppy disk, follow these steps:

1. Insert the floppy disk.
2. Start DoubleSpace.
3. Pull down the Compress menu and choose Existing Drive.
4. Move the cursor to the drive that holds the disk you want to compress and press Enter.
5. Type c to compress.

■ **Note:** The disk must be inserted and the drive you start closed before you start DoubleSpace. The program checks the system to see which drives can be compressed.

▶ Your Turn

Follow these steps to compress one of your floppy disks. (Make sure the disk is a formatted disk with .65M or more of free space. Do not use a 360K disk.)

1. Insert the floppy disk, making sure that the disk drive is closed.
2. Start DoubleSpace.
3. Pull down the Compress menu and choose Existing Drive. This dialog box appears:

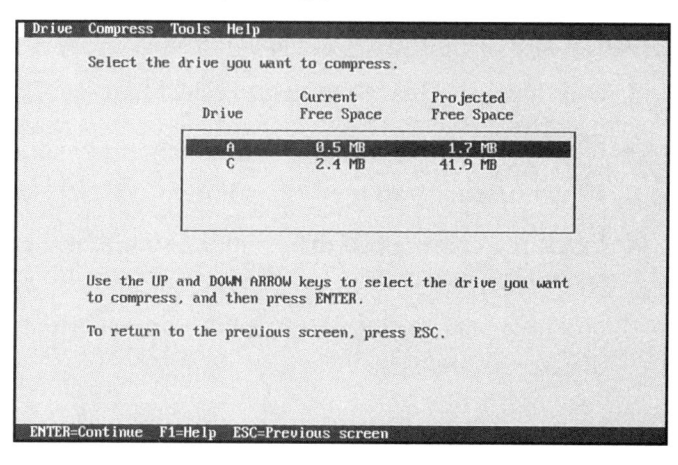

✘ **Warning:** After the disk is compressed, it can only be used on a PC that has DoubleSpace.

```
Drive  Compress  Tools  Help

        Select the drive you want to compress.

                         Current         Projected
                Drive    Free Space      Free Space

                  A        0.5 MB          1.7 MB
                  C        2.4 MB         41.9 MB


        Use the UP and DOWN ARROW keys to select the drive you want
        to compress, and then press ENTER.

        To return to the previous screen, press ESC.



 ENTER=Continue   F1=Help   ESC=Previous screen
```

Increasing Disk Space with DoubleSpace: Compressing Floppy Disks **231**

4 Select the drive that holds the disk you want to compress.

> **If you have problems...** If DOS does not display the drive you want to compress, make sure the disk in the drive is not a 360K disk, that it is formatted, and that it has a minimum of .65M of free space.

5 Type **c** to compress.

Using Compressed Floppy Disks

Immediately after a floppy disk is compressed, it is recognized by DOS and is ready for use. If you change the floppy disk or reboot the PC, DOS no longer recognizes the compressed floppy, and you must *mount* the disk.

To mount a compressed floppy disk, follow these steps:

1 Insert the disk.

2 Pull down the Drive menu and choose Mount.

3 Move the cursor to the appropriate CVF from the list.

4 Choose OK.

▶ Your Turn

Follow these steps to mount the SureSteps disk:

1 Pull down the Drive menu and select Exit.

2 Remove the compressed floppy disk.

3 Type **dblspace** and then press Enter.

4 Insert the compressed disk, making sure that the drive is closed.

5 Pull down the Drive menu and choose Mount. This dialog box appears:

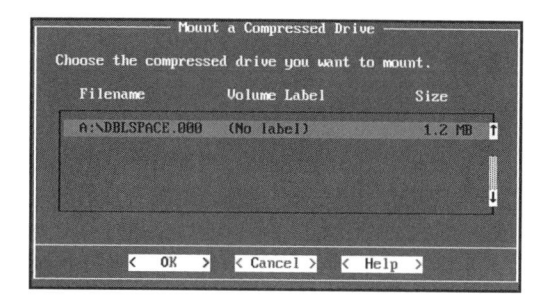

```
┌──────── Mount a Compressed Drive ────────┐
│ Choose the compressed drive you want to mount. │
│                                          │
│   Filename      Volume Label      Size   │
│  ┌────────────────────────────────────┐  │
│  │ A:\DBLSPACE.000  (No label)  1.2 MB│▓ │
│  │                                    │  │
│  │                                    │▓ │
│  └────────────────────────────────────┘  │
│                                          │
│        < OK >   < Cancel >   < Help >    │
└──────────────────────────────────────────┘
```

6 Move the cursor to the CVF for the SureSteps disk. The disk drive will help you identify the CVF.

7 Choose OK.

8 Exit DoubleSpace by pulling down the Drive menu and selecting Exit.

Troubleshooting

If you are using a compressed disk and you get the message A CVF is damaged when you boot, you probably have two files that are cross-linked. Files are *cross-linked* if they are recorded in the File Allocation Table (FAT) as occupying the same space on the disk. To correct the problem, follow these steps:

1 At the DOS prompt, type **dblspace** and press Enter.

2 Move the cursor to the compressed drive on the hard disk.

3 Pull down the Tools menu and choose Chkdsk. The CHKDSK command reports the names of files that are cross-linked.

4 A dialog box appears. If no cross-linked files are found, choose OK.

5 If DOS finds cross-linked files, note the names of the cross-linked files.

6 Exit DoubleSpace.

7 Copy the files to another location (a different drive or directory).

■ **Note:** Some data may be lost.

8 Delete the original files.

Increasing Disk Space with DoubleSpace: Troubleshooting

Removing DoubleSpace

If you encounter problems after installing DoubleSpace, you may want to remove it. There is no quick and easy way to remove DoubleSpace.

You can perform a full backup on all compressed drives, remove DoubleSpace, and then restore the backed-up files to the uncompressed drive. (It is possible, though, that the uncompressed disk will not hold all the files.)

Alternatively, you can move files from the compressed drives to the uncompressed drives, decrease the size of the compressed drives and increase the size of the uncompressed drives, and continue to move files and shrink compressed drives until all files are moved. Then remove DoubleSpace.

If you have many files and directories on the compressed disks, removing DoubleSpace with the first method is easier. If you have only a few files to move to an uncompressed disk, the second method is easier.

To remove DoubleSpace by using the backup-and-restore method, follow these steps:

1 Delete any unnecessary files from the compressed drives.

■ **Note:** If you have never used Microsoft Backup, you will not have the SET file, the INI file, the LOG file, or the RST file.

2 Back up the files on all compressed drives. If your backup program is located on a compressed drive, make sure that you copy these backup program files to an uncompressed drive or floppy disk:

MSBACKUP.EXE	MSBACKUP.OVL
MSBACKUP.INI	MSBACKDB.OVL
MSBACKDR.OVL	MSBACKFB.OVL
MSBACKFR.OVL	MSBCONFG.OVL
DEFAULT.SET	MSBACKUP.LOG
MSBACKUP.RST	

■ **Note:** You can determine the uncompressed drive by typing **dblespace /list** and pressing Enter. The uncompressed drive is listed under the heading CVF Filename.

3 Make your uncompressed drive the current drive. If drive H is your uncompressed drive, type **H:** at the DOS prompt and press Enter.

234 DOS 6 SureSteps

4 Type **cd ** and press Enter.

5 Use the ATTRIB command to change the system, read-only, and hidden attributes of DBLSPACE.000 by typing the following:

attrib dblspace.000 -s -r -h

6 To delete all of your DoubleSpace drives, type **deltree dblspace** and press Enter. If you want to delete just one of your DoubleSpace drives, type **deltree**, followed by the name of the CVF file. Type **deltree dblspace.000**, for example.

7 Restart your computer.

8 Restore your backup files. If you copied the backup program files to a floppy disk, copy them to the hard disk, and then run the backup program from your hard disk.

9 Delete all references to DoubleSpace in the AUTOEXEC.BAT and CONFIG.SYS files.

■ **Note:** If you are removing DoubleSpace from your startup drive, copy COMMAND.COM, AUTOEXEC.BAT, and CONFIG.SYS from your compressed drive to the root directory of your uncompressed drive before issuing the command in step 6.

To remove DoubleSpace by using the move-and-resize method, follow these steps:

1 Delete any unnecessary files from your compressed drives.

2 Delete unnecessary files from the uncompressed drive.

3 Change to the compressed drive (using the CD command).

4 Type **dblspace /size** at the DOS prompt to reduce the drive size as much as possible.

5 Repeat steps 3 and 4 for all compressed drives.

6 Move files from the compressed drive to the uncompressed drive (using the MOVE command) until only .5M of free space remains on the uncompressed drive.

7 Continue moving and resizing (steps 3, 4, 5, and 6) until all files are moved from the compressed drives.

8 Make the uncompressed drive the current drive and change to the root.

■ **Tip:** The Windows permanent swap file also can be deleted.

■ **Note:** You may have to run the Defragment command if DoubleSpace cannot reduce a compressed drive's size because the drive is too fragmented.

Increasing Disk Space with DoubleSpace: Removing DoubleSpace

■ **Note:** If you are removing DoubleSpace from your startup drive, copy the COMMAND.COM file from your compressed drive to the root directory of your uncompressed drive before issuing the command in Step 9.

9 To delete all your DoubleSpace drives, type **deltree dblspace** and press Enter. If you want to delete just one DoubleSpace drive, type **deltree**, followed by the name of the CVF file. Type **deltree dblspace.000**, for example.

10 Remove all references to DoubleSpace in the AUTOEXEC.BAT and CONFIG.SYS files.

11 Restart your computer.

▶ Your Turn

To remove DoubleSpace from all drives with the Microsoft Backup method, follow these steps from the DOS prompt:

1 Make a bootable disk using the SYS command. Copy the AUTOEXEC.BAT and the CONFIG.SYS files to the disk.

2 Back up all compressed drives with MS-Backup.

3 If the Microsoft Backup program files are stored on a compressed drive, change to the compressed drive with the CD command and copy the files to the bootable disk with these two commands:

copy msb*.* a:

copy default.set a:

4 Type **dblspace /list** and press Enter. A screen like this appears:

■ **Note:** If the compressed drive is C (the startup drive), copy COMMAND.COM, AUTOEXEC.BAT, and CONFIG.SYS to the uncompressed drive.

5 Look at the CVF Filename column. The uncompressed drive is listed with the name of the CVF file. Write down the name of this file. (In the figure, the uncompressed drive is H. Your system may be different.)

6 Change to the uncompressed drive. If the uncompressed drive is H, type h: and press Enter.

7 Type cd \ and press Enter to ensure that you are in the root directory.

8 Type **attrib** *filename* **-s -r -h** where *filename* is the name you wrote down in step 5.

9 Type **delete** *filename*, using the file name in steps 5 and 9.

10 Restart your computer.

> **If you have problems...** Use the bootable disk created in Step 1 to start the computer if the PC will not reboot.

11 Restore all files to the hard disk. If you suspect that all the files will not fit on the uncompressed disk, select the files that you want to restore.

12 Edit your CONFIG.SYS file, removing any commands that refer to DoubleSpace.

13 Edit your AUTOEXEC.BAT file, removing any commands that refer to DoubleSpace.

■ **Note**: If you had to copy the Microsoft Backup program files to the bootable disk, copy them back to the hard drive before step 11.

Lesson Summary

To	Do this
Install DoubleSpace	Exit all programs that are running. At the DOS prompt, type **dblspace** and press Enter. Press Enter after the Welcome screen displays. Choose Express Setup or Custom Setup. If you choose Express Setup, type **c** to compress. If you choose Custom Setup, choose Compress an Existing Drive, or choose Create a New Empty Compressed Drive. Press Enter and type **c**.
Get information about a compressed disk	From the DoubleSpace menu, select the desired drive, pull down the **D**rive menu, and then choose Info. Choose OK when finished.
Change the size of a compressed disk	From the DoubleSpace menu, select the desired drive, pull down the **D**rive menu, and then choose Change **S**ize. Type the desired size of the host disk and choose OK.

> continues

Increasing Disk Space with DoubleSpace: Lesson Summary

> **continued**

To	Do this
Change the compression ratio of a compressed disk	From the DoubleSpace menu, select the desired drive, pull down the Drive menu, and then choose Change Ratio. Type the desired ratio and choose OK.
Defragment a compressed disk	From the DoubleSpace menu, select the desired drive, pull down the Tools menu, and then choose Defragment. Choose Yes.
Format a compressed disk	From the DoubleSpace menu, select the desired drive, pull down the Tools menu, and then choose Format. Choose OK and then choose Yes.
Delete a compressed drive	From the DoubleSpace menu, select the desired drive, pull down the Drive menu, and then choose Delete. Choose OK and then choose Yes.
Compress a floppy disk	Insert the floppy disk. From the DoubleSpace menu, pull down the Compress menu, and then choose Existing Drive. Move the cursor to the desired drive and press Enter. Type **c** to compress.
Mount a floppy disk	Insert the disk. From the DoubleSpace menu, pull down the Drive menu, and then choose Mount. Move the cursor to the appropriate CVF. Choose OK.

If You Want to Stop Now

If you want to stop now, exit all programs that are running and turn off your system.

From Here

If you have decided to use DoubleSpace, be sure to study Lesson 11, "Optimizing Memory and Speed." The discussion of upper memory and the device driver DOUBLESPACE.SYS is very helpful.

SURESTEPS LESSON 11

Optimizing Memory and Speed

In this lesson, you learn how to do the following:

- Distinguish the types of system memory
- Use memory management
- Use MemMaker
- Use techniques to speed system processing

Lesson time: 30–45 minutes

As you learned in Lesson 1, memory is that part of the computer that temporarily holds programs and your work. If your PC has a large amount of memory, you can work with several programs at once and work with very large files. Don't be misled into thinking, however, that a large amount of memory automatically guarantees you these opportunities. If you want to work with several programs at the same time, you must have program and memory manager software that enables you to do so. One of the most popular programs of this type is Microsoft Windows.

Distinguishing Types of Memory

■ **Note:** Programs that are written to work with Windows do not have a 640K limitation.

The topic of computer memory can be very confusing if you do not have all the facts about your PC's memory and the memory requirements of the programs you use. You can have a computer with 8M of RAM, for example, and still not have enough memory to open a 200K file with a program that uses only 512K of memory. On the surface, this seems impossible. If you add 200K and 512K, the sum is much less than 8M, so why isn't there enough memory? The answer might be that the program you are using can access no more than 640K of memory, regardless of how much memory you have. Another possible answer is that your program can use only expanded memory and your computer has extended memory.

Understanding and properly configuring the memory within a system can enhance the performance of that system, but you must know the difference between the different types of memory. Following are the types of memory:

- Conventional Memory
- Upper Memory
- Extended Memory (XMS)
- High Memory Area (HMA)
- Expanded Memory (EMS)

If you are not sure what kind and how much memory your computer has, use the MEM command with the /C parameter (Classification). The report lists the programs currently loaded into memory, and the amount and type of memory used by each. The report also summarizes the overall use of memory.

```
80286 LIMIT = 16M
80386 LIMIT = 4G
```

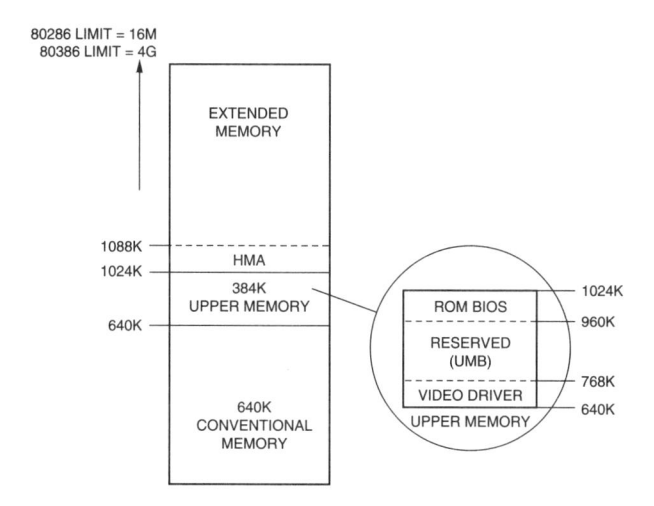

```
                    EXTENDED
                    MEMORY

1088K          ----------
               |   HMA   |
1024K          ----------                      1024K
                    384K          ROM BIOS
                UPPER MEMORY                    960K
 640K                             RESERVED
                                   (UMB)
                                                768K
                                  VIDEO DRIVER
                    640K                        640K
                CONVENTIONAL      UPPER MEMORY
                  MEMORY
```

▶ Your Turn

To find out about the memory in your system and to print the report, follow these steps:

1 At the DOS prompt, type **mem /c |more** and press Enter.

Your screen should look similar to (but not identical to) the following figure because you will have different programs running in memory.

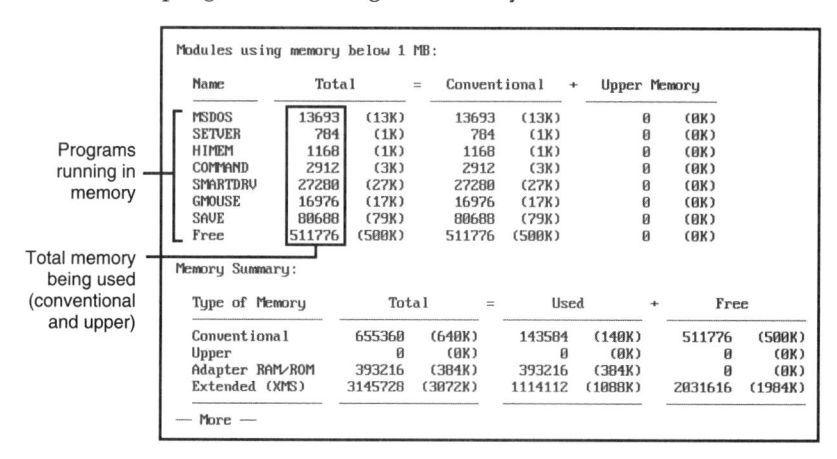

```
Modules using memory below 1 MB:

Name        Total        =    Conventional    +   Upper Memory

MSDOS       13693   (13K)       13693   (13K)       0   (0K)
SETVER        704    (1K)         704    (1K)       0   (0K)
HIMEM        1168    (1K)        1168    (1K)       0   (0K)
COMMAND      2912    (3K)        2912    (3K)       0   (0K)
SMARTDRV    27280   (27K)       27280   (27K)       0   (0K)
GMOUSE      16976   (17K)       16976   (17K)       0   (0K)
SAVE        80688   (79K)       80688   (79K)       0   (0K)
Free       511776  (500K)      511776  (500K)       0   (0K)

Memory Summary:

Type of Memory      Total       =       Used        +       Free

Conventional       655360   (640K)    143584   (140K)   511776  (500K)
Upper                   0     (0K)         0     (0K)        0    (0K)
Adapter RAM/ROM    393216   (384K)    393216   (384K)        0    (0K)
Extended (XMS)    3145728  (3072K)   1114112  (1088K)  2031616 (1984K)

— More —
```

- Programs running in memory
- Total memory being used (conventional and upper)

Optimizing Memory and Speed: Distinguishing Types of Memory   **243**

2 Press any key to continue.

3 To print the report, type **mem /c >prn** and press Enter.

Conventional Memory

Conventional memory is the basic memory found in all computers before additional memory is added. Early computers had 64K of conventional memory. Now most systems have the maximum amount of conventional memory possible, 640K. Conventional memory is used by DOS, by some device drivers that are loaded by the CONFIG.SYS and AUTOEXEC.BAT files, and by application programs that are executed with DOS.

Conventional memory requires no additional memory management software to interface with application programs. The other types of memory discussed later in this lesson do require special memory management before they can be accessed by application programs.

Conventional memory must be shared by DOS and by some of the device drivers and commands in CONFIG.SYS and AUTOEXEC.BAT. The memory that is left can be used by application programs and data files.

▶ Your Turn

Follow these steps to see how much conventional memory your computer is using:

1 Exit all programs that are running, including the DOS Shell.

2 At the DOS prompt, type **mem** and press Enter. Your screen should look similar to the following figure.

```
C:\>mem

Memory Type        Total  =   Used   +   Free
 
Conventional        640K       140K       500K
Upper                 0K         0K         0K
Adapter RAM/ROM     384K       384K         0K
Extended (XMS)     3072K      1088K      1984K

Total memory       4096K      1612K      2484K

Total under 1 MB    640K       140K       500K

Largest executable program size      500K  (511584 bytes)
Largest free upper memory block        0K       (0 bytes)
MS-DOS is resident in the high memory area.

C:\>
```

3 Study the report and determine how much conventional memory is being used.

Upper Memory Area

Most systems have a portion of memory, 384K in size, called the upper memory area. This area resides between the 640K and 1M memory addresses. Even though the upper memory area is present, it is not usually considered part of the total memory because it is normally reserved for running the hardware for the system (usually the monitor). In most cases, however, the hardware does not use all this memory area. The leftover memory is referred to as upper memory blocks (UMBs). DOS can load into the UMBs any programs that fit. Only systems that use an 80386 or 80486 processor, however, can conserve conventional memory by running programs in the upper memory area. Due to the way some programs handle memory addresses, however, not all memory programs can be properly processed in the upper memory area.

▶ Your Turn

Follow these steps to see how much upper memory is available for use:

1 Refer to the report that should still be on-screen, or run the report again by typing **mem** and pressing Enter.

2. Determine how much upper memory is available and how much is used.

3. Confirm your findings by typing **mem /free** and pressing Enter. A report similar to the following figure should appear:

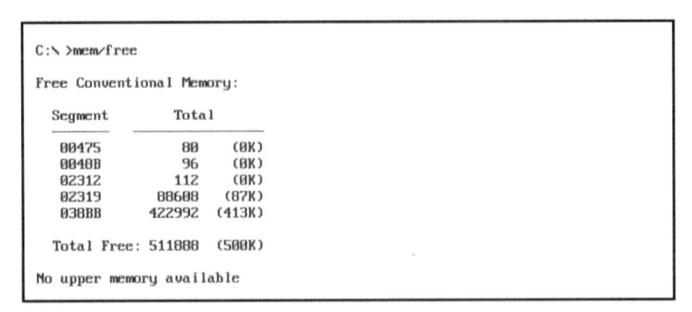

```
C:\ >mem/free

Free Conventional Memory:

  Segment        Total
   00475           80      (0K)
   0040B           96      (0K)
   02312          112      (0K)
   02319        88608     (87K)
   038BB       422992    (413K)

  Total Free: 511808    (500K)

No upper memory available
```

Extended and Expanded Memory

Extended memory (XMS) is any memory beyond 1M (640K conventional plus 384K upper memory). Not all computers can have extended memory; only those PCs with an 80286 or higher processor can use it. The amount of extended memory that a PC can use also is limited. An 80286 processor can address up to 16M of extended memory, and an 80386 processors can address up to 4G (4000M) of extended memory. Most application programs cannot use extended memory, however, without the assistance of a memory management program, such as the DOS extended memory manager called HIMEM.SYS, which is discussed in more detail later in this lesson.

Expanded memory (EMS) was the first type of memory beyond the 640K conventional memory. It uses a very complicated system of addressing memory above 1M. Expanded memory does not actually give an application direct access to the extra memory addresses. Rather, when an application requests access to data, a 16K block (page) of data is mapped into an area called a *page frame*. The application program then is given access to the addresses in the page frame. When additional information is requested, additional pages are added to the page frame. Because of this paging routine, expanded memory operates more slowly than extended memory.

To use expanded memory, older PCs need an expanded memory board and an expanded memory manager. The Lotus/Intel/Microsoft Expanded Memory Specifications (LIM EMS) designates how programs are to make use of expanded memory. Newer PCs can configure extended memory as expanded and use the DOS program called EMM386.EXE to simulate expanded memory. This program is discussed later in this section.

▶ Your Turn

See how much extended and expanded memory you have by following these steps:

1 Type **mem** and press Enter. The report that you have seen before is displayed.

2 Look for Extended (XMS) in the Memory Type Column.

3 See how much memory is listed in the total column.

4 See if you have any expanded memory.

High Memory Area (HMA)

The first 64K of extended memory is called the high memory area (HMA). By design, only one program may use the HMA at a time; however, very few programs, except DOS, have been written to use this area of memory. To free up more conventional memory for application programs, the setup program of DOS 6 automatically installs DOS in the High Memory Area if the PC has extended memory.

▶ Your Turn

Follow these steps to see if DOS is loaded in high memory:

1 Type **mem** /c and press Enter.

2 Look at the last line of the report.

3 If DOS is loaded in high memory, the report looks similar to the following figure:

```
HIMEM         1168    (1K)      1168    (1K)       0    (0K)
COMMAND       2912    (3K)      2912    (3K)       0    (0K)
SMARTDRV     27280   (27K)     27280   (27K)       0    (0K)
GMOUSE       16976   (17K)     16976   (17K)       0    (0K)
SAVE         80688   (79K)     80688   (79K)       0    (0K)
Free        511776  (500K)    511776  (500K)       0    (0K)

Memory Summary:

Type of Memory          Total       =       Used       +      Free

Conventional           655360    (640K)    143584   (140K)    511776   (500K)
Upper                       0      (0K)         0     (0K)         0     (0K)
Adapter RAM/ROM        393216    (384K)    393216   (384K)         0     (0K)
Extended (XMS)        3145728   (3072K)   1114112  (1088K)   2031616  (1984K)

Total memory          4194304   (4096K)   1650912  (1612K)   2543392  (2484K)

Total under 1 MB       655360    (640K)    143584   (140K)    511776   (500K)

Largest executable program size            511584   (500K)
Largest free upper memory block                 0     (0K)
MS-DOS is resident in the high memory area.
```

Managing Memory with DOS

Each type of available memory requires a distinct method of management. DOS provides device drivers and commands that control the use of upper memory blocks, extended memory, high memory area, and expanded memory. Before trying to make any adjustments to the memory management on a PC, the user should have a clear understanding of the current memory configuration. Refer to the report you printed in the earlier exercise as you read the rest of this lesson.

The CONFIG.SYS and AUTOEXEC.BAT files can load the DOS memory management commands and device drivers into memory for use. The order in which device drivers are loaded into memory can affect the performance of the system and can impact how the memory is used.

Follow this general order for loading device drivers:

1 Load HIMEM.SYS in the CONFIG.SYS file by using the following statement:

    DEVICE=C:\DOS\HIMEM.SYS

2 Load the expanded memory manager in the CONFIG.SYS file if the system has a special expanded memory manager that comes with an expanded memory board.

3 Load all device drivers in the CONFIG.SYS file that use extended memory.

4 Load EMM386.EXE if any applications are to be run that can access expanded memory. Do not use EMM386 if an expanded memory manager has already been loaded in step 2, and be sure that HIMEM.SYS is loaded before EMM386.EXE.

5 Load all device drivers in the CONFIG.SYS file that use expanded memory.

6 Load any device drivers or programs in the CONFIG.SYS file that use the upper memory areas by using one of the following commands, for example:

```
DEVICEHIGH    C:\TOOLS\MOUSE.COM
```

or

```
LOADHIGH      C:\DOS\DOSKEY
```

Using MemMaker

You can use the MemMaker program to free conventional memory on an 80386 or an 80486 computer by modifying the CONFIG.SYS and AUTOEXEC.BAT files. MemMaker adds or edits statements and commands that load device drivers and other memory-resident programs in the upper memory area so that they function more efficiently.

It is generally safe to say that MemMaker can optimize the system's memory better than the user can because it analyzes each device driver and memory-resident program to determine exactly how much memory each requires. Then it fits the device drivers and programs into the UMBs as efficiently as possible. To determine the most efficient configuration, MemMaker considers thousands of possibilities in a matter of seconds.

Before using the MEMMAKER command, follow these procedures:

1 Ensure that the system hardware and memory work properly; that is, make sure that all parts of the PC and all programs are running without problems or error messages.

2 Delete any unnecessary programs or drivers from the CONFIG.SYS and AUTOEXEC.BAT files—that is, programs or drivers you really are not using any more.

3 Exit any application programs that are running.

4 Start any hardware or memory-resident programs that are normally used (like a network).

Running the Express Setup

You can run MemMaker using the Express Setup or the Custom Setup. When you use the Express Setup to run MemMaker, you have fewer choices to make, but you also have less control. The Custom Setup gives the user more opportunity for input in the procedure. Generally speaking, however, the Express Setup optimizes the memory in a highly efficient way. The MemMaker program can be run over and over again, so if you start by using the Express Setup and you think the process could be performed better, try the Custom Setup.

Use the following steps to run the Express Setup:

1 Type **memmaker** at the DOS prompt and press Enter. A Welcome screen is displayed.

2 Press Enter to continue.

3 Select Express Setup.

4 Answer the question concerning the use of expanded memory.

5 If you use Windows, provide information if prompted. (Even if you have Windows on your PC, you may not be prompted to answer any questions about it.)

6 Press Enter to restart the computer.

7 Observe the startup process. DOS asks if the system appears to be working properly. If the PC seems to be starting properly, answer Yes. If there were error messages during the startup or there appears to be a problem, answer No and follow the instructions on-screen.

8 If the startup was successful, press Enter to quit MemMaker.

▶ Your Turn

With the following steps, you use MemMaker to optimize the memory in your PC:

1 Exit all programs that are running.

2 Type **memmaker** and press Enter. This screen appears:

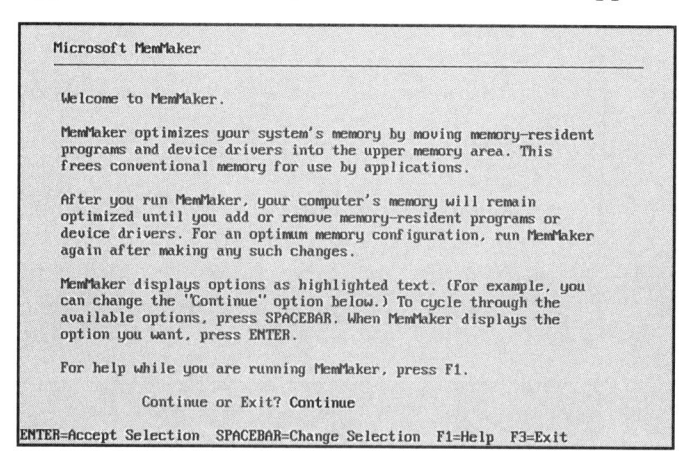

```
Microsoft MemMaker

Welcome to MemMaker.

MemMaker optimizes your system's memory by moving memory-resident
programs and device drivers into the upper memory area. This
frees conventional memory for use by applications.

After you run MemMaker, your computer's memory will remain
optimized until you add or remove memory-resident programs or
device drivers. For an optimum memory configuration, run MemMaker
again after making any such changes.

MemMaker displays options as highlighted text. (For example, you
can change the "Continue" option below.) To cycle through the
available options, press SPACEBAR. When MemMaker displays the
option you want, press ENTER.

For help while you are running MemMaker, press F1.

            Continue or Exit? Continue
ENTER=Accept Selection  SPACEBAR=Change Selection  F1=Help  F3=Exit
```

3 Press Enter to continue. This screen displays:

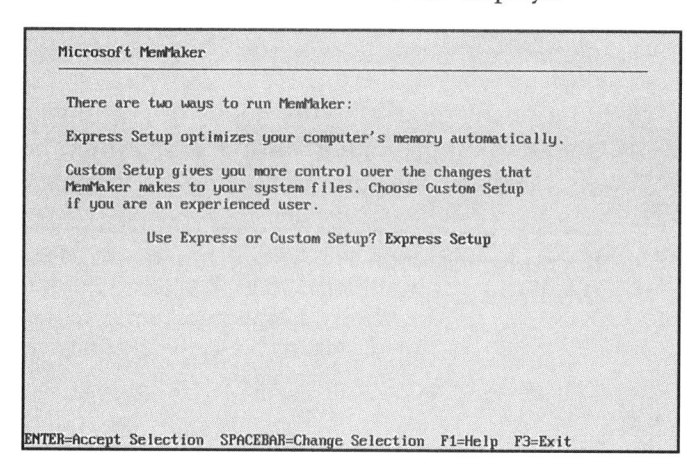

```
Microsoft MemMaker

There are two ways to run MemMaker:

Express Setup optimizes your computer's memory automatically.

Custom Setup gives you more control over the changes that
MemMaker makes to your system files. Choose Custom Setup
if you are an experienced user.

        Use Express or Custom Setup? Express Setup




ENTER=Accept Selection  SPACEBAR=Change Selection  F1=Help  F3=Exit
```

4 Press Enter to run the Express Setup. This screen about expanded memory displays:

Optimizing Memory and Speed: Using MemMaker

```
Microsoft MemMaker

If you use any programs that require expanded memory (EMS), answer
Yes to the following question. Answering Yes makes expanded memory
available, but might not free as much conventional memory.

If none of your programs need expanded memory, answer No to the
following question. Answering No makes expanded memory unavailable,
but can free more conventional memory.

If you are not sure whether your programs require expanded memory,
answer No. If you later discover that a program needs expanded
memory, run MemMaker again and answer Yes to this question.

Do you use any programs that need expanded memory (EMS)? No




ENTER=Accept Selection   SPACEBAR=Change Selection   F1=Help   F3=Exit
```

5 Press the space bar to toggle between Yes and No. If you do not use expanded memory, choose No. If you do use expanded memory, choose Yes and then press Enter. Regardless of your choice, this screen displays:

```
MemMaker will now restart your computer.

If your computer doesn't start properly, just turn it off
and on again, and MemMaker will recover automatically.
If a program other than MemMaker starts after your computer
restarts, exit the program so that MemMaker can continue.

  • Remove any disks from your floppy-disk drives and
    then press ENTER. Your computer will restart.
```

6 Remove any disks from the floppy drives and press Enter as prompted. MemMaker reboots your system and calculates the optimum memory configuration.

If you have problems... If the PC locks up, turn it off and then on again. MemMaker will automatically recover. If an application program starts after the system reboots, exit the program so that MemMaker can continue.

Finally another screen displays, telling you that MemMaker will reboot the system as soon as you remove floppy disks and press Enter.

7 Press Enter and observe the system closely, watching for error messages.

If you have problems... If the PC locks up, turn it off and then on again. MemMaker will automatically recover. If an application is loaded when the system reboots, exit the program so that MemMaker can continue.

8 When MemMaker asks you if your system seems to be working properly, press Enter for Yes. MemMaker displays a table summarizing the "before and after" use of memory.

9 Press Enter to exit.

▶ On Your Own

Revise the new AUTOEXEC.BAT file with MS-DOS Editor and compare it to the old version, AUTOEXEC.UMB. Compare the new CONFIG.SYS with the old CONFIG.UMB. Use the command MEM /C /page to see how the memory is currently being used.

Undoing Changes

If the system is not satisfactory after using MemMaker, MemMaker can undo its changes. To undo the changes made by MemMaker, follow these steps:

1 Exit any application programs that are running.

2 Type **memmaker /undo** at the DOS prompt and press Enter.

3 Press Enter to restore the original files.

▶ Your Turn

Use these steps to undo the changes made by MemMaker:

1 Exit all programs that are running.

2 Type **memmaker /undo** and press Enter. This screen displays:

Optimizing Memory and Speed: Using MemMaker

```
Microsoft MemMaker

You have specified that you want to undo the changes MemMaker made
to your system files.

When you started MemMaker, it made backup copies of your CONFIG.SYS
and AUTOEXEC.BAT files (and, if necessary, your Windows SYSTEM.INI
file).  MemMaker restores these files by replacing the current files
with the backup copies it made earlier.  If the files have changed
since MemMaker made the backup copies, those changes will be lost
when you restore the original files.

              Restore original system files or exit? Restore files now




ENTER=Accept Selection  SPACEBAR=Change Selection  F1=Help  F3=Exit
```

■ **Note:** If changes have been made to the CONFIG.SYS or the AUTOEXEC.BAT file after MemMaker was run, MemMaker warns that the changes in the files will be lost. At that time, the user can choose not to restore the files.

3 Press Enter to select Restore files now. MemMaker displays this screen:

```
MemMaker has finished restoring your original CONFIG.SYS and
AUTOEXEC.BAT files (and, if necessary, your Windows SYSTEM.INI
file).

  • To restart your computer with its original memory
    configuration, remove any disks from your floppy-disk
    drives, and then press ENTER.
```

4 Remove all floppy disks and press Enter. The system reboots.

▶ On Your Own

Run the Express Setup for MemMaker again so that your system uses memory efficiently.

Optimizing the Order in CONFIG.SYS and AUTOEXEC.BAT

Although MemMaker can add statements and commands to the CONFIG.SYS and AUTOEXEC.BAT files and can fine-tune existing commands and statements, it cannot change the order of the lines in these files. You can ensure the best use of memory if you load programs requiring more memory before programs requiring less memory. Programs are loaded in the order in which they are listed in the CONFIG.SYS file.

To determine the amount of memory each program or driver requires, print the MEMMAKER.STS file created by MemMaker during the optimization process. (The file is located in the same directory as MEMMAKER.EXE.) For each driver and program, the file lists a MaxSize. Make note of the memory requirements and arrange these drivers and programs in order by size in the CONFIG.SYS file, but remember that HIMEM.SYS and EMM386 must precede the commands.

▶ Your Turn

To optimize the order of the commands and drivers in your system, follow these steps:

1 Print the file MEMMAKER.STS by selecting the file in the DOS Shell, pulling down the File menu, and choosing Print.

> **If you have problems...** If you cannot find this file to print it, it is in the same directory as MEMMAKER, usually the DOS directory.

2 Note the MaxSize listed for each command or driver.

3 Save a copy of CONFIG.SYS and AUTOEXEC.BAT, changing the extensions to BAK, to use as a backup. You can type **copy autoexec.bat autoexec.bak**, for example.

4 Type **mem /c >prn** and press Enter to print a memory report.

5 Edit the CONFIG.SYS file and change the order of programs and drivers so that the commands and drivers are listed in descending order (from largest to smallest) by MaxSize. Remember, however, that HIMEM.SYS and EMM386 (if present) must precede the commands and drivers.

6 Save the file.

7 Follow the same procedure to rearrange the commands in the AUTOEXEC.BAT file. Save the file.

8 Reboot the system.

■ **Note:** If you want to use the MS-DOS Editor to make these changes, see Lesson 12. Alternatively, you can use any word processing program with which you are familiar, but remember that you must save the file in ASCII format.

Optimizing Memory and Speed: Using MemMaker

9 Type **mem /c >prn** and press Enter to print another memory report.

10 Compare the "before" and "after" reports to see if there is an improvement in memory.

11 If less memory is available to DOS after rearranging the commands and drivers, delete the AUTOEXEC.BAT and CONFIG.SYS files and rename the old files (now called AUTOEXEC.BAK and CONFIG.BAK). Reboot the system.

> **If you have problems...** Some device drivers and commands are very fussy about the order in which they are executed in AUTOEXEC.BAT and CONFIG.SYS. If you have problems with your system that you didn't have before rearranging the commands and drivers, delete AUTOEXEC.BAT and CONFIG.SYS and rename your backup files created in step 3 to their original names. Reboot the system.

Optimizing System Speed

■ **Note:** Many times the speed of a system must be balanced with memory limitations.

As the configuration of systems becomes more complex, the processing speed of a system may slow down. This section examines some common ways to enhance the speed with which programs are executed.

Optimizing speed can be accomplished with one or more of these methods: cleaning up directory structures, using the CHKDSK /F command, streamlining the path, using the DEFRAG command, using buffers effectively, using the FASTOPEN.EXE program, using the SMARTDRV.SYS device driver, and using the RAMDRIVE.SYS device driver.

Cleaning Up Directory Structures

Processing speed can be slowed down by the sheer number of files on a disk. The number of files stored in a directory also has impact on processing time. As a general rule, you should limit the number of files stored in a directory to 150 or less.

You should look for unused directories and files and delete them on a regular basis. Specifically look for old application programs and for temporary files created by some applications. Also look for program video drivers and printer drivers that you do not need. Even some DOS programs can be deleted. Check the following list for DOS program files that you might be able to delete.

■ **Tip:** Rather than delete the DOS files, move them to a floppy disk so that you know exactly which files you removed. You can always move a file back if your needs change.

File name	Description
APPEND.EXE	Allows programs to open files even though they are not in the current directory.
NLSFUNC.EXE, KEYB.COM, *.CPI, COUNTRY.SYS, DISPLAY.SYS, KEYBOARD.SYS	All these files are used to support foreign language characters. If you never used foreign characters like the Spanish tilde or the German umlaut, delete all these files.
RAMDRIVE.SYS	This program creates a RAM disk in extended memory. If you have only conventional memory, delete this program.
DOSSHELL.*, *.VID	If you plan to use DOS from the DOS prompt exclusively, delete these two files which are used with the DOS Shell.
POWER.EXE	This program is used to conserve power on a laptop computer. Obviously, you do not need this program if you are not using a laptop.
INTERLNK.*, INTERSVR.*	These two programs are used when you connect two computers by means of a parallel or serial cable (generally for the purpose of transferring files). If you never intend to link your computer with another one, delete these two files.
EMM386.EXE, MEMMAKER.*, SIZER.EXE, CHKSTATE.SYS	All these files are used to manage or maximize memory use on an 80386 or higher PC. If you do not have an 80386 or higher computer, you can delete these files.
SMARTDRV.EXE	This program is used with extended memory to create a disk cache. Delete the file if you do not have extended memory.

Optimizing Memory and Speed: Optimizing System Speed

Several other ways of speeding up your system have been covered in preceding lessons. These include the following:

- Run CHCKDSK /F. This recovers lost space on your hard drive. See Lesson 7.
- Streamline the path. See Lesson 7.
- Defragment the disk. See Lesson 6.
- Make sure that the BUFFERS command is correct in the CONFIG.SYS file. See Lesson 7.

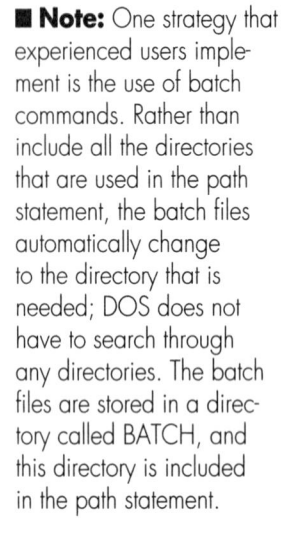

■ **Note:** One strategy that experienced users implement is the use of batch commands. Rather than include all the directories that are used in the path statement, the batch files automatically change to the directory that is needed; DOS does not have to search through any directories. The batch files are stored in a directory called BATCH, and this directory is included in the path statement.

▶ **On Your Own**

Take time to delete unnecessary files, starting with DOS files. Before deleting other program files, research the documentation that comes with each program to see if the program itself recommends files that can be deleted. Some programs include all the video drivers and printer drivers that they support. Delete the ones that you are not using.

Next, use the CHKDSK /F command. If lost clusters are recovered, delete them and then defragment the disk.

Examine the path statement in the AUTOEXEC.BAT file and rearrange the order of directories if necessary. Implement the batch file strategy.

Examine the BUFFERS statement in the CONFIG.SYS file and change the statement if it has a large number of buffers specified and you are unable to substantiate the number.

Using Programs for Extended Memory

If you have extended memory, you can use three additional DOS programs to speed up your system. They are the following:

    FASTOPEN

    SMARTDRV

    RAMDRIVE

The FASTOPEN program decreases processing time by creating a name cache for files that are opened frequently. The name cache is maintained in memory so that DOS does not have to consult the File Allocation Table on the disk. Use the FASTOPEN program if you are working with programs that often require accessing multiple files, such as databases. Loading the FASTOPEN program in upper memory increases processing speed even more.

The SMARTDRV.SYS device driver, loaded in the CONFIG.SYS file, creates a disk cache in either extended or expanded memory. A disk cache speeds processing time by storing disk-sector data in RAM, thereby reducing the number of times the PC must access the disk for the information.

■ **Note:** Do not use SMARTDRV.SYS if the system is already using a disk-caching program.

The RAMDRIVE.SYS program creates a RAM disk in extended or expanded memory that simulates a real disk. Although RAM disks are much faster than mechanical disks because the files and data are already stored in memory, they do have their disadvantages. Any data stored on a RAM disk is lost when the computer is turned off or restarted.

■ **Tip:** If you are using a RAM, you might want to save the data in RAM to a permanent disk more frequently than you normally would. This prevents loss of data in case the system loses power.

When DOS is booted, the RAM disk is created and the next available drive letter (after the currently assigned drives) is used to name the drive. The new RAM drive can be used just like a physical disk drive.

■ **Tip:** RAMDRIVE.SYS does not operate properly in expanded memory if the EMM386 program is being run.

▶ Your Turn

If you have extended memory, follow these steps to add FASTOPEN, SMARTDRV, or RAMDRIVE to your configuration.

1 To add FASTOPEN.EXE to your CONFIG.SYS file, add this line:

   install=c:\dos\fastopen.exe c:=50

2 To load SMARTDRV.SYS in extended memory with a cache size of 2M (the optimum size), use this statement in the CONFIG.SYS file:

   device=c:\dos\smartdrv.sys 2048

■ **Tip:** Before using SMARTDRV.SYS with extended or expanded memory, be sure that the proper memory manager has been loaded.

3 To create a RAM disk in extended memory with 4M, use the following statement in the CONFIG.SYS file:

device=c:\dos\ramdrive.sys 4096 /e

Or to create a RAM drive in expanded memory using the default size of 64K, use this statement in the CONFIG.SYS file:

device=c:\dos\ramdrive.sys /a

Lesson Summary

To	Do this
Use MemMaker	At the DOS prompt, type **memmaker** and press Enter.
Undo the changes made by MemMaker	At the DOS prompt, type **memmaker /undo** and press Enter.
Optimize the system speed	Delete all unnecessary files and directories. Use the CHKDSK /F command periodically to convert lost chains to files and then delete them. Streamline the path statement. Use the DEFRAG command periodically. Make sure that the correct numbers of buffers is specified in the CONFIG.SYS file. Use applicable device drivers that are intended to increase speed like FASTOPEN.EXE, SMARTDRV.SYS, and RAMDRIVE.SYS.

If You Want to Stop Now

If you want to stop now, exit all programs that are running and turn off your system.

From Here

At this point, you should be on a self-directed path. Only two lessons remain. The next lesson on the DOS text editor is helpful if you create and edit batch files frequently, and the last lesson explains how to link two computers.

Section Four

Productivity Tools

4

12. Using the MS-DOS Editor

13. Connecting Two PCs with Interlnk

SURESTEPS LESSON 12

Using the MS-DOS Editor

The MS-DOS Editor is a very simple text-editing program that is used primarily for creating and revising batch files and the CONFIG.SYS file. You might think of the MS-DOS Editor as a stripped-down word processing program. Unlike a word processing program, the MS-DOS Editor does not have features for margins, underlining, bold, spell checking, and so on. Files can be saved in only one format—ASCII.

Text in the MS-DOS Editor does not even wrap from line to line; each line must be ended with a Return (Enter). Thus, the MS-DOS Editor is often referred to as a *line editor*. Remember that each command that is included in a batch file or the CONFIG.SYS file must be typed on a line by itself, so you really don't need a text-wrapping feature in the MS-DOS Editor.

Prior to the introduction of the MS-DOS Editor with DOS 5, DOS provided an even less-sophisticated line-editing program called Edlin. In DOS 6, you have the option of using this program rather than the MS-DOS Editor. Some users may be so familiar with Edlin that they are reluctant to switch to the MS-DOS Editor. If those users would try using the MS-DOS Editor just once, they would never use Edlin again; the MS-DOS Editor is so much better.

In this lesson, you learn how to do the following:

- Start the MS-DOS Editor
- Create a file
- Enter and edit text
- Find and change text
- Save a file
- Print a file
- Open a file
- Exit the MS-DOS Editor

Lesson time:
30–40 minutes

Starting the MS-DOS Editor

You can start the MS-DOS Editor from the DOS Shell or the DOS prompt. You can edit an existing file (such as your AUTOEXEC.BAT file if you have one) or you can create a new file to edit.

Editing an Existing File

To start the program from the DOS Shell, follow these steps:

1 Activate the DOS Shell.

2 Display the Main group in the Program List area.

3 Select Editor.

4 Choose OK. The Editor opens with a Welcome screen.

5 Press Esc to close the dialog box and go to the editing screen.

6 Pull down the File menu and choose **Open**.

7 Select a drive and directory in the Dirs/Drives box. If the files you want are not displayed, change the search pattern in the File Name box from *.TXT to **.***.

8 Select a file in the Files box.

9 Choose OK to open the file.

■ **Tip:** If you type a name of the file you want to edit before choosing OK in step 4, DOS starts the program with this file open and skips the Welcome screen. You then can skip steps 5 through 9.

To start the MS-DOS Editor from the DOS prompt, follow these steps if you want to revise or create a new file:

1 From the DOS prompt, type **edit** and press Enter.

2 Press Esc to close the dialog box and go to the editing screen.

3 Follow steps 6 through 9 above to open a file.

Notice that the Welcome screen tells you to press Enter if you want to see the Survival Guide. The Survival Guide covers all the features and keystrokes associated with the MS-DOS Editor.

■ **Tip:** If you type **edit**, followed by a space and the name of the file you want to edit, before step 2, DOS starts the program with this file open and skips the Welcome screen. You do not need to perform any more steps to open the file.

▶ Your Turn

In this exercise, you edit the file called EMPSEP.ASC in the MANUAL directory of the lesson disk. Insert the disk in the disk drive and then follow these steps:

1 Start the DOS Shell.

2 Select the icon for the drive that holds the SureSteps disk (a: or b:).

3 Display the Main group in the Program List if it is not displayed.

4 Select Editor. The File to Edit dialog box appears:

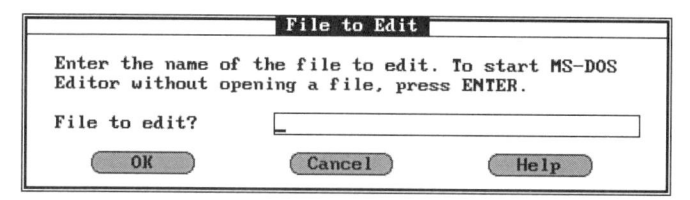

```
┌─────────────── File to Edit ───────────────┐
│ Enter the name of the file to edit. To start MS-DOS │
│ Editor without opening a file, press ENTER.         │
│                                                      │
│ File to edit?    [                              ]    │
│                                                      │
│   ( OK )        ( Cancel )        ( Help )           │
└──────────────────────────────────────────────┘
```

5 Choose OK.

6 Press Esc when the Welcome screen appears.

7 Pull down the File menu and select Open. This dialog box appears:

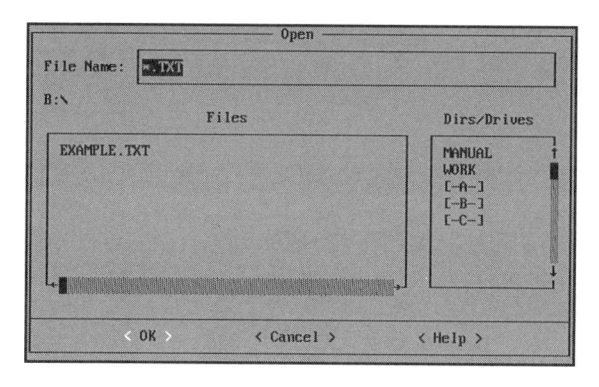

```
─────────────── Open ───────────────
File Name: [*.TXT]
B:\
              Files              Dirs/Drives
 EXAMPLE.TXT                     MANUAL
                                 WORK
                                 [-A-]
                                 [-B-]
                                 [-C-]

       < OK >    < Cancel >    < Help >
```

8 Type *.* in the File Name box.

9 Select MANUAL from the Dirs/Drives box and choose OK.

Using the MS-DOS Editor: Starting the MS-DOS Editor

10 Select EMPSEP.ASC by highlighting it and choosing OK. Your screen should look like the following figure:

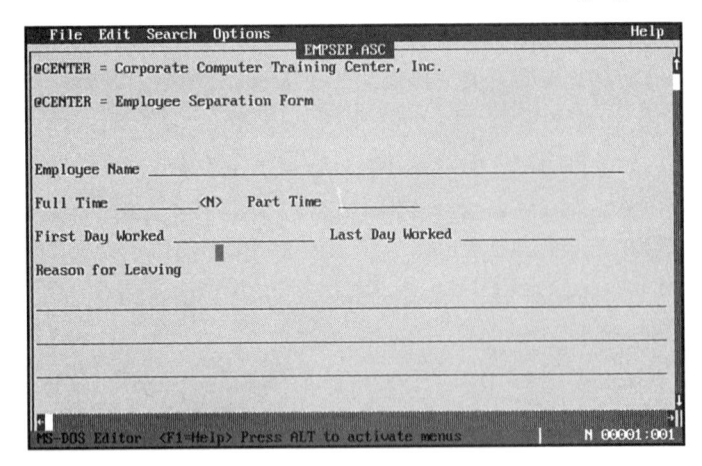

```
  File  Edit  Search  Options                                    Help
                        ┌──────EMPSEP.ASC──────┐
@CENTER = Corporate Computer Training Center, Inc.
@CENTER = Employee Separation Form

Employee Name _____

Full Time _____ <N>  Part Time _____
First Day Worked _____     Last Day Worked _____
Reason for Leaving
_____
_____
_____

MS-DOS Editor  <F1=Help> Press ALT to activate menus      N 00001:001
```

11 Pull down the File menu and choose Exit to return to the DOS Shell.

> **If you have problems...** If you couldn't resist the temptation and changed something in the file, the MS-DOS Editor knows that a change has been made and displays this message:
>
> ```
> ┌──────────────────────────────────────────┐
> │  Loaded file is not saved. Save it now?  │
> │                                          │
> │   < Yes >   < No >   <Cancel>   < Help > │
> └──────────────────────────────────────────┘
> ```
>
> Choose No.

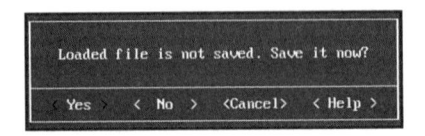

▶ On Your Own

If you have an AUTOEXEC.BAT or CONFIG.SYS file, use the MS-DOS Editor to open one of them. Don't make any changes to the file at this time.

Creating a New File to Edit

The easiest way to create a new file to edit is to open it when you start the MS-DOS Editor.

1. Display the Main group in the Program List area.
2. Select Editor.
3. Type the name of the file you want to create and choose OK.

▶ Your Turn

In this exercise, you create a new file. Follow these steps:

1. Select Editor from the DOS Shell.
2. Type **\work\letters\example.txt** and press Enter. This file, called EXAMPLE.TXT, will be stored in the LETTERS directory, a subdirectory of the WORK directory.

   If you have problems... If DOS displays the message `Path not found. Press any key to continue`, press any key and begin again with step 1. Be careful to type the file name and path correctly.

3. Type this line and press Enter twice:

   The following topics are covered in this lesson:

4. Press the Tab key.
5. Type **Starting MS-DOS** and press Enter.
6. Type the following lines, pressing Enter after each line:

   Creating a File

   Editing a File

   Searching for Text

   Replacing Text

7. Press Enter and then press Backspace.
8. Type **The lesson will take approximately 25 minutes**. Your screen should look exactly like this (if you are an outstanding typist):

```
 File  Edit  Search  Options                                    Help
                       ┌──────EXAMPLE.TXT──────┐
The following topics are covered in this lesson:

        Starting MS-DOS
        Creating a File
        Editing a File
        Searching for Text
        Replacing Text

The lesson will take approximately 25 minutes.




MS-DOS Editor   <F1=Help> Press ALT to activate menus      N 00009:047
```

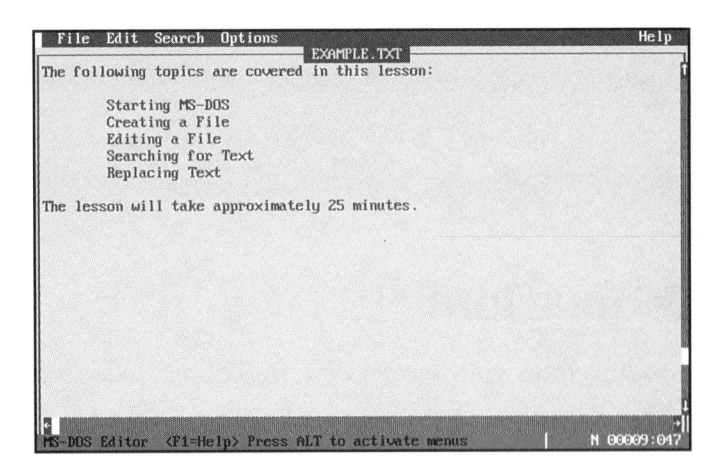

If you have some typographical errors, do not worry about them now. You learn how to make corrections and revisions later in this lesson.

■ Tip: You can use this shortcut for steps 8 and 9: pull down the **F**ile menu, choose E**x**it, and then choose **Y**es to save.

9 Pull down the File menu and choose **S**ave.

10 Pull down the File menu and choose Exit.

Getting Familiar with the Screen and Menu

The MS-DOS Editor screen has a menu bar at the top with the options File, Edit, Search, Options, and Help. Below the menu bar is the name of the file. If you have started the MS-DOS Editor without opening a file, the word Untitled appears on this line, not a file name. As you have already seen, the area under the file name is the typing area. On the right and below the typing area are scroll bars. Below the scroll bar at the bottom of the screen is an information line which displays information such as the line number and column number of the cursor (at the far right). If you have a menu option highlighted, the information line explains the purpose of the option.

Preceding exercises in this lesson assume that you already know how to use the menus in the MS-DOS Editor. This is true if you have read Lesson 2. The menu in the MS-DOS Editor is used in exactly the same way as the DOS Shell menu. To review, the menu is activated from the keyboard by pressing Alt. To choose a menu option, type the emphasized character for the option or use an arrow key to move the cursor to the desired option and press Enter. (If you are using a mouse, you don't need to activate the menu. Simply click the option.) A pull-down menu is displayed when you choose an option. You can choose pull-down menu options the same way you choose options from the menu bar.

To cancel an option or menu that you have chosen, press Esc or click the mouse in a non-menu area. To cancel a dialog box, press Esc or choose the Cancel button.

▶ Your Turn

Practice using the menu by following these steps:

1 Select Editor from the DOS Shell.

2 Choose OK and then press Esc.

3 Press Alt to activate the menu.

4 Type **e**. The Edit pull-down menu is displayed.

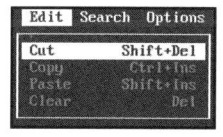

```
Edit  Search  Options
Cut          Shift+Del
Copy         Ctrl+Ins
Paste        Shift+Ins
Clear        Del
```

5 Press the right arrow to display the Search menu.

6 Press Esc.

Using Help

Using the Help system in the MS-DOS Editor is very similar to using Help in the DOS Shell. You can access Help by using the following methods:

■ Press F1 at any time to display a Help screen about the current task.

■ Choose the Help button if it is displayed in a dialog box.

▶ Your Turn

You should still be in the MS-DOS Editor. Practice using Help by following these steps:

1 Press Alt to activate the menu.

2 Press F1. This Help screen is displayed:

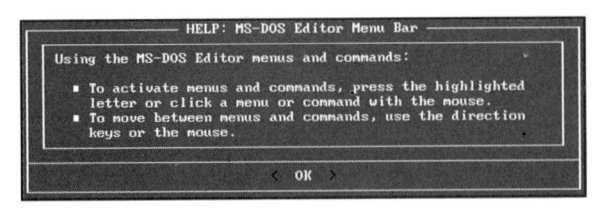

3 Press Esc.

4 Press F1 and select Getting Started. This Help screen appears:

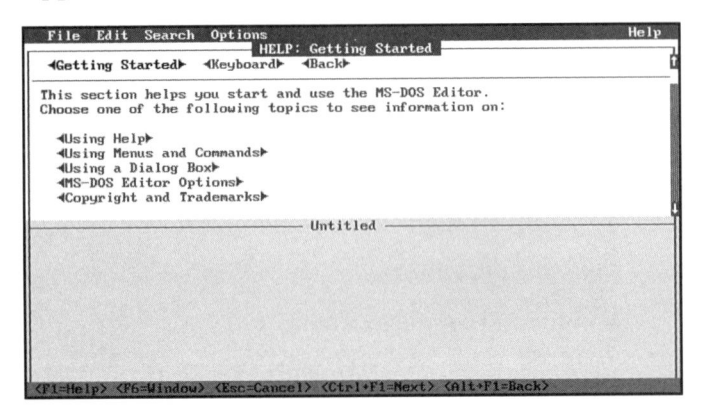

You then can select from the topics that are listed.

5 Press Esc.

6 Pull down the File menu and choose Save As to display this dialog box:

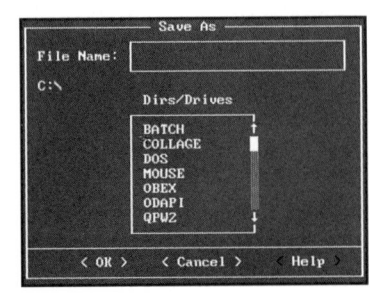

---

270 DOS 6 SureSteps

7 Choose the Help button. This Help screen appears:

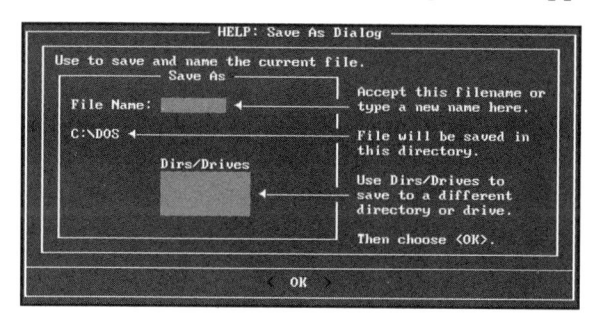

```
┌─────────────── HELP: Save As Dialog ───────────────┐
│ Use to save and name the current file.             │
│   ┌─ Save As ──────────────┐                       │
│   │ File Name: ▓▓▓▓▓▓  ◄── │ Accept this filename or│
│   │                        │ type a new name here.  │
│   │ C:\DOS ◄──             │ File will be saved in  │
│   │         Dirs/Drives    │ this directory.        │
│   │        ┌──────────┐    │                        │
│   │        │          │    │ Use Dirs/Drives to     │
│   │        │          │◄── │ save to a different    │
│   │        │          │    │ directory or drive.    │
│   │        └──────────┘    │                        │
│   │                        │ Then choose <OK>.      │
│   └────────────────────────┘                        │
│                  < OK >                             │
└─────────────────────────────────────────────────────┘
```

8 Press Esc twice to exit the Help screen and return to the typing area of the MS-DOS Editor.

Entering and Editing Text

As mentioned in a preceding section, text is typed line by line—that is, you must press Enter at the end of each line. If you make a mistake while you are typing, you can use Backspace to erase the character to the left of the cursor and continue typing. If you spot a mistake that you have made on another line, you can use the arrow keys to move the cursor to the mistake and correct it in various ways, depending on the mistake.

Another way to delete text is to use the Delete key. If you have typed a character that should be deleted, move the cursor to the character and press Del. To delete all or part of a word, position the cursor on the first character to be deleted and press Ctrl+T. To delete leading spaces on a line, position the cursor anywhere on the line and press Shift+Tab. To delete the current line (storing it in the Clipboard which is discussed later in this lesson), press Ctrl+Y. To delete from the current cursor position to the end of the line, press Ctrl+Q, Y.

To indent text, press Tab. The cursor advances the number of spaces specified in the Display dialog box. (To set the number of spaces that Tab indents, pull down the **O**ptions menu and choose **D**isplay. Type the number of spaces to indent and then choose OK.) After you have pressed Tab, typed the text on the line, and pressed Enter, the cursor moves to the first indention on the next line, not to the left edge of the screen. If you do not want the next line indented, press Backspace to move the cursor to the left edge.

Using the MS-DOS Editor: Entering and Editing Text

You know how to use the arrow keys to move around in the text, of course, but that is the slowest way to move the cursor. Table 12.1 lists all the cursor movement keys. Some of the keystrokes listed are much faster than using only the arrow keys.

Table 12.1. Cursor movement keystrokes

To move to	Press
Character on the left	left arrow
Character on the right	right arrow
Word on the left	Ctrl+left arrow
Word on the right	Ctrl+right arrow
Line above	up arrow
Line below	down arrow
First character on the line	Home
Beginning of line	Ctrl+Q, S
End of line	End
First character in the next line	Ctrl+Enter
Beginning of file	Ctrl+Home
End of file	Ctrl+End
Next screen	Pg Dn
Preceding screen	Pg Up

■ **Note:** Insert is the default mode for the MS-DOS Editor, but you can turn it on and off with the Ins key. When DOS has Overstrike mode activated, the cursor is a flashing rectangle rather than an Underline.

If you have omitted a character, move the cursor to where the character should be and type the character. The MS-DOS Editor inserts the character. To replace a character, press Ins to activate the Overstrike mode and type the correct character over the incorrect character.

To insert a blank line above the current line, press Home or Ctrl+Q, S to get to the beginning of the line and then press Enter. To insert a blank line below the current line, press End to move to the end of the line and then press Enter.

▶ Your Turn

You should still be in the MS-DOS Editor. Follow these instructions to practice moving around in the text to make simple corrections:

1 Pull down the File menu and choose Open.

2 Select WORK in the Dirs/Drives box.

3 Select LETTERS in the Dirs/Drives box.

4 Type *.* in the File Name box and press Enter.

5 Select EXAMPLE.TXT in the Files box and choose OK.

■ **Note:** Rather than complete steps 2, 3, 4, and 5, you can type **\work\letters\example.text** in the File Name box and then press Enter.

If you have problems... If you have added text to the current document that has been used to practice using the menus and the Help screens, the MS-DOS Editor displays this dialog box:

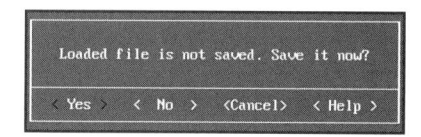

```
Loaded file is not saved. Save it now?

 < Yes >   < No >   <Cancel>   < Help >
```

Choose Yes if you want to save the changes or No if you do not.

6 Move the cursor to the *S* in Starting and press Backspace. When you press Backspace, you must be on the first character of the line, not on the left margin.

7 Delete the indentations in the next four lines.

8 Delete the word *topics* in the first line.

9 Change 25 minutes to **25-30 minutes**.

10 Insert the word **topics** in the first line again.

11 Move the cursor to the word this in the first line. Delete *i* and *s* and insert **e**, changing *this* to *the*.

12 Move the cursor to the end of the file. Move the cursor to the beginning of the file.

13 Move the cursor to the end of the line and then back to the beginning of the line.

Using the MS-DOS Editor: Entering and Editing Text

Selecting and Editing Blocks of Text

You frequently will want to delete, copy, or move a portion of text. Before doing so, you must select the text. (When text is *selected*, it is highlighted.) To select text by using the keyboard, hold down the Shift key while you use the cursor movement keys to move to the end of the desired text. To select part of a line from some point in the middle of the line to the end of the line, for example, position the cursor on the first character that you want to select, hold down the Shift key, and then press End. (Table 12.1 indicates that the End key moves the cursor to the end of the line.) To deselect text, press Esc.

If you are using a mouse, you can select text by pointing to the first character, holding down the left mouse button, dragging the cursor to the last character, and then releasing the mouse button. To deselect text, simply move the cursor in any direction or click the mouse at any location.

After you have the desired text selected, you can edit it in these ways:

- Delete
- Copy
- Move

To delete a selected block of text, press Del or pull down the Edit menu and choose Clear.

To copy selected text, press Ctrl+Ins. (When you press Ctrl+Ins, DOS copies the text to a memory area called the Clipboard, and it can be recalled or *pasted* later.) Move the cursor to the new location and press Shift+Ins.

If you prefer to use the menu, follow these steps to copy text:

1. Select the text.
2. Pull down the Edit menu and choose **Copy**.
3. Move the cursor to the new location.
4. Pull down the Edit menu and choose **Paste**.

> **Tip:** Notice that the keyboard shortcuts are shown on the pull-down menu.

To move selected text, press Shift+Del. (When you press Shift+Del, the text is held in the Clipboard just like copied text.) Move the cursor to the new location and then press Shift+Ins; DOS inserts the text.

If you prefer to use the menu, follow these steps to move text:

1 Select the text.

2 Pull down the Edit menu and choose **Cut**.

3 Move the cursor to the new location.

4 Pull down the Edit menu and choose **Paste**.

■ **Note:** The Clipboard can hold only one block of text at a time. When you copy or cut selected text to the Clipboard, the text that was being held there is replaced by the new text. On the other hand, after you have pasted text from the Clipboard, the text is not removed. It remains in the Clipboard and can be pasted over and over again.

▶ **Your Turn**

To practice selecting, copying, and moving text, follow these steps:

1 Select the last sentence.

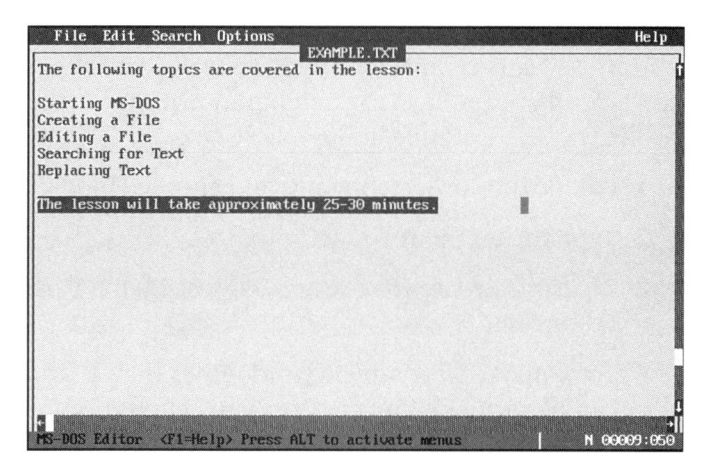

```
 File  Edit  Search  Options                                    Help
                        ┌──────EXAMPLE.TXT──────┐
 The following topics are covered in the lesson:

 Starting MS-DOS
 Creating a File
 Editing a File
 Searching for Text
 Replacing Text

 The lesson will take approximately 25-30 minutes.

 MS-DOS Editor  <F1=Help> Press ALT to activate menus      N 00009:050
```

2 Move to the first sentence and delete it.

3 Select the second topic in the list.

4 Insert it before the first topic in the list by pressing Shift+Del and Shift+Ins. Your screen should look like this:

Using the MS-DOS Editor: Entering and Editing Text   **275**

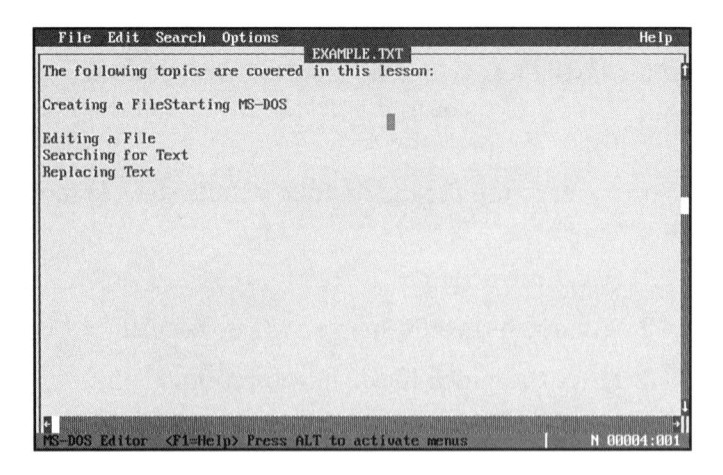

```
 File  Edit  Search  Options                                    Help
                          ┌─ EXAMPLE.TXT ─┐
 The following topics are covered in this lesson:

 Creating a FileStarting MS-DOS

 Editing a File
 Searching for Text
 Replacing Text




 MS-DOS Editor   <F1=Help> Press ALT to activate menus       N 00004:001
```

5 Move the cursor to the *S* in Starting and press Enter to move the topic to the next line.

6 Move the cursor to the blank line above Editing a File and press Backspace.

Finding Text

To move the cursor quickly to a character or character string, use the Find option in the Search pull-down menu. To find specific text, for example, follow these steps:

1 Pull down the Search menu and choose Find.

2 Type the text that you wish to find.

3 To do a case-sensitive search, choose Match Upper/Lowercase.

4 To search for a complete word rather than a string that can be contained in a larger string, choose Whole Word.

5 Choose OK. The cursor moves to the first occurrence of the text.

■ **Note:** The Find and Repeat Last Find commands search the complete file, regardless of the cursor position when the command is invoked.

To move the cursor to the next occurrence of the text, pull down the Search menu and choose Repeat Last Find. The keyboard shortcut to repeat the last find is F3.

▶ Your Turn

Practice using the Find and Repeat Last Find features by following these steps:

■ Tip: The keyboard shortcut for finding text is Ctrl+Q, F.

1 Pull down the Search menu and choose Find. The Find dialog box displays:

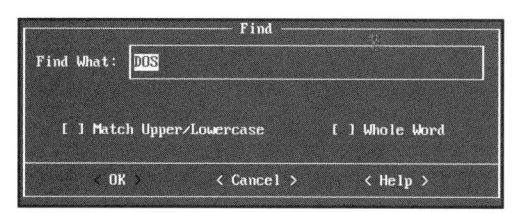

2 Type **in** and press Enter. The cursor moves to the first occurrence of *in*.

3 Press F3 to find the next occurrence.

4 Press F3 again.

5 Pull down the Search menu and choose Find.

6 Tab to Whole Word, press the space bar, and choose OK.

7 Press F3. The cursor should not move because there are no other occurrences of the whole word.

8 Pull down the Search menu and select Find.

9 Type **text**, select Match Upper/Lowercase, and choose OK. Because all occurrences of *Text* have the first letter capitalized, this message displays:

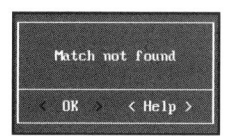

10 Choose OK.

Using the MS-DOS Editor: Entering and Editing Text

Finding and Changing Text

If you have typed the same text several times in a file and misspelled the text, you can use the Change option to find all occurrences of the text and change it.

To change all occurrences of a specified text without confirming each change, follow these steps:

1 Pull down the Search menu and choose Change.

2 Type the text to find in the Find What box.

3 Move to the Change To box.

4 Type the new text.

5 Choose Change All. When the changes are complete, a change complete message is displayed.

6 Choose OK.

■ **Note:** The Change option searches the complete file, regardless of the cursor position when the option is invoked.

■ **Tip:** The keyboard shortcut to change text is Ctrl+Q, A.

To selectively change the occurrences of a specified text, follow these steps:

1 Pull down the Search menu and choose Change.

2 Type the text to find.

3 Move to the Change To box.

4 Type the new text.

5 Choose Find and Verify. A dialog box is displayed when DOS locates the first occurrence.

6 To change the first occurrence, select Change. To skip this one and go to the next occurrence, select Skip.

7 When the last occurrence has been changed or skipped, a Change Complete message is displayed.

8 Choose OK.

▶ Your Turn

Practice finding and changing text with this exercise:

1 Pull down the Search menu and choose Change. This dialog box displays:

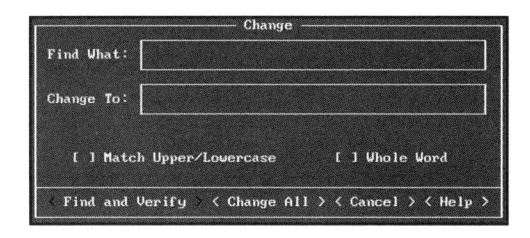

2 Type **Text** in the Find what box.

3 Tab to the Change To box and type **Strings**.

4 Choose Change All. This message displays:

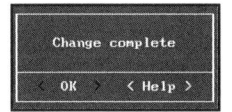

5 Choose OK.

6 Pull down the Search menu and choose Change.

7 Type **Strings** in the Find What box.

8 Tab to the Change To box and type **Text**.

9 Choose Find and Verify. The MS-DOS Editor displays this dialog box when the cursor locates the first occurrence of *Strings*:

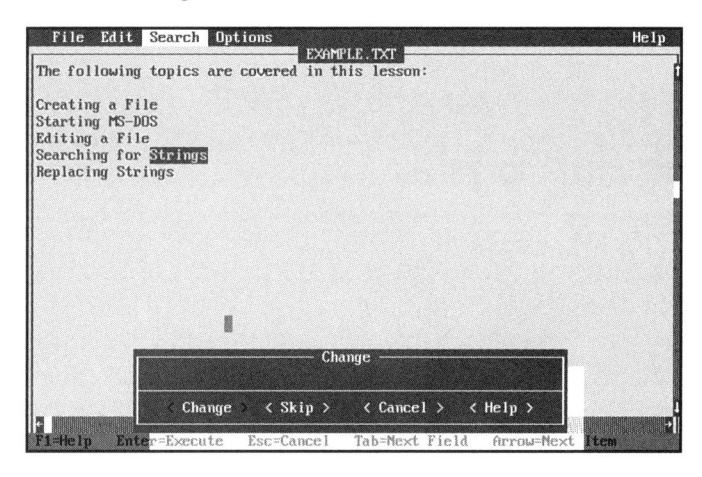

10 Choose Skip. The cursor moves to the next occurrence of *Strings*.

Using the MS-DOS Editor: Entering and Editing Text **279**

11 Choose Change. The Change Complete message displays.

12 Choose OK.

Setting Bookmarks

> **■ Note:** The MS-DOS Editor can move to the marker whether the cursor is above or below it.

A bookmark is an invisible marker or placeholder that you can set in a file. After you set the marker, you can move the cursor quickly to it.

To set a marker, position the cursor and press Ctrl+K, followed by a number from zero to three. (A maximum of four markers can be set in a single file.) To move to the marker, press Ctrl+Q, followed by the number of the marker.

▶ Your Turn

Practice using bookmarks by following these steps.

1 Place the cursor on the third line of the file that is open (EXAMPLE.TXT).

2 Press Ctrl+K and type **2** to set a marker.

3 Move the cursor to the end of the file.

4 Press Ctrl+Q and type **2**. The cursor then moves to the marker you inserted.

Saving a File

After you finish typing a file, you must save it to store it permanently on a disk. To save a file, pull down the File menu and choose **Save**. If the file is labeled *Untitled* because you did not name the file when you began, the MS-DOS Editor displays the Save As dialog box when you try to save the file. Type the name of the file (including the path if necessary) and then choose OK.

> **■ Tip:** Use the Save As option to save the same file under a different name if you need a copy of it.

If you type a file name that already exists in the path, the MS-DOS Editor asks if you want to overwrite the old file. You can overwrite the file by choosing Yes. If you choose No, the Save As dialog box is displayed and you can enter a different file name.

▶ Your Turn

You have made many revisions to the EXAMPLE.TXT file. Follow these steps to save the revised file:

1 Pull down the File menu and choose **S**ave.

2 To make another copy of the file, pull down the File menu and choose Save As. The Save As dialog box displays.

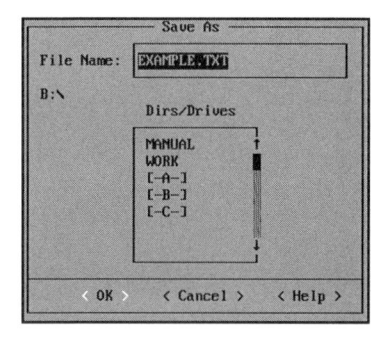

```
─────────── Save As ───────────
File Name: EXAMPLE.TXT
B:\
            Dirs/Drives
         MANUAL
         WORK
         [-A-]
         [-B-]
         [-C-]

   < OK >    < Cancel >    < Help >
```

3 Press the left arrow key four times, type **2**, and press Enter.

4 Pull down the File menu and choose Save As again.

5 Press the left arrow key five times, press Del, and then press Enter. This error message box displays:

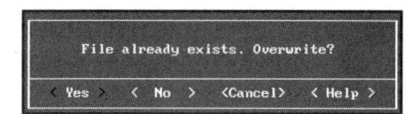

```
   File already exists. Overwrite?
< Yes >   < No >   <Cancel>   < Help >
```

6 Choose No and then choose Cancel.

Printing a File

When you print a file, the output is sent to the attached printer. You cannot adjust any printer settings or select a different printer. You can choose, however, to print all of a file or selected text only.

Using the MS-DOS Editor: Printing a File   **281**

To print a complete file, follow these steps:

1 Pull down the File menu and choose **Print**.

2 Select Complete Document.

3 Choose OK.

To print a portion of the file, follow these steps:

1 Select the desired text.

2 Pull down the File menu and choose **Print**.

3 Make sure that Selected Text Only is selected.

4 Choose OK.

▶ Your Turn

Practice printing the EXAMPLE.TXT file with this brief exercise:

1 Highlight the five topics as shown in the figure:

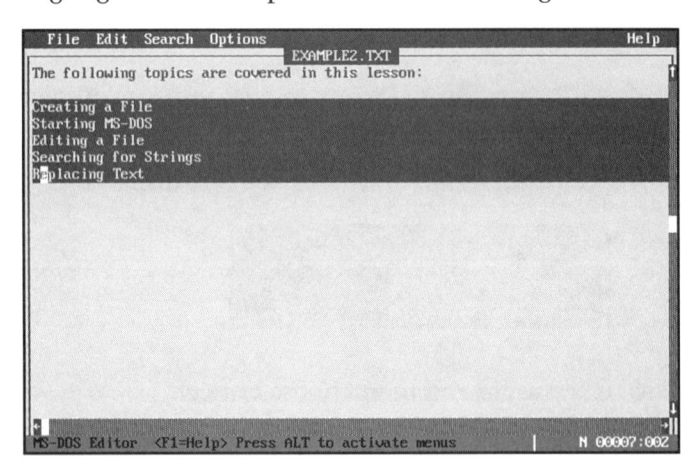

```
 File  Edit  Search  Options                                    Help
┌────────────────────────── EXAMPLE2.TXT ──────────────────────────┐
The following topics are covered in this lesson:

Creating a File
Starting MS-DOS
Editing a File
Searching for Strings
Replacing Text




MS-DOS Editor   <F1=Help> Press ALT to activate menus    N 00007:002
```

2 Pull down the File menu and choose **Print**. This dialog box displays:

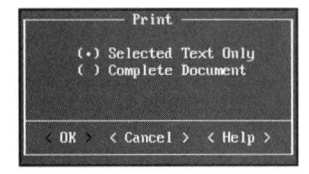

```
┌──────── Print ────────┐
│ (•) Selected Text Only │
│ ( ) Complete Document  │
│                        │
│ < OK >  < Cancel >  < Help > │
└────────────────────────┘
```

282 *DOS 6 SureSteps*

3 Choose OK.

4 Pull down the File menu and choose Print again.

5 Select Complete Document and choose OK.

Exiting the MS-DOS Editor

To exit the MS-DOS Editor, pull down the File menu and choose Exit. If you are working on a file that has not been saved since the last keyboard entry, DOS displays this message:

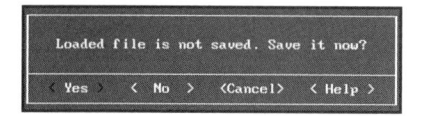

```
Loaded file is not saved. Save it now?
  < Yes >   < No >   <Cancel>   < Help >
```

If you choose Yes, the file is saved and you are returned to the DOS prompt. If you choose No, you return to the DOS prompt without saving the file.

▶ Your Turn

Exit the MS-DOS Editor by pulling down the File menu and then choosing Exit.

Lesson Summary

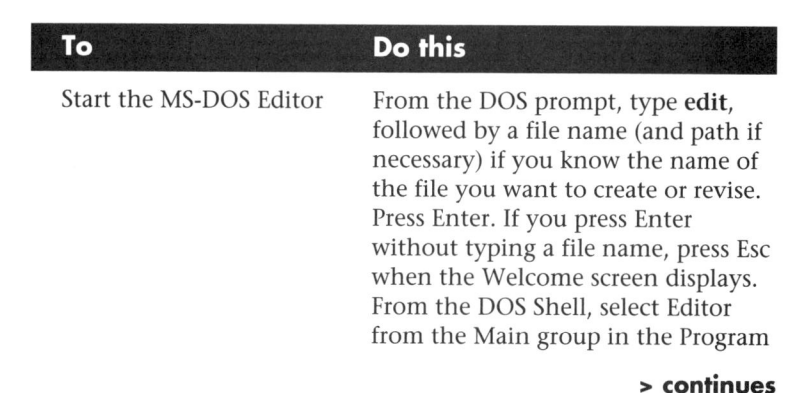

To	Do this
Start the MS-DOS Editor	From the DOS prompt, type **edit**, followed by a file name (and path if necessary) if you know the name of the file you want to create or revise. Press Enter. If you press Enter without typing a file name, press Esc when the Welcome screen displays. From the DOS Shell, select Editor from the Main group in the Program

> continues

> continued

To	Do this
	List box. Type the name of the file you want to create or revise and choose OK. If you do not type a file name, press Esc when the Welcome screen is displayed.
To indent	Press Tab.
Toggle between Insert and Overstrike mode	Press Ins.
Select Text	Hold down the Shift key while you move the cursor through the desired text or use the mouse to drag the cursor across the text.
Delete Text	Press Backspace to delete the character to the left. Press Del to delete the character at the cursor position. Select the text and press Del.
Copy text	Select the text. Press Ctrl+Ins. Move the cursor to the new location and press Shift+Ins.
Move text	Select the text. Press Shift+Del. Move the cursor to the new location and press Shift+Ins.
Find Text	Pull down the Search menu and choose Find. Type the desired text, select other options as desired, and choose OK.
Change Text	Pull down the Search menu and choose Change. Type the text to find. Move to the Change To box and type the new text. Make other selections as desired and choose OK.
Set a bookmark	Position the cursor and press Ctrl+K followed by a number from zero to three.
To go to a bookmark	Press Ctrl+Q followed by the number of the desired bookmark.

To	Do this
Save a New File	Pull down the File menu and choose **Save** or **Save As**. Type the name of the file and choose OK.
Print a file	Pull down the File menu and choose **Print**. Choose Complete Document and OK.
Print a portion of a file	Select the text. Pull down the File menu and choose **Print**. Choose Selected Text Only (if it is not already selected) and choose OK.
Exit the MS-DOS Editor	Pull down the File menu and choose **Exit**.

If You Want to Stop Now

If you want to stop now, exit all programs that are running and turn off your system.

From Here

The last lesson in this book deals with linking two PCs for the purpose of transferring files. Even if you do not intend to link PCs, it might be interesting for you to look at the lesson summary to get a quick idea about the procedure. Then you might want to look at Appendix B to review several commands that are available in DOS.

SURESTEPS LESSON 13

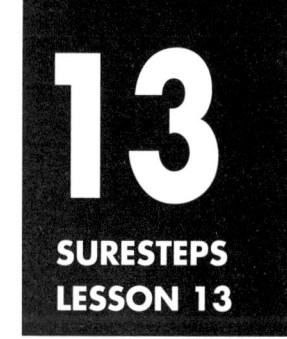

Connecting Two PCs with InterInk

In this lesson, you learn how to do the following:

- Connect two computers
- Copy files from one PC to another
- Disconnect the PCs

Lesson time:
15 minutes

The popularity of laptop computers has increased the need for connecting two computers so that files can be copied from one PC to the other. You can purchase several different programs that allow you to connect two PCs, and most of them come with a parallel cable and a serial cable. DOS 6 also includes a utility, called InterInk, that allows you to connect two PCs, but you have to supply your own cable.

The InterInk program not only allows you to copy files from one PC to another, it also allows you to operate one PC by using the other. This means that all the keystrokes can be performed at one computer.

Understanding the Relationship of the Two PCs

■ **Note:** Any two PCs can be connected. A laptop does not have to be involved.

When a connection is made between two computers, one is called the client and the other is called the server. The *client* PC controls the server PC and is used for all the keyboard input. The *server* is only used to break the connection.

The disk drives and printer ports of the server become extensions of the client. In other words, if the client PC has two disk drives and the server has three disk drives, InterInk sees the client PC as having five disk drives.

The drive letters are assigned to the client on the basis of the last used hard drive. If the client has one hard drive (drive C), for example, the three server drives become D, E, and F.

Preparing to Use InterInk

Before you decide to use InterInk, you must ensure that all requirements for both PCs are satisfied. To use InterInk successfully, the following conditions must be met:

- One computer must use DOS 6. The other can use any version between 3.0 and 6.0.
- Both computers must have the file INTERLNK.EXE.
- The client PC must have at least 16K of available memory.
- The server must have at least 130K of available memory.

■ **Note:** You can specify the port that InterInk uses for data transfer. If you do not specify a port, the client PC uses the first port (either parallel or serial, whichever you are using) that it finds on the server.

- The client PC must have a device driver statement in the CONFIG.SYS file like the following:

    device=[path]interlnk.exe.

▶ On Your Own

Use the VER and MEM commands to check the DOS versions and memory of both the client and server. Use the MS-DOS

Editor to add the needed device driver statement to the CONFIG.SYS file.

Making and Breaking the Connection

To connect two PCs, first attach the cable to both PCs and then follow these steps:

1 On the server, type **intersvr** and press Enter.

2 On the client, type **interlnk** and press Enter.

After the two PCs are connected, the client can issue DOS commands or use programs on the server—provided the client has the proper configuration for the programs. A few DOS commands cannot be used when Interlnk is in use. These include CHKDSK, DEFRAG, DISKCOMP, DISKCOPY, FDISK, FORMAT, MIRROR, SYS, UNDELETE, and UNFORMAT.

To break the connection between the two PCs, press Alt+F4 on the server keyboard. This is the only time the server keyboard is used after the server is started.

■ **Note:** Rather than complete step 2, you can start the client by rebooting or by changing to a disk drive for the server. Following this example, you could type **d:** and press Enter.

▶ Your Turn

If you have two computers that meet the Interlnk requirements and a parallel-to-parallel or serial-to-serial cable, connect the two PCs and follow these steps:

1 On the server, type **intersvr** and press Enter. The screen displays this table:

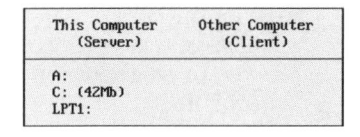

```
This Computer     Other Computer
  (Server)           (Client)

A:
C: (42Mb)
LPT1:
```

2 On the client, type **interlnk** and press Enter. The client screen displays a table like this:

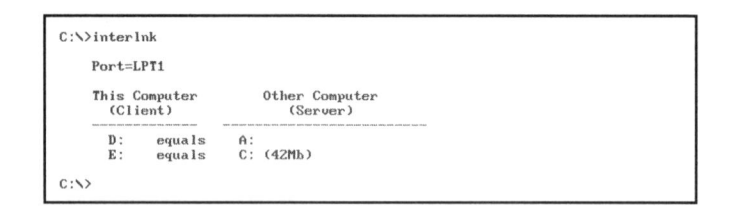

```
C:\>interlnk

    Port=LPT1

    This Computer        Other Computer
       (Client)             (Server)

       D:    equals    A:
       E:    equals    C: (42Mb)

C:\>
```

and the server screen changes to this:

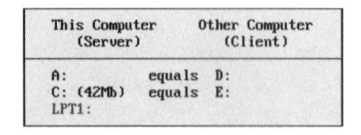

```
This Computer        Other Computer
   (Server)             (Client)

A:              equals   D:
C: (42Mb)       equals   E:
LPT1:
```

3 Copy a file from the client PC to the server. For example, if the client PC has drive A and C and the server has two drives A and C (drives D and E in Interlnk), use the COPY command like this:

copy a:readme.doc e:

4 Change to the hard drive of the server. For example, type **e:** and press Enter.

5 Start a program on the server (from the client PC).

6 Exit the program.

7 On the server, press Alt+F4, to break the connection.

Lesson Summary

To	Do this
Start Interlnk on the server	Type **intersvr** and press Enter.
Start Interlnk on the client	Do one of the following: reboot the client, change to a disk drive that belongs to the server, or type **interlnk** and press Enter.
Break the connection	Press Alt+F4 on the server.

A
SURESTEPS APPENDIX A

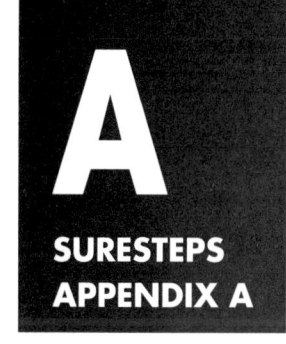

Getting Ready to Use *DOS 6 SureSteps*

Two versions of the DOS 6 program can be purchased. One is for installation on new computers and one is for upgrading computers. Unless you are in the business of building new computers, you will most likely be using the DOS 6 Upgrade program to replace an older version of DOS. (If you purchase a new computer, it will probably have DOS already loaded.)

Preparing to Install DOS 6

Before you install the DOS 6 upgrade, you should make a backup of your hard disk so that you can restore it if anything goes wrong during the upgrade process. To back up your hard disk, format as many disks as you will need and then, at the C prompt, type one of these commands (depending on which disk drive you will be using for backup):

> backup c:*.* a:/s

or

> backup c:*.* b:/s

■ **Note:** See the documentation for your old DOS version for details about using BACKUP and the number of disks you will need.

This command backs up drive C including all the directories. If you have more than one hard drive, you should perform a backup on each drive.

After backing up the hard disk, format one more disk to be used as the Uninstall disk in drive A. (If you are using 360K disks, format two disks.) During the installation of the DOS 6 upgrade, your old version of DOS will be stored on the Uninstall disk. If you have any problems with DOS 6 during or after the installation, you can use the Uninstall disk to restore your former version of DOS.

■ **Note:** If you do not feel that you are sufficiently trained to back up the hard disk before upgrading, you can rely on the fact that the DOS 6 Upgrade installation procedure does take steps to restore your old version of DOS should anything go wrong during the upgrade. Although relying on this process is not as good as backing up the hard drive, you can count on the restoration of the system with a high degree of confidence.

Next, you should disable any automatic messages that pop up on-screen, such as printing notification messages or appointment reminders. You will have to disable the messages in the programs that generate the messages.

Finally, Microsoft recommends that you disable any memory-resident programs. These programs can be disabled in the files called AUTOEXEC.BAT or CONFIG.SYS.

■ **Tip:** If you don't know how to edit these two files or don't understand them, see Lesson 7, "Commands and Files That Deal with the System."

To view and revise the content of these files, use the MS-DOS Editor or a word processing program. If you think you have found a memory-resident program, you should type **rem** at the beginning of the line that has the instruction to load the program. After changing and saving each file, restart your PC by pressing Ctrl+Alt+Del.

If you look at the AUTOEXEC.BAT and CONFIG.SYS files and feel uncertain about any of the commands, do not change them. If a memory-resident program interferes with the DOS installation, DOS tells you during the process. DOS 6 actually can be installed even when some memory-resident programs are not disabled.

Installing the Upgrade

To install the upgrade, follow these steps:

1 Return to the C prompt if the DOS Shell or Windows is running.

2 Insert the Setup Disk 1 in drive A or B.

3 Type **a:setup** if you inserted the disk in drive A or **b:setup** if you inserted the disk in drive B.

4 Press Enter. DOS displays a Welcome screen.

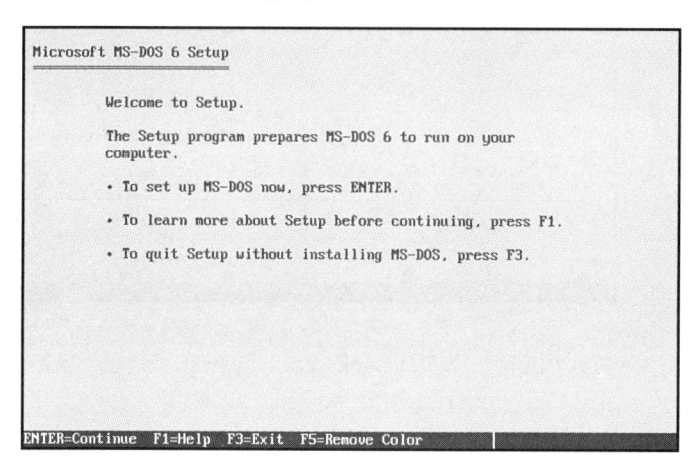

```
Microsoft MS-DOS 6 Setup

        Welcome to Setup.

        The Setup program prepares MS-DOS 6 to run on your
        computer.

         • To set up MS-DOS now, press ENTER.

         • To learn more about Setup before continuing, press F1.

         • To quit Setup without installing MS-DOS, press F3.










ENTER=Continue   F1=Help   F3=Exit   F5=Remove Color
```

5 Press F1 if you want to see more information about the installation process. Press Esc after you read the information.

Appendix A: Getting Ready to Use DOS 6 SureSteps   **293**

If you have problems... If Setup stops and displays a message that a program is running that is incompatible with DOS Setup, you need to disable this program and then run Setup again. Setup will display the name of the program. If you do not know how to disable the program, see Lesson 7 or call the technical support group for MS-DOS or the store where you purchased your computer.

6 Press Enter when you are ready to start the installation process.

DOS displays a screen that instructs you to label a disk as Uninstall #1. (If you are using 360K disks, you will need a second disk, labeled Uninstall #2.)

```
Microsoft MS-DOS 6 Setup

        During Setup, you will need to provide and label one
        or two floppy disks. Each disk can be unformatted
        or newly formatted and must work in drive A. (If you
        use 360K disks, you may need two disks; otherwise,
        you need only one disk.)

        Label the disk(s) as follows:

            UNINSTALL #1
            UNINSTALL #2 (if needed)

        Setup saves some of your original DOS files on the
        UNINSTALL disk(s), and others on your hard disk in a
        directory named OLD_DOS.x. With these files, you can
        restore your original DOS if necessary.

          • When you finish labeling your UNINSTALL disk(s),
            press ENTER to continue Setup.

ENTER=Continue   F1=Help   F3=Exit
```

■ **Note:** If DOS detects Windows on your system, it displays the same list of utility programs, but installs the programs in Windows only. You can install both the Windows version and the DOS version by moving the cursor to the desired utility and pressing Enter. Then highlight Windows and MS-DOS and press Enter. DOS may ask you to confirm the path that it finds for Windows. If the path it displays is correct, press Enter. If the path is not correct, type the correct path and press Enter.

7 Press Enter. DOS checks your system to see what type of DOS is currently installed and what type of monitor you are using. It reports its findings on-screen.

8 Press Enter. DOS displays a list of three utility programs that you can install. If you do not want to install a program, move the cursor to the program that you do not want to install and press Enter. Then move the cursor to None and press Enter.

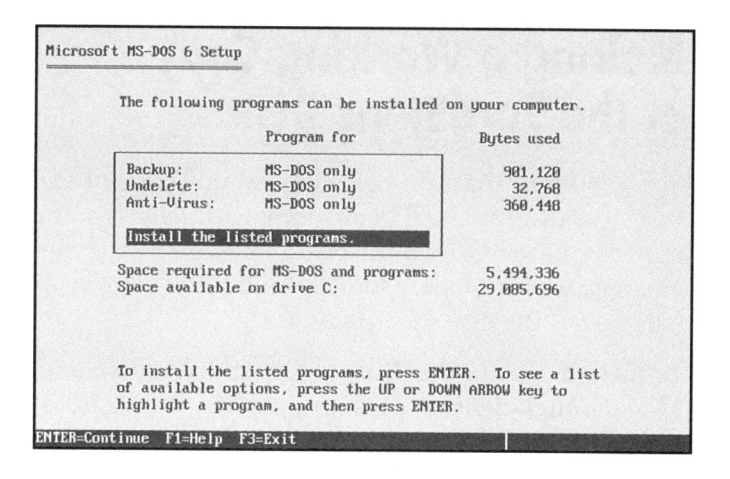

```
Microsoft MS-DOS 6 Setup

         The following programs can be installed on your computer.
                     Program for              Bytes used
         Backup:       MS-DOS only              901,120
         Undelete:     MS-DOS only               32,768
         Anti-Virus:   MS-DOS only              360,448
         Install the listed programs.

         Space required for MS-DOS and programs:  5,494,336
         Space available on drive C:             29,085,696


         To install the listed programs, press ENTER.  To see a list
         of available options, press the UP or DOWN ARROW key to
         highlight a program, and then press ENTER.

ENTER=Continue   F1=Help   F3=Exit
```

9 Press Enter to install the programs. DOS installs the Windows utilities and then asks whether you are ready to install the DOS upgrade.

10 Type y for Yes. DOS displays a bar at the bottom of the screen that shows the progress of the installation.

11 After about 2 percent of the installation is complete, DOS asks you to insert the Uninstall disk (if you are using a 360K disk, DOS also will ask you to insert a second disk).

12 After copying files to this disk, DOS asks for Setup Disk #1 again.

13 When finished with the first Setup disk, DOS prompts you to insert the next disk and continues prompting until all the necessary disks have been used.

When the installation process is complete, DOS tells you that your original AUTOEXEC.BAT and CONFIG.SYS files have been copied to the Uninstall disk and named AUTOEXEC.DAT and CONFIG.DAT.

14 When DOS tells you to restart your PC, remove all floppy disks and press Enter.

DOS 6 should now be installed on your system and ready for you to use.

Appendix A: Getting Ready to Use DOS 6 SureSteps   **295**

Making a Working Copy of the SureSteps Disk

It is important that you make at least one copy of the SureSteps disk; you will be working with its files and need to protect yourself against the possibility of deleting files. Also, you may want to repeat some lessons and will need an original copy of the disk each time.

To make a copy of the disk, you must first obtain another 3 1/2-inch high-density, 720K floppy disk. (If you have requested a 5 1/4-inch disk, make sure that you copy to a disk of the same size.) The disk doesn't have to be formatted. If it is formatted, it should be blank or contain data that you don't mind losing. Copying the SureSteps disk to another disk will destroy all data on the second disk.

If you have a computer with one floppy disk drive that is the size of the SureSteps disk, follow these steps to copy the disk:

■ **Note:** To follow these steps, you must be at the DOS prompt. If you reboot your computer and a screen titled DOS Shell is displayed, press Alt+F4 to return to the DOS prompt.

1 Insert the SureSteps disk in the floppy drive.

2 Type **diskcopy a: a:** (or **diskcopy b: b:**) and then press Enter.

> **If you have problems...** If you get the message Bad command or file name, type this command and then press Enter:
>
> **\dos\diskcopy a: a:**
>
> or
>
> **\dos\diskcopy b: b:**
>
> If you get the same error message, seek assistance from a more experienced user.

3 Watch the messages on-screen and follow the prompts. The SureSteps disk is the *source* disk, and the second disk is the *target*.

4 When you get the message Copy another diskette (Y/N) and you want to make only one copy, type **n**. If you want to make several copies, type **y** and follow the prompts.

If you have two identical floppy disk drives, follow these steps:

1 Insert the SureSteps disk in the top or left floppy drive.

2 Insert the second disk in the bottom or right floppy drive.

3 Type **diskcopy a: b:** and then press Enter.

> **If you have problems...** If you get the message Bad command or file name, type this command and then press Enter:
>
> **\dos\diskcopy a: b:**
>
> If you get the same error message, seek assistance from a more experienced user.

4 Watch the messages on-screen and follow the prompts. The SureSteps disk is the *source* disk and the second disk is the *target* disk.

5 When you get the message Copy another diskette (Y/N)? and you want to make only one copy, type **n**. If you want to make several copies, type **y** and follow the prompts.

Appendix A: Getting Ready to Use DOS 6 SureSteps

SURESTEPS APPENDIX B

Commands Used at the DOS Prompt and in Batch Files

This appendix lists the most commonly used DOS commands that can be typed at the DOS prompt and the commands and device drivers used in the CONFIG.SYS file. All the commands covered in this book are listed in this appendix with some of the most commonly used parameters. For a reference that lists all DOS 6 commands and their usage, see *Que's MS-DOS 6 Quick Reference*. For a more in-depth discussion of DOS 6, see *Using MS-DOS 6*, Special Edition.

CALL

Syntax: **CALL** *d:path***filename** *parameters*

Allows the execution of a batch file within a batch file. After the called batch is executed, the original batch file continues.

CD (CHDIR)

Syntax: **CD** *d:path*

Changes the current directory to a specified directory or displays the name of the current directory.

[handwritten note: Back to the Root Dir ⇒ CD_ D:\ ENTER]

CHKDSK

Syntax: **CHKDSK** *d:path\\filename* */F/V*

Displays a status report of the disk and fixes disk errors. The /F parameter fixes errors on the disk. The /V parameter displays the names of files in each directory as the disk is checked. CHKDSK /F should not be used when Windows and most other programs are running.

CHOICE

Syntax: **CHOICE** */c:keys text*

Prompts the user to make a choice between Y for Yes and N for No. Used only in batch files. The */c:keys* parameter enables you to specify other keys in addition to or in place of Y or N. The text parameter specifies the text that is displayed before the prompt.

CLS

Syntax: **CLS**

Clears the screen and lists the DOS prompt at the top.

COPY

Syntax: **COPY source** *destination*

Copies one or more files to the specified location (optionally with the specified name).

DATE

Syntax: **DATE** *mm-dd-yy*

Displays the date and prompts you for a new date.

DBLSPACE

Syntax: **DBLSPACE** */CHKDSK*
DBLSPACE */COMPRESS*
DBLSPACE */CREATE*
DBLSPACE */DEFRAGMENT*
DBLSPACE */LIST*
DBLSPACE */MOUNT*

Compresses a hard or floppy disk. The parameters used with DBLSPACE perform these commands:

CHKDSK checks the disk.
COMPRESS compresses a hard or floppy disk.
CREATE creates a new compressed drive.
DEFRAGMENT defragments a drive.
LIST lists all the drives on the computer.
MOUNT mounts a compressed volume file (CVF).

DBLSPACE should not be used when Windows is running.

DEFRAG

Syntax: **DEFRAG** *d:*

Moves files to different locations to maximize disk space. Should not be used when Windows is running.

DEL (ERASE)

Syntax: **DEL** *d:path***filename**

Deletes one or more specified files.

DELTREE

Syntax: **DELTREE** *d:***path**

Deletes a directory and all its files and subdirectories.

DIR

Syntax: **DIR** *d:path\filename /P/W*

Displays a list of files and subdirectories in the specified drive and/or directory. The /P parameter pauses the display. The /W parameter shows the display in a wide version.

DISKCOMP

Syntax: **DISKCOMP** *d1: d2:*

Compares the contents of two floppy disks.

DISKCOPY

Syntax: **DISKCOPY** *d1: d2:*

Makes an exact copy of one floppy disk on another floppy disk of the same size.

DOSSHELL

Syntax: **DOSSHELL** */T/G/B*

Starts the DOS Shell. The /T parameter starts the DOS Shell in text mode. The /G parameter starts the DOS Shell in graphics mode. The /B parameter is used to display the DOS Shell on a monochrome monitor.

ECHO

Syntax: **ECHO** ON OFF

In batch files, displays or hides the text on a command line.

EDIT

Syntax: **EDIT** *d:path\filename*

Starts the MS-DOS Editor.

EXPAND

Syntax: **EXPAND** *d:path***filename destination**

Decompresses a compressed file.

FASTHELP

Syntax: **FASTHELP** *command*

Displays a list of all MS-DOS commands with a brief explanation of each.

FOR

Syntax: **FOR %%***variable* **IN** (*set*) **DO** *command*

Executes a specified command for each file listed in a set of files.

FASTOPEN

Syntax: **FASTOPEN d:**=*n*

Starts FASTOPEN, which creates a name cache in memory of frequently opened files, thus improving performance time. The =*n* parameter specifies the number of files that can be open. Should not be used when Windows is running.

FORMAT

Syntax: **FORMAT d:** */V/S/Q/U*

Formats a disk. The /V parameter prompts you for a name; /S transfers the system files and COMMAND.COM to the formatted disk; /Q performs a quick format; and /U performs a format that cannot be unformatted.

GOTO

Syntax: **GOTO label**

In batch files, directs DOS to a command line that begins with the specified label.

HELP

Syntax: **HELP** *command*

Starts MS-DOS Help.

Appendix B: Commands Used at the DOS Prompt and in Batch Files

IF

    Syntax: **IF** *not* **errorlevel number command**

               IF *not* **string1==string2 command**

               IF *not* **exist filename command**

In batch files, lists a condition and an action to perform if the condition is true.

INTERLNK

    Syntax: **INTERLNK** *client:=server:*

Starts the Interlnk program on the client machine, which connects two computers for the purpose of sharing disk drives and printer ports.

INTERSVR

    Syntax: **INTERSVR** *d:/RCOPY*

Starts the Interlnk server. The /RCOPY parameter copies the Interlnk files from one computer to another.

LOADHIGH (LH)

    Syntax: **LOADHIGH** *d:path***filename**

Loads and runs a program into upper memory.

MD (MKDIR)

    Syntax: **MD** *d:***path**

Makes a directory.

MEM

    Syntax: **MEM** /C

Displays the amount of used and available memory on your computer. The /C parameter lists the programs that are currently loaded in memory and shows how much memory is being used.

MEMMAKER

Syntax: **MEMMAKER** */UNDO*

Optimizes computer memory by configuring device drivers and memory-resident programs to run in upper memory. The /UNDO parameter reverses the last changes made by MEMMAKER.

MORE

Syntax: **MORE**

Pauses a screen display when the screen is full and displays the message - -More- - at the bottom.

MOVE

Syntax: **MOVE** *d:path***filename destination**

Copies one or more files to a specified location and deletes them from the original location.

MSAV

Syntax: **MSAV** *d:/C*

Scans the computer for known viruses. The /C parameter causes MSAV to clean a virus off the disk if one is found.

MSBACKUP

Syntax: **MSBACKUP**

Backs up or restores one or more files from one disk to another.

PATH

Syntax: **PATH** *d:path;d:path;...*

Indicates the directories DOS should search and the order in which DOS should search them when a command (executable program) is issued.

PAUSE

Syntax: **PAUSE**

In a batch file, pauses the processing of commands and displays a message to press any key to continue.

POWER

Syntax: **POWER** *OFF*

For a laptop, activates or deactivates power management and sets the level of conservation. Also used to report the status of power management.

PROMPT

Syntax: **PROMPT** *text*

Customizes the appearance of the DOS prompt.

RD (RMDIR)

Syntax: **RD** *d:***path**

Removes a directory.

REM

Syntax: **REM** *string*

In batch files, prevents a line from executing. Used to make comments (remarks).

REN (RENAME)

Syntax: **REN** *d:path***filename1 filename2**

Changes the name of a specified file or files.

REPLACE

Syntax: **REPLACE** *d1:path1***filename** *d2:path2*

Replaces files in a destination directory with files of the same name from a source directory.

RESTORE

Syntax: **RESTORE d1: d2:***path\filename*

Restores files that were backed up with the Backup command from earlier versions of DOS.

SMARTDRV

Syntax: **SMARTDRV**

Creates a disk cache in extended memory. Can be used at the DOS prompt or in AUTOEXEC.BAT. Should not be used when Windows is running.

SYS

Syntax: **SYS** *d1:path* **d2:**

Copies the hidden DOS system files and COMMAND.COM to a disk. The parameters d1:path specify the location of the system files if they are not located on the current drive.

TIME

Syntax: **TIME** *hours:minutes:seconds.hundredths A P*

Displays the system time and prompts you for a new time. The A parameter refers to a.m., and the P refers to p.m.

TREE

Syntax: **TREE** *d:path* /F

Displays the structure of a directory. The /F parameter lists the files in each directory.

TYPE

Syntax: **TYPE** *d:path***filename**

Displays the contents of a text file.

UNDELETE

Syntax: **UNDELETE** *d:path\filename*

Restores files that were previously deleted with the Del command.

UNFORMAT

Syntax: **UNFORMAT d:** */L/TEST*

Restores the data to a disk that has been formatted. The /L parameter lists every file and directory found by UNFORMAT. The /TEST parameter shows how UNFORMAT would re-create the information on the disk.

VSAFE

Syntax: **VSAFE**

Constantly monitors the computer for viruses and displays a warning if a virus is found. Should not be used when Windows is running.

XCOPY

Syntax: **XCOPY source** *destination /S/E*

Copies directories, their subdirectories, and files (except hidden and system files). The /S parameter copies directories and subdirectories unless they are empty. The /E parameter causes even empty directories and subdirectories to be copied.

Commands and Device Drivers Used Only in CONFIG.SYS

ANSI.SYS

A device driver used to set screen colors, employ graphics, and change the assignment of keys on the keyboard.

BREAK

Sets or clears checking for Ctrl+Break (Ctrl+C) during disk-access routines.

BUFFERS

Allocates memory for a specified number of disk buffers.

COUNTRY

Specifies country-specific conventions for dates, times, and currency, sort routines, and the characters that can be used in file names.

DBLSPACE.SYS

A device driver that moves DBLSPACE.BIN to its final location in memory. (DBLSPACE.BIN is created by the Dblspace command when a drive is compressed. This file must be loaded into memory when the PC is booted.)

DEVICE

Loads the specified device driver into memory.

DEVICEHIGH

Loads the specified device driver into upper memory.

DISPLAY.SYS

A device driver that displays international character sets on EGA, VGA, and LCD monitors.

DOS

Maintains a link to the upper memory area. Can load part of DOS into the high memory area (HMA).

DRIVER.SYS

A device driver that creates a logical drive used to refer to a physical floppy disk drive.

DRIVPARM

Defines parameters for devices such as disk and tape drives when you start MS-DOS.

EGA.SYS

A device driver that saves and restores the display when the DOS Shell Task Swapper is used with EGA monitors.

EMM386.EXE

A device driver that provides access to the upper memory area and uses extended memory to simulate expanded memory. Not for use on a PC with a processor less than an 80386.

FCBS

Specifies the number of file control blocks (FCBS).

FILES

Specifies the number of files that can be open at one time.

HIMEM.SYS

A device driver that manages extended memory.

INCLUDE

Includes one configuration block within another.

INSTALL

Loads a memory-resident program into memory.

INTERLNK.EXE

A device driver that redirects commands on the client PC to drives and printer ports on the server PC.

LASTDRIVE

Specifies the maximum number of drives you can access. You can use this command only in your CONFIG.SYS file.

MENUCOLOR

Specifies the text and background colors for the startup menu.

MENUDEFAULT

Specifies the item on the startup menu that is the default and (optionally) the number of seconds in which the default will be selected automatically if the user makes no choice.

MENUITEM

Defines an item on the startup menu.

NUMLOCK

Activates or deactivates Numlock when the PC is booted. Can be used only in a menu block.

POWER.EXE

A device driver that reduces power consumption on a laptop when applications and devices are idle.

RAMDRIVE.SYS

A device driver that uses part of the RAM to simulate a hard disk drive.

SETVER.EXE

A device driver that loads the DOS Version table into memory. Other device drivers that were designed to use earlier versions of DOS use this table to get the version of DOS.

Appendix B: Commands Used at the DOS Prompt and in Batch Files

SHELL

Specifies the name and location of the command interpreter you want DOS to use.

SMARTDRV.EXE

A device driver that provides compatibility for hard-disk controllers that cannot work with EMM386 and Microsoft Windows running in enhanced mode.

STACKS

Specifies the number and size of stacks used for hardware interrupts.

SUBMENU

Defines a submenu item on a startup menu.

SWITCHES

Specifies special options in MS-DOS.

SURESTEPS GLOSSARY

Glossary

allocation unit A cluster of sectors.

application A computer program such as dBASE, WordPerfect, Lotus 1-2-3, and so on.

AUTOEXEC.BAT A batch file that DOS executes automatically after it loads the system files and CONFIG.SYS.

batch file A file with an extension of BAT that contains several DOS commands. It is executed by typing the name of the file at the DOS prompt.

bit map A format for storing images. A bit-mapped image is stored as a pattern of pels, another term for pixels (or dots).

boot sector virus A virus that attaches itself to the boot sector. See *virus*.

branch A part of a directory tree that consists of the directory plus all subdirectories and files within the directory. See *collapse, directory tree, expand*.

buffer An area in memory used by DOS to store disk data for faster access.

cache See *disk cache*.

check box In a dialog box, a small square box that represents an option. An *X* in the box indicates a selected option; a blank box indicates that the option is not selected. To select the check box, click the box.

click Pressing and releasing the mouse button quickly. Clicking usually selects a menu, command, option, or object.

client When using Interlnk, the PC that is attached to the server and performs all the keyboard activity.

clipboard In the DOS Shell, a holding area in memory that stores text that has been cut or copied.

collapse In the DOS Shell, to hide subdirectories below a selected directory.

COM port The serial port of your computer, usually COM1 and COM2. See *parallel port* and *serial port*.

command A word or phrase that carries out an action.

command prompt In DOS, the system prompt (C:\>).

COMMAND.COM The command interpreter file for DOS.

compressed drive A drive that has been compressed by a program such as DoubleSpace.

CONFIG.SYS A file that is automatically loaded by DOS when the computer is booted. The file contains statements that configure the PC.

configuration block A block of commands in the CONFIG.SYS file that are executed if the menu item that represents them is selected from the startup menu.

conventional memory The memory in a computer from 0 to 640K.

current directory The directory in which you are working or the directory selected in the DOS Shell.

current drive The drive on which you are working or the drive that is selected in the DOS Shell.

cursor A blinking line in a document or text box that indicates where the next typed character will appear. Also, refers to the mouse pointer when it is used in any text area.

CVF The Compressed Volume File that contains all the information about files on a compressed drive.

default A setting that an application uses unless you specify another setting—such as a default typeface, page margin, column width, and so on. You can change the defaults of most programs.

defragment To reorganize files on a disk so that space is optimized.

destination The target of a command. When copying a file, for example, the file is copied from the source to the destination.

device driver A program that must be loaded into memory to operate a hardware or software device.

dialog box A window that requests the user to provide information. You must select an option in the dialog box before you can continue working in the application.

dimmed In the DOS Shell, a dimmed option that indicates that the option is currently unavailable.

directory A part of an organizational structure for managing files, applications, and so on.

directory tree In the DOS Shell, a way of viewing the directory structure.

disk A medium for storing information. See *floppy disk* and *hard disk*.

disk cache A large disk buffer used to speed access time.

disk partition A division of a disk that can hold an operating system. DOS allows four partitions, but only one is needed if you are not using another operating system in addition to DOS.

double-click To press and release the mouse button twice in rapid succession without moving the mouse.

drag The action of positioning the mouse pointer, holding down the mouse button, and then moving the mouse. Dragging can select text, move scroll boxes, and so on.

drive A device that holds a disk.

drive icon In the DOS Shell, an icon that represents a floppy drive, hard disk drive, CD-ROM drive, and so on.

expand In the DOS Shell, an option that shows hidden directories in a directory tree. See *collapse*. Also, a command used at the DOS prompt to expand a compressed file from the original DOS disk.

expanded memory Memory provided by an expansion board, in addition to conventional memory. Uses a complicated paging routine, defined by the Lotus/Intel/Microsoft Extended Memory Specification, to address memory.

extended memory Memory, provided in addition to the conventional memory, that requires a memory manager like HIMEM.SYS.

extension The three characters that follow a period in a file name.

file Data that is stored on a disk under a specific name.

file infector virus A virus that attacks files. See *virus*.

file name The name of a file. File names can use eight or less characters, followed by a period and three or less characters.

floppy disk A medium for storing files; a disk—either 3 1/2- or 5 1/4-inch—that is placed in a floppy drive. Also, a drive that holds a disk is called a floppy. See *disk* and *hard disk*.

format To prepare a disk to accept information.

fragmentation The random storage of files in different sectors on a disk, resulting in unused space being inaccessible. See *defragment*.

group A window in the Program List area of the DOS Shell.

hard disk A permanent medium in the computer for storing files and programs; accessed through C:\, D:\, or so on. See *disk* and *floppy disk*.

hidden file A file with the file attribute set to hidden and thus does not display in a list of files in a directory. Usually applied to program files such as IO.SYS and MSDOS.SYS.

high memory area The first 64K of memory in extended memory.

highlighted Text in a document, dialog box, or window that is selected. See *select*.

icon A small graphical image representing an application, document, or other object.

interrupt A call for immediate attention by a hardware device, stopping DOS from performing the current task.

list box In a dialog box window, a kind of box that lists choices—such as a file list or a directory list.

LPT port The parallel printer port. See *parallel port*.

memory-resident program A program that stays resident in memory and is available at all times.

menu A grouping of commands.

menu bar The horizontal bar, usually at the top of the screen, that contains menu commands.

mount A command that must be performed so that DOS recognizes a compressed floppy disk.

open In the MS-DOS Editor, to display the contents of a file in the typing area.

option A choice in a menu or a dialog box.

parallel port The receptacle on a computer into which you plug a parallel cable and, thus, a parallel printer. The parallel port names are LPT1, LPT2, and LPT3.

parameter A variation on a command. The /W parameter for the DIR command, for example, displays a wide version of the directory list.

partition See *disk partition*.

paste In the MS-DOS Editor, to place copied or cut material from the Clipboard at the location of the cursor. See *clipboard*.

path Maps the location of a file by listing the drive and directories. The path of the file APPEND.EXE may be C:\DOS, for example.

point To move the mouse pointer (arrow) to a position on-screen.

pointer The arrow that is moved by the mouse.

printer driver   A file of information about your printer—such as font description, printing interface, and printer features. The printer driver controls how your computer and the printer interact.

RAM drive   A logical drive created in memory that acts like a physical drive.

root directory   The top level of directories on a disk; always indicated by the backslash (\).

scroll   To move through parts of a document or list to view the material that is not displayed on-screen. See *scroll bar*.

scroll arrows   Arrows at either end of the scroll bar, which enable you to move in the direction of the arrow you click.

scroll bar   A bar appearing on the bottom or right of the window.

select   To mark an object—text, file name, menu option, and so on—for an action. Selected items are highlighted.

serial port   A computer receptacle in which you plug a cable for a serial device. Serial ports are named COM1, COM2, and so on.

stack   An area in memory used by DOS to store information about a current routine when the routine must stop because of a hardware interrupt.

subdirectory   A directory within a directory.

system time and date   The time and date according to your computer's internal clock.

Task List   In the DOS Shell, a window that shows all open programs and enables you to switch from program to program.

text box   In a dialog box, a box in which you type the needed information. A text box may be blank or may contain text when the dialog box opens.

Trojan horse virus   A virus that is hidden in another program.

UMB Upper Memory Blocks. Blocks of unused memory in the upper memory area that can be used by memory-resident programs.

upper memory The 384K of memory above 640K of memory.

virus A computer program that replicates itself and spreads to other disks. Viruses usually destroy files and can even erase an entire disk.

wild card A character used to represent one or more characters in a file name. The asterisk (*) represents more than one character; the question mark (?) represents one character.

Index

Symbols

* (asterisk) wild card character, 68
? (question mark) wild card character, 68
@ command, 168
@ECHO OFF command, 166

A

/A parameter. REPLACE command, 112
accessing
    Help, DOS Shell, 45-46
    menus, 37-38
Add mode (Shift+F8) keyboard combination, 98-99
allocation units, 313
Alt key, 17
ANSI.SYS command, 308
Anti-Virus, 203-207
    configuring, 206-208
    information about viruses, 208-209
    menu options
        Create Report, 207-208
        Detect and Clean, 204-208
        Options, 206-208
        Select New Drive, 204-205
    Windows version, 212-213

ASC (ASCII) file extension, 64
ASCII files, 161-162
AUTOEXEC.BAT file, 25-28, 160-161, 169-171, 313
    creating, 163-166
    optimizing order of programs, 254-256

B

backing up hard disk files, 184-187, 192-196
    comparing with originals, 187-189
    Microsoft Backup, Windows, 197-198
backup catalogs, 195-197
BACKUP command, 178-179, 184-186, 192-194
    Compare, 187-189
    Restore, 189-191
Backup Fixed Disk, 33
Backup menu options, 184-187
    Compare, 187-191
    Restore, 189-191
backup sets, restoring, 189-191
backup strategy, 192-193
backup-and-restore method, removing DoubleSpace program, 234-237
Bad command or file name error message, 205, 296-297

batch files, 160-161, 313
　commands, 168-171
　creating, 166-167
bit-mapped images, 313
blocks of text
　editing, 274-276
　selecting, 274-276
bookmarks, MS-DOS Editor, 280
boot sector computer viruses, 203, 313
bootable disks, 202-203
booting PCs, 11-12, 23-24
　cold, 24-26
　interrupting process, 27-28
　warm, 26-27
Bootstrap Loader, 24, 160
branches, directory tree, 313
BREAK command, 309
buffers, 313
BUFFERS command, 172, 309
bytes, 13

C

/C parameter, Mem command, 242-244
cache memory, 10, 313-315
CALL command, 168, 300
Caps Lock key, 16-19
catalogs
　backup, 195-197
　master, 197
ccMail, 22
CD command, 80, 300
Central Processing Unit (CPU), 10
Change Ratio option (DoubleSpace Drive menu), 226-227
Change Size option (DoubleSpace Drive menu), 225
changing directories, 79
　at DOS prompt, 80-81
　in DOS Shell, 79-80
CHDIR command, 300
check boxes, 313
CHKDSK command, 126-127, 164, 217, 233, 256-258, 300
　parameters, 127-129
Chkdsk option (DoubleSpace Tools menu), 233

CHKLIST.MS file, 206
CHOICE command, 168, 300
cleaning hard disks, 256-258
Clear option (MS-DOS Editor Edit menu), 274
clicking with mouse, 20-21, 313
client servers, 288, 314
clipboard, 314
clocks
　date, 153-154
　time, 154-155
CLS command, 300
codes
　backup catalog names, 196
　customizing DOS prompt, 158-159
cold booting, 24-26
collapsing directories, 314
COM port, 314
command prompt, 33, 314
Command Prompt Syntax Help, 44-45
COMMAND.COM file, 25, 160, 314
commands, 168, 303, 314
　@ECHO OFF, 166
　ANSI.SYS, 308
　BACKUP, 178-179, 184-186, 192-194
　　Compare, 187-189
　　Restore, 189-191
　batch file, 168-171
　BREAK, 309
　BUFFERS, 172, 309
　CALL, 168, 300
　CD (CHDIR) 80, 300
　CHKDSK, 126-127, 164, 217, 233, 256-258, 300
　　parameters, 127-129
　CHOICE, 168, 300
　CLS, 300
　COMPARE, 178
　COPY, 103, 107, 300
　COPY CON, 161-171
　COUNTRY, 309
　DATE, 153-154, 301
　DBLSPACE, 301
　DBLSPACE.SYS, 309
　DEFRAG, 129-131, 256, 301
　DEL, 301
　DELETE, 114-115

322   *DOS 6 SureSteps*

DELTREE, 88-89, 301
DEVICE, 172, 309
DEVICEHIGH, 309
DIR, 65-66, 302
    wild cards, 68-69
DISKCOMP, 134-135, 302
DISKCOPY, 131-134, 302
DISPLAY.SYS, 309
DOSSHELL, 302
DOUBLESPACE, 218-224
DRIVPARM, 310
ECHO, 168, 302
ECHO OFF, 166
EDIT, 302
ERASE, 68, 301
EXPAND, 302
FASTHELP, 303
FASTOPEN, 303
FCBS, 310
FILES, 172, 310
FOR, 168, 303
FORMAT, 136-139, 303
    parameters, 139-142
GOTO, 168, 303
HELP, 51, 303
HIMEM.SYS, 310
IF, 168, 304
INCLUDE, 310
INSTALL, 172, 310
INTERLNK, 304
INTERLNK.EXE, 310
INTERSVR, 304
LABEL, 145-146
LASTDRIVE, 311
LOADHIGH (LH), 304
MD (MKDIR), 83, 304
MEM, 242-244, 288, 304
MEMMAKER, 249, 305
MENU, 170
MENUCOLOR, 311
MENUDEFAULT, 311
MENUITEM, 311
MORE, 305
MOVE, 305
MSAV, 305
MSBACKUP, 305
NUMLOCK, 311
PATH, 155-157, 305
PAUSE, 164-165, 169, 306
POWER, 306
PROMPT, 158-159, 306
QUICK FORMAT, 136-139

QUIT, 178
RD (RMDIR), 86, 306
REM, 169, 173, 306
REN (RENAME), 306
REPLACE, 112-113, 306
RESTORE, 178, 307
SEARCH, 100
SHELL, 312
SMARTDRV, 307
STACKS, 172, 312
SUBMENU, 312
SWITCHES, 312
SYS, 307
TIME, 154-155, 307
TREE, 87-88, 307
TYPE, 307
UNDELETE, 116-119, 308
UNFORMAT, 136, 142-144, 308
    parameters, 144-145
VER, 152, 288
VOL, 145-146
VSAFE, 308
    options, 211-212
XCOPY, 108-110, 308
see also options
communications software, 22
COMPARE command, 178
Compare option (Backup menu), 187-188, 191
comparing
    floppy disks, 134-135
    hard disk files with originals, 187-189
compressed drives, 314
    defragmenting, 227-228
    deleting, 229-230
    formatting, 228-229
    maintaining, 223-224
    ratio, 226-227
    sizes, changing, 225-226
    troubleshooting, 233
compressed floppy disks, 232-233
    troubleshooting, 233
Compressed Volume File (CVF), 314
compressing
    floppy disks, 230-232
    hard disk drives, 216-223
        compression ratio, 226-227

Index

computer viruses, 319
  boot sector, 313
  detecting
    false alarms, 209-210
    with Anti-Virus, 203-207
    with Anti-Virus Windows
      version,
      212-213
    with VSafe, 211-212
  file infector, 203, 316
  information in Anti-Virus
    program, 208-209
  Michelangelo, 153
  preventing, 202-203
  Trojan horse, 203, 318
CONFIG.SYS file, 25-28, 160,
  169-173, 314
  Anti-Virus alarm, 209-210
  optimizing order of programs,
    254-256
  troubleshooting, 173-174
configuration blocks, 314
configuring
  Anti-Virus, 206-208
  hardware/memory,
    172-173
  Microsoft Basic, 179
Confirmation option (Options
  menu), 49
context-sensitive Help, 45
conventional memory,
  244-245, 314
COPY command, 103, 107, 300
COPY CON command,
  161-171
Copy option (File menu),
  102-103
Copy option (MS-DOS Editor
  Edit menu), 274
copying
  directories at DOS prompt,
    108-110
  disks, SureSteps, 296-297
  files, 102
    at DOS prompt, 107-110
    in DOS Shell, 102-105
    with mouse, 105-106
  floppy disks, 131-134
COUNTRY command, 309
CPU (Central Processing Unit),
  10

Create Directory option (File
  menu), 82
Create Report option (Anti-
  Virus menu), 207-208
creating
  directories, 81-82
    at DOS prompt, 83
    in DOS Shell, 82-83
  files, 161-162
    AUTOEXEC.BAT, 163-166
    batch, 166-167
cross references, DOS Prompt
  Help, 55-56
CrossTalk, 22
Ctrl key, 17
current directory, 79
cursor keys, 17-18
cursor movement keystrokes,
  MS-DOS Editor, 272
cursors, 314
  moving, MS-DOS Editor, 272
Custom Setup, installing
  DoubleSpace, 220-223
Cut option (MS-DOS Editor
  Edit menu), 275
CVF (Compressed Volume File),
  314

D

daisywheel printers, 21
database management
  applications, file extensions,
    22, 62-71
date and time, system, 318
  setting on internal clock,
    153-154
DATE command, 153-154, 301
date-stamping files, 153-154
DBLSPACE command, 301
DBLSPACE.SYS command, 309
defaults, 314
DEFRAG command, 129-131,
  256, 301
Defragment option
  (DoubleSpace Tools menu),
  227-228
defragmenting
  files, 315
  hard disks, 129-131
    compressed, 227-228

324   DOS 6 SureSteps

DEL command, 301
DELETE command, 114-115
Delete option (DoubleSpace Drive menu), 229-230
Delete option (File menu), 114-115
Delete Sentry program, 116-118
Delete Tracker program, 116-118
deleting
    files in DOS Shell, 114-115
    hard disk drives, compressed, 229-230
    see also removing
DELTREE command, 88-89, 301
Deselect All (Ctrl+\) key combination, 98
Detect and Clean option (Anti-Virus menu), 204-205, 208
detecting computer viruses
    false alarms, 209-210
    with Anti-Virus, 203-207
    with Anti-Virus Windows version, 212-213
    with VSafe, 211-212
DEVICE command, 172, 309
device drivers, 315
    loading, 248-249
    RAMDRIVE.SYS, 256, 259
    SMARTDRV.SYS, 256, 259
DEVICEHIGH command, 309
dialog boxes, 38-39, 315
    Help buttons, 49-50
differential backups, 192
dimmed options, 315
DIR command, 65-66, 302
    wild cards, 68-69
directories, 315
    changing, 79
        at DOS prompt, 80-81
        in DOS Shell, 79-80
        views, 94-96
    collapsing, 314
    copying at DOS prompt, 108-110
    creating, 81-82
        at DOS prompt, 83
        in DOS Shell, 82-83
    current, 33, 79, 314
    expanding, 315
        views, 94-96

files
    finding, 100-101
    moving from one to another, 110-111
paths, 317
removing, 84
    at DOS prompt, 85-86
    in DOS Shell, 84-86
    trees at DOS prompt, 88-89
restoring on disks, 142-145
root, 76-78, 318
    clearing for formatting, 136
viewing, 94
    trees at DOS prompt, 88
Directory Tree, 33-36, 77-78, 315
    branches, 313
    directories
        changing, 79-80
        creating, 82-83
        removing, 84-86
        viewing, 87, 94-96
disk caches, 313-315
Disk Copy, 33
disk drives, 11-16
disk labels, 145-146
Disk Utilities group, 33-34, 37, 116-119
DISKCOMP command, 134-135, 302
DISKCOPY command, 131-134, 302
disks
    bootable, 202-203
    compressed, 314
    copying, SureSteps, 296-297
    formatting, 316
    mounting, 317
    partitions, 315-317
    source, 297
    target, 297
    see also floppy disks; hard disks
Display option (MS-DOS Editor Options menu), 271
Display option (Options menu), 40
DISPLAY.SYS command, 309

Index **325**

DOS 6
    functions, 23-24
    installing, 292-293
        upgrades, 293-295
    system software, 22
DOS command, 309
DOS prompt, 42-45
    customizing, 158-159
    directories
        changing, 80-81
        copying, 108-110
        creating, 83
        removing, 85-86
        viewing tree, 87-88
    directory trees, removing, 88-89
    files
        AUTOEXEC.BAT, 160-161
        copying, 107-110
        creating, 161-166
        replacing, 112-113
        undeleting, 117
    Help, 50-52
        cross references, 55-56
        menus, 53-55
    versions of DOS, 152-153
DOS Shell, 32-34
    directories
        changing, 79-80
        creating, 82-83
        removing, 84-86
        viewing, 87
    disks
        copying, 132-134
        formatting, 137-140
    exiting, 32
    files
        copying, 102-105
        deleting, 114-115
        moving, 110-111
        renaming, 120-121
    Help, 45
    modes, text/graphics, 39-41
    navigating, 35-37
    starting, 32
    starting MS-DOS Editor, 264-266
    views, 41-42
DOSSHELL command, 302
dot-matrix printers, 21
double-clicking with mouse, 20-21, 315

DoubleSpace
    Compress menu options, Existing Drive, 231
    Drive menu options
        Change Ratio, 226-227
        Change Size, 225
        Delete, 229-230
        Format, 228
        Info, 224
        Mount, 232
    Tools menu options
        Chkdsk, 233
        Defragment, 227-228
DOUBLESPACE command, 218-224
DoubleSpace program, 216-217, 230-233
    installing, 217-223
    removing, 234-237
dragging with mouse, 20-21, 315
drive icons, 315
DRIVER.SYS command, 309
drivers
    device, 315
        loading, 248-249
        RAMDRIVE.SYS, 256, 259
        SMARTDRV.SYS, 256, 259
    optimizing order in CONFIG.SYS and AUTOEXEC.BAT files, 254-255
    printer, 317
drives, 315
    compressed
        compression ratio, 226-227
        defragmenting, 227-228
        deleting, 229-230
        formatting, 228-229
        information, 223-224
        maintaining, 223-224
        sizes, changing, 225-226
        troubleshooting, 233
    current, 33, 314
    RAM, 317
    removing DoubleSpace program, 234-237
    see also disk drives
DRIVPARM command, 310
Dual File List option (View menu), 41

326 *DOS 6 SureSteps*

E

E-mail software, 22
ECHO command, 168, 302
ECHO OFF command, 166
echoing to screens, 166
EDIT command, 302
editing in MS-DOS Editor, 33
   files , 264-267
   text, 271-276
EGA.SYS command, 310
ellipsis (...), 38
EMM386.EXE
   command, 310
   file, 249
EMS (expanded memory), 10,
   246-247, 316
End key, 18
enhanced keyboards, 18
Enter key, 17-19
ERASE command, 68, 301
error messages, Bad command or
   file name, 205, 296-297
Esc key, 18-19
Existing Drive option
   (DoubleSpace Compress menu),
   231
Exit option (DOS Prompt Help
   File menu), 53-55
Exit option (MS-DOS Editor File
   menu), 283
exiting
   DOS Shell, 32
   MS-DOS Editor, 283
Expand All option (Tree menu),
   95
Expand Branch option (Tree
   menu), 95
EXPAND command, 302
Expand One Level option (Tree
   menu), 95
expanded memory (EMS), 10,
   246-247, 316
expanded memory manager, LIM
   EMS (Lotus/Intel/Microsoft
   Expanded Memory
   Specifications), 247
expanding directories, 315
Express Setup, MemMaker
   program, 250-253
extended memory (XMS), 10,
   246-247

   programs to speed system,
      258-260
extended memory manager,
   HIMEM.SYS, 246-248
extensions, file name, 60-65

F

/F parameter, commands
   CHKDSK, 127-129,
      256-258
   TREE, 87-88
/F:size parameter, FORMAT
   command, 140
FASTHELP command, 303
FASTOPEN command, 303
FASTOPEN program, 256,
   259-260
FCBS command, 310
File Allocation Table (FAT),
   clearing for formatting, 136
File Display Options option
   (Options menu), 39, 96
file infector computer virus,
   203, 316
File List, 33-37
   files, selecting/deselecting,
      98-99
File menu options
   Copy, 102-103
   Create Directory, 82
   Delete, 114-115
   Deselect All, 98
   Move, 110-111
   Print, 255
   Rename, 120-121
   Run, 50
   Save Setup As, 193-195
   Search Entire Disk, 100-101
   Select All, 98
File menu (DOS Prompt Help)
  options
   Exit, 53-55
   Print, 53
file names, 60-61, 316
   extensions, 62-65, 316
   wild cards, 66-68
file specifications, 60-61
files, 33, 316
   AUTOEXEC.BAT, 25-28,
      160-161, 169-171, 313
      creating, 163-166

Index **327**

optimizing order of
   programs, 254-256
batch, 160-161, 166-167, 313
   commands, 168-171
CHKLIST.MS, 206
COMMAND.COM, 25, 160,
   314
CONFIG.SYS, 25-28, 160,
   169-173, 314
   Anti-Virus alarm, 209-210
   optimizing order of
      programs, 254-256
   troubleshooting, 173-174
copying, 102
   at DOS prompt, 107-110
   in DOS Shell, 102-105
   with mouse, 105-106
date-stamping, 153-154
defragmenting, 129-131, 315
deleting in DOS Shell,
   114-115
deleting from hard disks,
   256-258
editing in MS-DOS Editor,
   264-267
EMM386.EXE, 249
finding, 100-101
floppy disk, compressing,
   230-232
fragmented, 316
hard disk
   backing up, 184-187,
      192-196
   backing up with Microsoft
      Backup, Windows,
      197-198
   comparing backups with
      originals, 187-189
   compressing, 216-223
   restoring, 189-191
hidden, 316
IO.SYS, 24, 160
MEMMAKER.STS, 255
MENU.BAT, 169-171
moving in DOS Shell,
   110-111
MSAV.RPT, 208
MSDOS.SYS, 24, 160
opening, 317
order, 96-98
paths, 80, 155-157, 317

printing, MS-DOS Editor,
   281-283
renaming in DOS Shell,
   120-121
replacing at DOS prompt,
   112-113
restoring on disks, 142-145
saving, MS-DOS Editor,
   280-281
selecting, 98-100
setup, 193
time-stamping, 154-155
undeleting, 116-118,
   118-119
viewing list, 65-68, 94-96
FILES command, 172, 310
Find option (DOS Prompt Help
   Search menu), 54-55
Find option (MS-DOS Editor
   Search menu), 276-277
finding
   files, 100-101
   text, MS-DOS Editor,
      276-280
   topics, DOS Prompt Help,
      53-56
floppy disks, 13-16, 315-316
   checking, 127
   checking for viruses
      with Anti-Virus, 203-207
      with Windows version of
         Anti-Virus, 212-213
   comparing, 134-135
   compressed, 232-233
      troubleshooting, 233
   compressing, 230-232
   copying, 131-134
   formatting, 136-142
   naming, 145-146
   unformatting, 142-145
FOR command, 168, 303
Format, 33
FORMAT command, 136-139,
   303
   parameters, 139-142
Format option (DoubleSpace
   Drive menu), 228
formatting
   disks, 316
   floppy disks, 136-142
   hard disk drives,
      compressed, 228-229

328   *DOS 6 SureSteps*

see also unformatting floppy disks
fragmented files, 316
frames, page, 246
full backups, 192
function keys, 17

G

gigabytes (G, GB, or gigs), 13
GOTO command, 168, 303
graphics mode, DOS Shell, 39-41
graphing applications, 22
    file extensions, 63-71
groups, 316
    Disk Utilities, 33-34, 37
    Main, 33-34, 37

H

hard disks, 13-16, 315-316
    checking, 126-129
    checking for viruses
        with Anti-Virus, 203-207
        with VSafe, 211-212
        with Windows version of Anti-Virus, 212-213
    cleaning, 256-258
    compressed
        defragmenting, 227-228
        deleting, 229-230
        formatting, 228-229
        maintaining, 223-224
        sizes, changing, 225-226
        troubleshooting, 233
    compressing, 216-221
    compression ratio, 226-227
    defragmenting, 129-131
    directories, 76-77
    files
        backing up, 184-187, 192-196
        backing up with Microsoft Backup, Windows, 197-198
        comparing backups with originals, 187-189
        compressing, 221-223
        restoring, 189-191
    optimizing speed, 256

removing, DoubleSpace program, 234-237
hardware
    configuring, 172-173
    disk drives, 13-16
    keyboards, 16-20
    monitors, 12
    mouse, 20-21
    printers, 21-22
    system units, 10-11
        turning off, 28-29
Help, 43-45
    dialog box buttons, 49-50
    DOS prompt, 50-52
        cross references, 55-56
        menus, 53-55
    DOS Shell, 45
    MS-DOS Editor, 269-271
    navigating screen, 47-48, 52-53
    printing sections, 53
Help (F1) shortcut key, 45-46
HELP command, 51, 303
Help menu options, 45-46
hidden files, 316
high memory area (HMA), 247, 316
highlighting text, *see* selecting text
HIMEM.SYS command, 310
HIMEM.SYS extended memory manager, 246-248, 316
Home key, 18
hot keys, 37

I

icons, 316
    drive, 315
IF command, 168, 304
INCLUDE command, 310
incremental backups, 192-194
Info option (DoubleSpace Drive menu), 224
inkjet printers, 21
Ins key, 19
INSTALL command, 172, 310
installing
    DOS 6, 292-293
        upgrades, 293-295
    DoubleSpace, 217-223

Index **329**

integrated applications, 22
    file extensions, 63-71
Intel, 10
INTERLNK command, 304
Interlnk program, 288-290
INTERLNK.EXE command, 310
interrupts, 316
INTERSVR command, 304
IO.SYS file, 24, 160

J-K

key combinations
    Add mode (Shift+F8), 98-99
    Deselect All (Ctrl+\), 98
    Help (F1), 45-46
keyboards, 11, 16-20
    enhanced, 18
    selecting files, 98-99
kilobytes (K), 13

L

LABEL command, 145-146
laser printers, 21
LASTDRIVE command, 311
LIM memory specification, 10
line editors, MS-DOS Editor, 263
list boxes, 317
list of files, viewing, 94-96, 65-68
LOADHIGH (LH) command, 304
loading device drivers,
    248-249
lost clusters, fixing, 128
Lotus/Intel/Microsoft Expanded
    Memory Specifications (LIM
    EMS), 247, 316
LPT port, 317

M

Main group, 33-34, 37
managing memory
    DOS, 248-249
    HIMEM.SYS, 246-248, 316
    LIM EMS, 247
master catalogs, 197
math coprocessing units, 10
MD (MKDIR) command, 83, 304
megabytes (M, MB, or megs), 13
MEM command, 242-244, 288,
    304

MEMMAKER command, 249,
    305
MemMaker program, 249-250
    Express Setup, 250-253
    undoing changes, 253-254
MEMMAKER.STS file, 255
memory, 10, 242-244
    configuring, 172-173
    conventional, 244-245, 314
    expanded memory (EMS),
        246-247, 316
    extended (XMS), 246-247,
        316
        programs to speed system,
            258-260
    HMA (high memory area),
        247
    increasing with
        DoubleSpace, 216-223
    managing
        DOS, 248-249
        HIMEM.SYS, 246-248, 316
        LIM EMS, 10, 247
    optimizing with MemMaker,
        250-253
    stacks, 318
    upper area (UMBs),
        245-246, 318
memory-resident programs,
    317
    VSafe, 211-212
menu bar, DOS Shell, 33, 317
MENU command, 170
MENU.BAT file, 169-171
MENUCOLOR command, 311
MENUDEFAULT command,
    311
MENUITEM command, 311
menus, 38-39, 317
    accessing, 37-38
    DOS Prompt Help, 53-55
    MS-DOS Editor, 268-269
Michelangelo computer virus,
    153
Microsoft, 10
Microsoft Backup
    configuring, 179-183
    functions, 178
    hard disk files
        backing up, 184-187,
            192-196

330 *DOS 6 SureSteps*

comparing backup with
  originals, 187-189
  restoring, 189-191
  Windows, 197-198
modems, 11
modes
  graphics (DOS Shell), 39-41
  text (DOS Shell), 39-41
monitors, 11-12
MORE command, 305
Mount option (DoubleSpace
  Drive menu), 232
mounting floppy disks,
  232-233, 317
mouse, 11, 20-21
  files
    copying, 105-106
    selecting, 98-100
  navigating Help screens, 52-53
MOVE command, 305
Move option (File menu),
  110-111
moving
  cursors, MS-DOS Editor, 272
  files, in DOS Shell, 110-111
MS-DOS Editor, 165, 169-171,
  263
  Edit menu options
    Clear, 274
    Copy, 274
    Cut, 275
    Paste, 274, 275
  exiting, 283
  File menu options
    Exit, 283
    Open, 264-265
    Print, 282
    Save, 280-281
  files
    editing, 264-267
    printing, 281-282,
      282-283
    saving, 280-281
  Help system, 269-271
  menus, 268-269
  Options menu options,
    Display, 271
  Search menu options
    Change, 278
    Find, 276-277
    Repeat Last Find, 276

starting, 264-266
text
  bookmarks, 280
  changing, 278-280
  editing, 271-276
  entering, 271-273
  finding, 276-280
MS-DOS QBasic, 33
MSAV command, 305
MSAV.RPT file, 208
MSBACKUP command, 305
MSDOS.SYS file, 24, 160

N

naming
  files, 60-61
  floppy disks, 145-146
navigating
  DOS Shell, 35-37
  Help screen, 47-48, 52-53
Norton Utilities, 23
Notes section, Help screen,
  commands, 51
Num Lock key, 16-18
NUMLOCK command, 311

O

Open option (MS-DOS Editor
  File menu), 264-265
opening files, 317
optimizing
  hard disk
    memory with MemMaker,
      250-253
    space, 129
    speed, 256
  order of programs
    AUTOEXEC.BAT file,
      254-256
    CONFIG.SYS file,
      254-256
options, 317
  Anti-Virus menu
    Create Report, 207-208
    Detect and Clean,
      204-205, 208
    Options, 206-208
    Select New Drive,
      204-205

Index **331**

options (continued)
  Backup menu, 184-187
    Compare, 187-191
    Restore, 189-191
  dimmed, 315
  Compress menu
    (DoubleSpace), Existing
    Drive, 231
  Drive menu (DoubleSpace)
    Change Ratio, 226-227
    Change Size, 225
    Delete, 229-230
    Format, 228
    Info, 224
    Mount, 232
  Edit menu (MS-DOS Editor)
    Clear, 274
    Copy, 274
    Cut, 275
    Paste, 274, 275
  File menu
    Copy, 102-103
    Create Directory, 82
    Delete, 114-115
    Deselect All, 98
    Move, 110-111
    Rename, 120-121
    Run, 50
    Save Setup As, 193-195
    Search Entire Disk,
      100-101
    Select All, 98
  File menu (DOS Prompt Help)
    Exit, 53, 55
    Print, 53
  File menu (MS-DOS Editor)
    Exit, 283
    Open, 264-265
    Print, 282
    Save, 280-281
  Help menu, 45-46
  Options menu
    Confirmation, 49
    Display, 40
    File Display Options, 39, 96
    Preview, 40
    Select Across Directories, 39
  Options menu (MS-DOS
    Editor), Display, 271
  Search menu (DOS Prompt
    Help)
    Find, 54-55
    Repeat Last Find, 54
  Search menu (MS-DOS
    Editor)
    Change, 278
    Find, 276-277
    Repeat Last Find, 276
  Tools menu (DoubleSpace)
    Chkdsk, 233
    Defragment, 227-228
  Tree menu
    Expand All, 95
    Expand Branch, 95
    Expand One Level, 95
  View menu
    Dual File List, 41
    Single File List, 41
  see also commands
Options option (Anti-Virus
  menu), 206-208
order of files, 96-98

P

/P parameter, DIR commands,
  66
page frames, 246
parallel ports, 317
parameters, 51, 317
  /A, REPLACE command, 112
  /C, MEM command, 242,
    244
  /F
    CHKDSK command,
      127-129, 256-258
    TREE command, 87-88
  /F:size, FORMAT command,
    140
  /P, DIR command, 66
  /Q, FORMAT command, 139
  /S, REPLACE command, 112
  /S, FORMAT command, 139
  /TEST, UNFORMAT
    command, 144
  /U, FORMAT command, 139
  /U, REPLACE command, 112
  /W, DIR command, 65
parent directories, 76
partitions, disks, 315-317
Paste option (MS-DOS Editor
  Edit menu), 274-275
pasting text, 317
PATH command, 155-157, 305

paths, 317
   files, 80, 155-157
PAUSE command, 164-165, 169, 306
PCs
   booting, 23-24
      cold, 24-26
         interrupting process, 27-28
      warm, 26-27
   clients/servers, 288
   connecting, 288-290
   hardware, 10-11
      disk drives, 13-16
      keyboards, 16-21
      monitors, 12
      mouse, 20-21
      printers, 21-22
   memory, 242
   software, 22-23
   turning off, 28-29
peripherals, 11
Pg Dn key, 18, 35
Pg Up key, 18, 35
pointing with mouse, 20, 317
ports
   COM, 314
   LPT, 317
   parallel, 317
   serial, 318
POWER command, 306
Power On Self Test (POST), 24-26, 160
POWER.EXE command, 311
Preview option (Options menu), 40
Print option (File menu), 255
Print option (DOS Prompt Help File menu), 53
Print option (MS-DOS Editor File menu), 282
Print Screen key, 19-20
printer drivers, 317
printers, 11, 21-22
printing
   files, MS-DOS Editor, 281-283
   Help sections, 53
Program List, 33-36
programs
   Anti-Virus, 203-207
      configuring, 206-208

      information about viruses, 208-209
      Windows version, 212-213
   Delete Sentry, 116-118
   Delete Tracker, 116-118
   deleting from hard disks, 256-258
   DoubleSpace, 216-217, 230-233
      installing, 217-223
      removing, 234-237
   FASTOPEN, 259-260
   Interlnk, 288-290
   MemMaker, 249-250
      Express Setup, 251-253
      undoing changes, 253-254
   memory-resident, 317
   RAMDRIVE, 259
   SMARTDRV, 259
   VSafe, 211-212
   see also applications; software
PROMPT command, 158-159, 306
prompts, DOS, 42-45
   customizing, 158-159
   directories
      changing, 80-81
      copying, 108-110
      creating, 83
      removing, 86-86
      removing trees, 88-89
      viewing tree, 87-88
   files
      AUTOEXEC.BAT, 160-161
      copying, 107-110
      creating, 161-166
      replacing, 112-113
      undeleting, 117
   Help, 50-52
      cross references, 55-56
      menus, 53-55
   versions of DOS, 152-153

Q

/Q parameters, FORMAT command, 139
Quick Format, 33

Index **333**

QUICK FORMAT command,
   136-139
QUIT command, 178

R

RAM (Random Access Memory),
   10
   drives, 317
RAMDRIVE.SYS device driver,
   256, 259, 311
RD (RMDIR) command,
   86, 306
REM command, 169, 173, 306
removing
   directories, 84
      at DOS prompt, 85-86
      in DOS Shell, 84-86
   directory tree at DOS prompt,
      88-89
   disk names, 145-146
   programs, DoubleSpace,
      234-237
REN (RENAME) command, 306
Rename option (File menu), 120,
   121
renaming
   disks, 145-146
   files in DOS Shell, 120-121
Repeat Last Find option (DOS
   Prompt Help Search menu), 54
Repeat Last Find option (MS-
   DOS Editor Search menu), 276
REPLACE command, 112-113,
   306
RESTORE command, 178, 307
Restore Fixed Disk, 33
Restore option (Backup menu),
   189
restoring hard disk files,
   189-191
ROM (Read Only Memory), 10
root directories, 76-78, 318
   clearing for formatting, 136
rules, file names, 61-64
Run option (File menu), 50

S

/S parameters, FORMAT
   command, 139

/S parameter, REPLACE
   command, 112
Save option (MS-DOS Editor
   File menu), 280-281
Save Setup As option (File
   menu), 193-195
saving files, MS-DOS Editor,
   280-281
Screen Display mode (DOS
   Shell), 40
screens, MS-DOS Editor,
   268-269
scroll arrows, 318
scroll bars, 318
Scroll Lock key, 16-18
scrolling, 318
SEARCH command, 100
Search Entire Disk option (File
   menu), 100-101
Search menu (DOS Prompt
   Help) options
   Find, 54, 55
   Repeat Last Find, 54
Search option (MS-DOS Editor
   Search menu), 278
searching, *see* finding
Select Across Directories option
   (Options menu), 39
Select All option (Ctrl+/) key
   combination, 98
Select New Drive option (Anti-
   Virus menu), 204, 205
selecting
   files, 98-100
   items, 318
   text, 316-319
      blocks, 274-276
serial ports, 318
servers, 288
   client, 314
setup files, 193
SETVER.EXE command, 311
SHELL command, 312
Shift key, 20
shortcut keys, *see* key
   combinations
Single File List option (View
   menu), 41
SMARTDRV command, 307
SMARTDRV.EXE command,
   312

SMARTDRV.SYS device driver, 256, 259
software
　application, 22-23
　system, 22-23
　　DOS, 23-24
source disks, 297
　copying files, 108
speed, hard disk, optimizing, 256
SSF (Enable) file extension, 63
Stacker, 23
stacks, memory, 318
STACKS command, 172, 312
starting
　DOS Shell, 32
　MS-DOS Editor, 264-266
　see also booting PCs
status bar, DOS Shell, 33
subdirectories, 76, 318
SUBMENU command, 312
Super VGA monitors, 12
switches, 51
SWITCHES command, 312
SYS command, 307
system time and date, 318
system disks, formatting, 139
system software, 22-23
　DOS, 23-24
system units, 10-11
　booting, 11-12

T

T$0 (TimeLine) file extension, 63
Tab key, 35-36
target disks, 297
targets, copying files, 108
Task List, 318
/TEST parameter, UNFORMAT command, 144
text
　boxes, 318
　mode, DOS Shell, 39-41
　MS-DOS Editor
　　bookmarks, 280
　　changing, 278-280
　　editing, 271-276
　　entering, 271-273
　　finding, 276-280
　pasting, 317
　selecting, 316
time and date, system, 318

setting an internal clock, 154-155
TIME command, 154-155, 307
time-stamping files, 154-155
TimeLine, 22
title bar, DOS Shell, 33
TREE command, 87-88, 307
Tree menu options
　Expand All, 95
　Expand Branch, 95
　Expand One Level, 95
trees, see Directory Tree
Trojan horse virus, 203, 318
troubleshooting
　compressed drives, 233
　files, CONFIG.SYS, 173-174
TYPE command, 307

U

/U parameters, FORMAT command, 139
/U parameter, REPLACE command, 112
UMBs (upper memory blocks), 245-246, 318
Undelete, 33
UNDELETE command, 116-119, 308
undeleting files, 116-119
UNFORMAT command, 136, 142-144, 308
　parameters, 144-145
unformatting floppy disks, 142-145
　see also formatting
upgrades, installing DOS 6, 293-295
upper memory, 318
upper memory blocks (UMBs), 245-246, 318

V

VER command, 152, 288
versions of DOS, 152-153
vertical market software, 23
VGA monitors, 12
View menu options
　Dual File List, 41
　Single File List, 41

Index **335**

viewing
    directories, 94
        in DOS Shell, 87
    directory tree at DOS prompt, 87-88
    lists of files, 65-68, 94-96
views in directories,
    expanding/changing, 94-96
    DOS Shell, 41-42
viruses, *see* computer viruses
VOL command, 145-146
VSAFE command, 308
    options, 211-212
VSafe program, 211-212

W

/W parameter, DIR command, 65
warm booting, 26-27
wild cards, 319
    file names, 66-68
Windows, 22
    Microsoft Backup, 197-198
    Anit-Virus, 212, 213

X-Z

XCOPY command, 108-110, 308
XMS (extended memory), 246-247
    programs to speed system, 258-260

If your computer uses 5 1/4-inch disks...

DOS 6 SureSteps comes with a 3 1/2-inch, double-density, 720K floppy disk. If your computer uses 5 1/4-inch disks, return this form to Que Corporation to obtain one 360K 5 1/4-inch disk to use with this book. Simply fill out the form below and mail this page to:

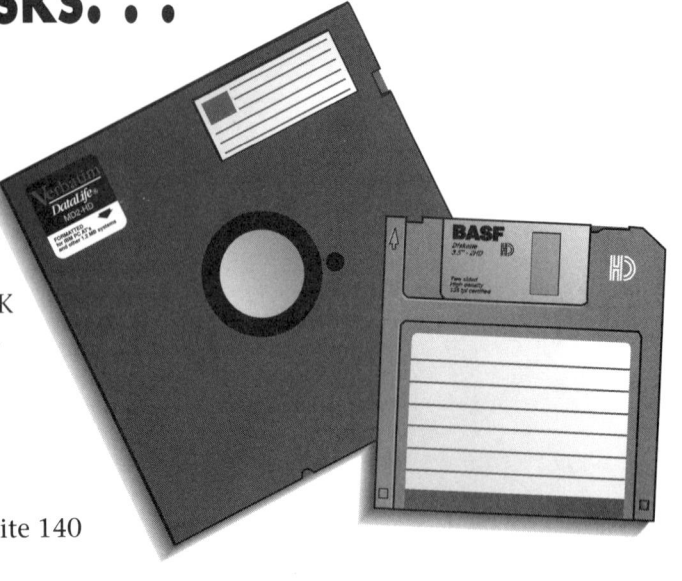

Book Disk Exchange
Que Corporation
11711 N. College Ave., Suite 140
Carmel, IN 46032

We will send you, free of charge, the 5 1/4-inch version of this book's software.

Name _____

Company _____ Title _____

Address _____

City _____ State _____

Zip _____ Phone _____